STRUCTURES OF SUBJUGATION IN DUTCH LITERATURE

LEGENDA

LEGENDA is the Modern Humanities Research Association's book imprint for new research in the Humanities. Founded in 1995 by Malcolm Bowie and others within the University of Oxford, Legenda has always been a collaborative publishing enterprise, directly governed by scholars. The Modern Humanities Research Association (MHRA) joined this collaboration in 1998, became half-owner in 2004, in partnership with Maney Publishing and then Routledge, and has since 2016 been sole owner. Titles range from medieval texts to contemporary cinema and form a widely comparative view of the modern humanities, including works on Arabic, Catalan, English, French, German, Greek, Italian, Portuguese, Russian, Spanish, and Yiddish literature. Editorial boards and committees of more than 60 leading academic specialists work in collaboration with bodies such as the Society for French Studies, the British Comparative Literature Association and the Association of Hispanists of Great Britain & Ireland.

The MHRA encourages and promotes advanced study and research in the field of the modern humanities, especially modern European languages and literature, including English, and also cinema. It aims to break down the barriers between scholars working in different disciplines and to maintain the unity of humanistic scholarship. The Association fulfils this purpose through the publication of journals, bibliographies, monographs, critical editions, and the MHRA Style Guide, and by making grants in support of research. Membership is open to all who work in the Humanities, whether independent or in a University post, and the participation of younger colleagues entering the field is especially welcomed.

ALSO PUBLISHED BY THE ASSOCIATION

Critical Texts
Tudor and Stuart Translations • *New Translations* • *European Translations*
MHRA Library of Medieval Welsh Literature

MHRA Bibliographies
Publications of the Modern Humanities Research Association

The Annual Bibliography of English Language & Literature
Austrian Studies
Modern Language Review
Portuguese Studies
The Slavonic and East European Review
Working Papers in the Humanities
The Yearbook of English Studies

www.mhra.org.uk
www.legendabooks.com

GERMANIC LITERATURES

Editorial Committee
Chair: Professor Ritchie Robertson (University of Oxford)
Dr Barbara Burns (Glasgow University)
Professor Jane Fenoulhet (University College London)
Professor Anne Fuchs (University of Warwick)
Dr Jakob Stougaard-Nielsen (University College London)
Professor Annette Volfing (University of Oxford)
Professor Susanne Kord (University College London)
Professor John Zilcosky (University of Toronto)

Germanic Literatures includes monographs and essay collections on literature originally written not only in German, but also in Dutch and the Scandinavian languages. Within the German-speaking area, it seeks also to publish studies of other national literatures such as those of Austria and Switzerland. The chronological scope of the series extends from the early Middle Ages down to the present day.

APPEARING IN THIS SERIES

1. *Yvan Goll: The Thwarted Pursuit of the Whole*, by Robert Vilain
2. *Sebald's Bachelors: Queer Resistance and the Unconforming Life*, by Helen Finch
3. *Goethe's Visual World*, by Pamela Currie
4. *German Narratives of Belonging: Writing Generation and Place in the Twenty-First Century*, by Linda Shortt
5. *The Very Late Goethe: Self-Consciousness and the Art of Ageing*, by Charlotte Lee
6. *Women, Emancipation and the German Novel 1871-1910: Protest Fiction in its Cultural Context*, by Charlotte Woodford
7. *Goethe's Poetry and the Philosophy of Nature: Gott und Welt 1798–1827*, by Regina Sachers
8. *Fontane and Cultural Mediation: Translation and Reception in Nineteenth-Century German Literature*, edited by Ritchie Robertson and Michael White
9. *Metamorphosis in Modern German Literature: Transforming Bodies, Identities and Affects*, by Tara Beaney
10. *Comedy and Trauma in Germany and Austria after 1945: The Inner Side of Mourning*, by Stephanie Bird
11. *E.T.A. Hoffmann's Orient: Romantic Aesthetics and the German Imagination*, by Joanna Neilly
12. *Structures of Subjugation in Dutch Literature*, by Judit Gera

Managing Editor
Dr Graham Nelson, 41 Wellington Square, Oxford OX1 2JF, UK
www.legendabooks.com

Structures of Subjugation in Dutch Literature

Judit Gera

Germanic Literatures 12
Modern Humanities Research Association
2016

Published by Legenda
An imprint of the Modern Humanities Research Association
Salisbury House, Station Road, Cambridge CB1 2LA

ISBN 978-1-910887-23-3 (HB)
ISBN 978-1-781883-06-8 (PB)

First published 2016

All rights reserved. No part of this publication may be reproduced or disseminated or transmitted in any form or by any means, electronic, mechanical, photocopying, recording or otherwise, or stored in any retrieval system, or otherwise used in any manner whatsoever without written permission of the copyright owner, except in accordance with the provisions of the Copyright, Designs and Patents Act 1988, or under the terms of a licence permitting restricted copying issued in the UK by the Copyright Licensing Agency Ltd, Saffron House, 6–10 Kirby Street, London EC1N 8TS, England, or in the USA by the Copyright Clearance Center, 222 Rosewood Drive, Danvers MA 01923. Application for the written permission of the copyright owner to reproduce any part of this publication must be made by email to legenda@mhra.org.uk.

Disclaimer: Statements of fact and opinion contained in this book are those of the author and not of the editors or the Modern Humanities Research Association. The publisher makes no representation, express or implied, in respect of the accuracy of the material in this book and cannot accept any legal responsibility or liability for any errors or omissions that may be made.

Trademark notice: Product or corporate names may be trademarks or registered trademarks, and are used only for identification and explanation without intent to infringe.

© Modern Humanities Research Association 2016

Printed in Great Britain

Copy-Editor: Nigel Hope

CONTENTS

	Preface	ix
	List of Illustrations	xi
	Introduction	1
1	The Colonial Subject as Subjugator: A Post-Colonial Reading of Bontekoe's *Journaal*	11
2	The Parvenu as Subjugator: Colonial Connotations of the Short Novel *De familie Kegge* by Nicolaas Beets	37
3	Speaking and Silence of the 'Other': Parallels of Colonial and Female Subjugation in Multatuli's Novel *Max Havelaar*	63
4	A Novel of Hybridity: Louis Couperus's *De stille kracht*	101
5	Victory of the 'Other' over Colonial Power: Madelon Székely-Lulofs: *Tjoet Nja Din*	121
6	The Subjugation of Female Subjectivity: A Feminist Reading of Karel van de Woestijne's 'De zwijnen van Kirkè'	149
7	Beatrijs and her Younger Sisters: Narrative Structures in Fictions of Female Development	161
	Bibliography	189
	Index	196

PREFACE

The publication of this work is due to the urge to produce something readable for a broader public than the two small but precious communities to which I am confined: the Dutch and the Hungarian. Writing in English helps to direct attention to lesser-known literatures and cultures.

The reason for choosing the subject of subjugation is that it is very often invisible both in society and in writing. When students ask me what literature is good for, I always answer that reading literary texts helps one to avoid getting into a subjugated situation without realizing it. Being conscious of literary narrative structures helps one to find one's way in the jungle of all other kinds of texts, discourses, and situations in which some are oppressed by others. Creating distance from what a literary text proposes at first sight means becoming alert and resistant to a variety of slyly oppressive strategies. No text, not even a short description of a landscape, is innocent. Texts are born as a result, and in the contexts, of ideologies. Ideologies try to make us accept things which they present as natural. But nothing is simply natural either in life or in literature. A text is always a network of human relations in which some are more visible, audible, and fathomable than others. Why is that, and what are the mechanisms of social and textual subjugation? These are the questions in which I am interested.

I wrote the book while teaching Modern Dutch Literature, Literary Translation, and other subjects in the Dutch Department of the Eötvös Loránd University Budapest. It was not easy to find time for writing, which was a difficulty I had to contend with all the time. On the other hand, my classes have helped me to think about things more thoroughly. Therefore I am grateful to my students for listening carefully, so that instead of robbing me of precious time they have rather helped the emergence of the book, albeit in an indirect way.

The inspiring atmosphere of the Institute for Germanic Studies and the Dutch Department at my university has contributed a great deal to my writing. Thank you, colleagues!

I am also very grateful to Bernard Adams, who has thoroughly and patiently corrected my English. My thanks go also to the Arnhem Department of the Orde van den Prince, and to the Algemeen Nederlands Verbond, which have generously contributed to the publishing costs. Anton van der Lem, curator of the Leiden University Libraries nicely surprized me by looking up and giving permission to publication of several illustrations for which I am very thankful. I am also obliged to Rosaly Klaver, copy editor of the Digital Library for Dutch Literature and Klaartje Groot, director of the Multatuli Museum Amsterdam for their helpfulness to find and put to disposal other visual material.

Last but not least I am very grateful to Jane Fenoulhet, professor at University College London for her critical remarks on the manuscript, and to Nigel Hope and Graham Nelson for their impeccable editing.

Translations in the text are my own unless otherwise stated. Shorter versions of chapters 1 and 2 have been published as parts of my handbook *Inleiding in de literatuurgeschiedenis voor de internationale neerlandistiek*, written together with A. Agnes Sneller (Hilversum: Verloren, 2010). Agnes Sneller is an acknowledged scholar in the Netherlands. She has been a colleague and friend for more than two decades now and a constant source of help, inspiration and encouragement.

J. G., Budapest, 28 March 2015.

Algemeen-Nederlands Verbond
Vereniging voor Nederlands-Vlaamse samenwerking

LIST OF ILLUSTRATIONS

❖

FIG. 1.1. 'WILLEM YSBRANTZ BONTEKOE VAN HOORN', portrait of the man, almost frontal, half shape, with globe, compasses and cramp, open sea in the background, author unknown, Paper, 13.8 x 17.5 cm, Collectie Westfries Museum

FIG. 1.2. The cover of the first Dutch edition of the *Journal* of Bontekoe. Paper, Leiden University Libraries 1365 G 62: 1

FIG. 1.3. The Dutchmen on the ship Santa Maria, at Madagascar. Paper, Leiden University Libraries 1365 G 62: 1

FIG. 1.4. The explosion of the ship Nieuw Hoorn. Paper, Leiden University Libraries 1365 G 62: 1

FIG. 2.1. Portrait of Nicolaas Beets by Johannes Philippus Lange, after William Grebner, published by Johannes Immerzeel, 1820–41, Steel-engraving, 13.5cm × 10.5cm, Digitale Bibliotheek voor de Nederlandse Letteren

FIG. 2.2. The title page of the fifth edition of the *Camera Obscura* by Karel Frederik Blombléd, 1857, Leiden University Libraries 1C01 C 20 001

FIG. 2.3. *Een onaangenaam mensch in den Haarlemmerhout* by Ch. Rochussen, Digitale Bibliotheek voor de Nederlandse Letteren

FIG. 3.1. Portrait of Multatuli by August Allebé, 1874, lithograph Collectie Documentatie Nederlandse Letterkunde

FIG. 3.2. Cover of the 1868 English edition of the *Max Havelaar*. Leiden University Libraries, M aa 186 001

FIG. 3.3. Multatuli's house in Java, Rangkas-Bitoeng. Multatuli Museum Amsterdam

FIG. 3.4. Portrait of Tine, Multatuli's wife. Multatuli Museum Amsterdam

FIG. 4.1. Portrait of Louis Couperus by Jan Veth, 1900, litograph, Collectie Documentatie Nederlandse Letterkunde

FIG. 4.2. Cover of the first edition of the *Stille kracht,* Leiden University Libraries, 22537 D 11 001

FIG. 5.1. The Monument East Indies — The Netherlands by Frits van Hall, 1935. Photograph by Wikimedia Commons user PjotrP.

FIG. 5.2. Portrait of Madelon Székely Lulofs, Collectie Documentatie Nederlandse Letterkunde

FIG. 5.3. Group portrait with Cut Nyak Dhien after she was taken prisoner, 1905, Tropenmuseum Amsterdam. © Tropenmuseum, part of the National Museum of World Cultures

FIG. 6.1. Portrait of Karel van de Woestijne by Gustave van de Woestijne, 1910, drawing, 29,5 x 26,5 cm, Digitale Bibliotheek voor de Nederlandse Letteren

FIG. 7.1. The first page from the c.1374 Manuscript of the *Beatrijs*

FIG. 7.2. The portrait of Aagje Deken en Betje Wolff by A. Cardon and W. Neering 1784, etching, Digitale Bibliotheek voor de Nederlandse Letteren

FIG. 7.3. The title page of the eighth edition of *Sara Burgerhart* 1891, VU University Library, Amsterdam, shelfmark XU.04474.-

FIG. 7.4. Portrait of Frederik van Eeden by Jan Veth, etching Digitale Bibliotheek van de Nederlandse Letterkunde

FIG. 7.5. Cover of the first edition of the *Van de koele meren des doods*, 1900, Leiden University Libraries 22544 D 40 001

FIG. 7.6. Portrait of Carry van Bruggen by Annie de Meester, drawing, 1915, Digitale Bibliotheek voor de Nederlandse Letteren

FIG. 7.7. The cover of the first edition of *Eva*, 1927 Leiden University Libraries, MTRB 5 E 001

FIG. 7.8. Portrait of Arthur Japin © Corbino

FIG. 7.9. Cover of *Een schitterend gebrek* by Steven van der Gouw. Henry Morland, De Arbeiderspers Amsterdam

INTRODUCTION

Subjugation as a concept is related to the subordinate as it is interpreted in post-colonial studies. I use the concept of post-colonialism, however, not only in the historical sense, but I extend it to other social relations where a person, a group, a culture are forced into a subjugated position by another person, group, or culture which has power.[1]

This monograph is based on my publications in Dutch, English, and Hungarian, which have appeared in different journals and books in the past several years and which all share a theoretical basis in ideology critique.[2] The book not only summarizes these findings but also contains new ones and views which I have revised since publishing them for the first time.

My analyses of Dutch prose works examine the literary representations of power and subjugation and the ways of rebelling against and resisting these. Literary representations are biased for several reasons; they are not mirrors of an objective reality, but constructions. Readers too are biased while they perceive and interpret literature: their past, knowledge, taste, and value-system delineate what they think of a certain literary work.

I examine two kinds of subjugation. One is the subjugation of women by men. The other is the subjugation of subjects by colonials. These two kinds of subjugation often go hand in hand. I try to explain how they may be related and intersect. Are actors conscious of having power or being powerless, and have literary scholars taken up these points in their analyses? Is subjugation visible, and to what extent does it seem to be something natural? I also argue that all forms of subjugation can be deduced from the dynamics of actual social and cultural circumstances. What are the structures of subjugation? How can someone be subjugated by deprivation of speech? How does a text depict *and* perform subjugation in its textuality?

If we speak of subjugation, the question arises: in whose name, in which institution's name, does it take place, what is the driving force behind it? To answer these questions, examination of ideologies is inevitable. Not only hierarchical relations but also their literary or other representations are operated by ideas and ideologies. Therefore I always look at the ideological connotations of literary representations.

Ideology can have several contents and positions. It also works in several different ways. Ideology can be positive or negative, manifest or hidden. Ideology is not pejorative from the first: if there were no ideologies with positive contents, there would be no ideologies whatsoever which could resist oppressive political regimes. Finding an ideology positive or negative is problematic because it is positive or negative only from a certain point of view. Therefore, thinking about ideology is itself ideological.

Positions of ideology have different forms. There are dominant ideologies in positions of power and there are confrontational, disputative, undermining, resistant ones. There are always several ideologies in a society and at a certain time existing in coordination and subordination. Not every dominant ideology is bad or dangerous and not every confrontational ideology is positive. Ideologies exist embedded in historical contexts, and assessment of them depends on several components which in turn can be considered the product of the same ideologies.

In addition, the working of ideologies can be different. As Terry Eagleton points out, ideology contains conscious, articulate, moral, and normative statements, but it also has an affective, unconscious, mythical, or symbolic character.[3] Individuals relate to the world in their everyday lives mostly spontaneously, directed by their 'cultural unconscious'. In literature, too, we meet these spontaneous, symbolic, very often hidden characters of ideology. One of the goals of this study is to recover and to negotiate these unspoken, seemingly invisible ideologies.

Subjects of ideologies can be different. Ideology is subject-centred on the one hand: subjects are constituted by it, but it is also the product of these subjects. On the other hand, ideology cannot be reduced to the activities of subjects. It also has influence through institutions such as parliament, schools, jurisdiction, and publishers.

Both dominant and confrontational ideologies use different strategies in order to be successful. These may be unifying, action-oriented, legitimating, universalizing, rationalizing, and naturalizing, as Eagleton argues. But not all ideologies make use of these strategies. It seems there is no definition of ideology which would be true in all circumstances, which is why it is such an elusive concept. According to Eagleton, different kinds of ideologies overlap with each other and form a network of family similarities. It is important to remember that an ideology is also a complicated network of conflicts and contradictions in itself.

Ideology is closely connected to discourse. Dominant power inscribes itself sometimes manifestly, sometimes invisibly into social utterances. An especially interesting task is to examine these utterances in the space of struggle for power.

Ideology can be located in literary works in different ways. In most of them we find empirical statements and referential elements. These are organized, however, in order to support a certain world-view offered by the text. In Eagleton's words: '"Constative" language, in other words, is harnessed to "performative" end.'[4]

From the 1970s and 1980s Dutch literary studies started to exchange structuralism as an approach for a contextual one. This development has to do, among other things, with the social changes in the Netherlands at the end of the 1960s, such as the dissolving of the social pillars and the Dutch second feminist wave.[5] Dutch literary studies were also influenced by international tendencies in literary theory such as poststructuralism, post-colonial, and gender studies. Dutch scholars articulated criticism of the male-centred, text-immanent practice of the literary journal *Merlyn* (1962–66). A good example of this reaction is Maaike Meijer's book *De lust tot lezen* [The Pleasure of Reading].[6] It expresses not only a comprehensive criticism of *Merlyn* and its circle, but is also an embodiment of a new approach.[7] The theme of research changed from a male approach to literary works written by men to women authors, and this was the time when women literary scholars appeared not only as accidental individuals but also as a group in the Dutch critical arena. When migration to the Netherlands raised the question of whether Dutch society was functioning in an adequate way politically and culturally, literary scholars began to analyse works of non-white authors and representations of non-European characters in literature. This also signals the beginnings of Dutch post-colonial criticism.[8]

Representatives of the new critical tendencies look at hidden meanings which do not strike us at first sight. In order to activate these meanings, critical — or in other words: resisting — reading is needed when literary works are examined in a network of social and cultural systems. At the end of this process astonishingly new interpretations become possible. Special significance is assigned to the scholar as reader who is also operating in his or her special social-cultural system. These scholars formulate their findings often in the first-person singular, underlining their own engagement and determination by their scholarly and cultural traditions and preferences.

In his theory of ideology critique, Ernst van Alphen interprets literature as a dynamic phenomenon, an articulate confrontation between work and reader.[9] Neither work nor reader exists in a vacuum: both move in a web of world-views, that is to say, ideologies. Authors, their characters, and readers always have some kind of conception of the world. These conceptions may clash, compete, strengthen, or weaken each other both inside and outside the literary work, which may even be ascribed new interpretations at each reading. Each work reflects and re-creates the ideologies of authors, characters, and readers. Readers perceive literary works — often unconsciously — in the space their ideology delineates. When a literary work and its reader confront each other, it is their ideological systems which really come face to face.

In this book I look upon canonized literature through the eyes of a twenty-first-century reader and I indicate ideological elements in literary texts which are not in accordance with the standard European political, cultural, and ideological value-system of our time. This is not intended as a reproach to the authors I consider, it is merely an assessment, a finding. Further, I bring back the author into the picture, arguing against his/her death. This is not because I want to discover any authorial intention — an author's purpose cannot be really known and is also irrelevant — but because an author's relation to his or her material adds an essential aspect to the evaluation of the work. This relation, more often than not, defines the ideological aspects of the work in question. The author's sociocultural context becomes, via several transformations, inscribed in the fabric of the text. Edward Said warns us to look at the so-called strategic position of the author and at the 'interest' in which literary works are born. Works, in their turn, elaborate on these interests in a hidden way or may even deny or exceed the assumptions of their author. In order to understand these mechanisms we cannot avoid looking at the author as a representative of certain interests, values, tastes, and world-views.[10] Dutch literature is studied here from the perspective of post-colonial and gender theories combined with post-classical narratology. All three are permeated with ideological issues, or rather are themselves ideologies.

Dutch society, culture, and literature were conspicuously influenced by having and losing the colonies, especially the East Indies. The branch of Dutch literature elaborating on this experience is called literature of or on the Dutch East Indies. Dutch literature on the Dutch Antilles and Surinam is called the literature of or on the West Indies. Non-colonial Dutch literature, too, is permeated by references, characters, and relations which point to colonial contexts. Therefore Dutch literature cannot be understood without knowing its colonial history and its deep embedding in Dutch culture. My choice of the literary works that I examine is partly explained by this fact.

In the critical analysis of ideology — as already mentioned — the subject plays a crucial role. The subject who interprets the world inside the text is the focalizer. This concept has been introduced by the Dutch literary scholar Mieke Bal in the theory of narratology. According to Bal focalization is the relationship between focalizing subjects and focalized objects.[11] The focalizer necessarily also manipulates the reader: his or her value-system and point of view colour the depicted world. However, the focalizer's view is also delimited and biased, having his or her own norms, values, and preferences.

Literary analysis in which the focalizer is not only a technical element of narratology, but in which the focalizer's ideology is the central question, is called post-classical narratology by Luc Herman and Bart Vervaeck.[12] They take Roland Barthes as an example: according to him there are codes in stories which directly or indirectly refer to social values, norms, and convictions. Classical narratology such as that of Genette does not deal with these; context is not an issue. According to Herman and Vervaeck, however, not only is the focalizer fully ideological but so are such elements as time-structure.

Herman and Vervaeck argue that it was feminist narratology which deepened narratology with ideology. One of the aims of feminist narratology was to show how gender defined whether a literary text was sexist or not.

In her article 'Toward a Feminist Narratology' Susan S. Lanser suggests the combination of narratology and feminist criticism.[13] Narratology created its critical apparatus based on texts written by men. This apparatus, however, did not prove applicable to texts written by women. Lanser emphasizes three aspects wherein narratology and feminist literary criticism differ from each other: (1) while the central category of feminist criticism is gender, narrative theory neglects this; (2) narration is considered mimetic in feminist criticism whereas the status of narration in narratology is semiotic; (3) context plays a crucial role in feminist criticism, while narratology ignores context.

Lanser proposes the reconciliation of the semiotic approach of narratology with the mimetic orientation of feminist criticism. Literature exists actually at the point of intersection of two systems: on the one hand it is the representation of life, it gives a report on reality and is a mimetic document; on the other hand it is a non-referential linguistic system, an utterance which supposes a narrator and a listener, basically a linguistic construction. Narratology ignores the referential aspects of literature and emphasizes only its semiotic character. This contradicts the basic supposition of feminist criticism according to which narrative texts are referential from several aspects, for example in depicting gender relations. Therefore feminist narratology should mix the mimetic and the semiotic status of literature by studying literature in its referential context, which is in itself a compound of linguistic, literary, historical, biographical, social, and political components.

Lanser illustrates her claim by means of a letter written by an anonymous person and published in 1832 in the journal *Atkinson's Casket*. She argues that the letter cannot be fully understood if analysed only by means of traditional narratology. It has at least two or three interpretations. Following Bakhtin, she warns that narratives always have more than one voice; there is always a polyphony of voices. One voice piles upon another, and these voices show a structure wherein others' discourses and discourses about others form the discourse of the 'I'.

The problem of voices is strongly related to the possible narrative levels of the text. Gérard Genette distinguishes the outermost level as extradiegetic. The narrative embedded in this level he calls intradiegetic and a further level embedded in the intradiegetic he calls metadiegetic.[14] The extradiegetic narrator is often the authorial narrator, a voice in the third-person singular which is at the same level as the public. Intradiegetic and metadiegetic narrators can only address those who are inside the narration. This model, however, only considers those relations which are inside the text. Individual narrative acts are ignored and the text is isolated from external, contextual relations.

As a complement to Genette's model, Lanser proposes the terminology of public and private narration. She argues that the question of public and private audience is a more complex problem in the case of women writers. Women's writings were not prohibited or controlled by men, while women wrote for themselves or for other women. Contradiction in the patriarchal order arises only when women write for men. This gives a historical explanation of why women preferred private genres for their writings, such as the letter, the diary, or the memoir. According to Lanser, public narration addresses an audience outside the text who can be identified with the public readers. In private narration the reader is given access to the text via a textual protagonist. The narration may be private, but with the tacit consent of the author readers other than the 'officially' designated ones can also read it. Lanser calls this a semi-private narrative act. In feminist narratology the meaning of narration is defined by the rhetorical context — when, on what occasion, where, in which medium, who is the addressee of the text — as well as by the relations of the narrative levels. The same text can gain different meanings if the rhetorical context is changed.

Lanser's third statement on the feminist version of traditional narratology concerns the plot. In literary works written by men, the plot is mostly related to action, change, adventure, and enterprise, while in those written by women these aspects often cannot be found because they are not consistent with female experience, whether historical or textual. Female narration can rather be characterized by stasis, waiting, and attempts to interpret the world. If the dynamic conception of plot used in traditional narratology cannot be applied to women's texts, it may mean that the traditional definition of the notion 'plot' is problematic. In a universe, Lanser argues, where passivity, acceptance, and resignation dominate, the acts of narration and writing themselves fulfil the desires of the hero(ine) and precisely these acts of narration and writing constitute the plot. When the narrator simply shares her experiences with her reader by the act of writing, then even this act of sharing can be considered as plot.

Although Lanser proposes feminist narratology because narratology proper does not offer an adequate apparatus for the interpretation of literary works written by women, in the following discussion I shall try to interpret also works written by men with the help of feminist narratology as described above. I take the social and rhetorical context and the referentiality of the narration into consideration, and I also examine voices and plots.

In the Dutch language area the work of Mieke Bal and Maaike Meijer, among several other feminist scholars, is essential.[15] They were the first to call attention to the systematic neglect of the female perspective up to their time, and to the importance of its role in textual analysis.

This book has a threefold aim. First of all, it deals with a relatively unfamiliar literature, that written in Dutch, which deserves more attention and promotion in the academic field. The American literary scholar Anna Balakian (1915–97), in her 1978 essay 'The Unfamiliar Literatures', elaborated on the methods by which these unfamiliar literatures could be brought to the attention of a wider public.[16] One possibility that she adumbrated was connecting an unfamiliar literature with what Comparative Literature usually offers: the study of international movements, genres, styles, and archetypes. Writing on Dutch literature in English, in the context of internationally deployed theories such as gender and post-colonial, can be a means of bringing the literature of the Low Countries into focus.

Secondly, this book aims to shed new light on canonical Dutch literary genres such as the novel, short story, historical novel, journal, and epic poetry by revealing hidden biases and mechanisms that have to do with dominant patriarchal and/or colonial ideologies. In their analyses, some Dutch scholars are inclined to neglect the ideological implications of literary works. This is understandable to some extent: ideology has been regarded as a corrupt concept since the Frankfurt School and Georg Lukács defined it as 'false consciousness'. However, neither literature nor reader functions outside ideologies. They both are born into and confronted by a network of ideologies. What is more, literature also produces and is responsible for ideologies, as Ernst van Alphen and others point out.[17] Therefore, my aim is to introduce innovative perspectives by holding up a mirror of ideology to literary works that have been analysed by other scholars from other points of departure.

Thirdly, the book aims to combine historical and biographical contexts with textual analysis. In Lanser's terms, the outside context will be combined with the rhetorical context and plot. Therefore each chapter begins with a short introduction to the historical background of the work under consideration. The author's biographical sketch then follows, with special attention being given to those elements which may have an essential role in the ideological conception(s) contained in the literary work under discussion. Finally, I analyse the text of the work in question looking for hidden and manifest ideologies of the period, of the author and of the text itself. These may differ from one another to a smaller or greater degree.

In Chapter 1 I investigate the *Journaal van Bontekoe* (*Bontekoe's Journal*, 1648) from a post-colonial perspective. I look at the journal of the seventeenth-century Dutch captain as a product of a colonial enterprise which served at the same time as a 'contact zone' of several cultures. The positions of these cultures are hierarchical, therefore their representatives do not have the same status in the journal, and they all look differently at the world. This point of departure may seem obvious, but it is quite new if compared to other Dutch reflections on the *Journaal* published so far. They set it either in the context of the economic and social history of its time, or in that of its literary antecedents, the conventions of its genre, and the taste of its contemporary readers. It is, of course, a legitimate alternative to read the *Journaal* as part of a certain literary convention of the seventeenth century; but it is just as legitimate to look back on it from the present day as a product of colonial history. In so doing I reproach neither the author nor the characters of the book, nor the way in which they look at the world. However, I consider the hierarchy of cultures represented in the work as a fact. I set out to understand and expose those episodes where peoples subjugate other peoples whom they brand barbarian, wild, and pagan. Nor do I seek to challenge the role of this work in the Dutch literary canon. At the same time, however, I cannot help speaking about the obvious or less obvious presence of power relations, about the mechanisms of oppression, discrimination, and stereotyping. I cannot pretend to be a seventeenth-century reader, unaware of the implications of colonialism. Therefore I ask my questions from a modern point of view and direct them to the modern reader. This does not mean neglecting the historical context of Dutch colonialism.

Chapter 2 analyses the short novel *De familie Kegge* (*The Kegge Family*, 1851) by Nicolaas Beets, placing it in its not so obvious colonial context. This work is a good example of how a story that is seemingly not about colonialism can still touch upon its practices. If this is considered, the interpretation of such a work can take a totally different direction. Edward Said showed a similar case in his analysis of *Mansfield Park* by Jane Austen. Literary works written during the colonial era often thematize the problems of colonialism only tangentially. It is up to the reader whether he or she sees the latent colonial aspects, and to what extent he/she gives way to these aspects during the interpreting process. Interestingly, Dutch scholars such as Van den Berg, Eijssens, Kloek, and Van Zonneveld pay no attention to the colonial background of the story;[18] the only exception is Jacqueline Bel, who analyses this work with emphasis on the colonial aspect.[19] My analysis has the same point of departure as Bel's but remains closer to the text and to its details in an attempt to offer further evidence of the colonial interpretation of the work.

Chapter 3 examines Multatuli's novel, *Max Havelaar*, published in the Netherlands in 1860.[20] In this chapter I analyse the parallels between female and colonial subjugations. The elements of both kinds of subjugation are similar: deprivation of name and individuality, replacing the representation of an individual with the characteristics of a group, silencing, objectification. Besides indicating contradictory elements in the text, I also call attention to verbal and non-verbal manifestations of protest against the suppression of women and of colonized subjects.

The fourth chapter provides an analysis of Louis Couperus's novel *De stille kracht*

(*The Hidden Force*, 1900) which is based on Homi Bhabha's concepts: ambivalence, mimicry, hybridity. Another source of inspiration has been an article by Pamela Pattynama, in which she examines the novel and its contemporary Dutch cultural background in terms of interracial sexuality.[21] Ambivalence permeates and destabilizes the social positions, actions, thoughts, emotions, and physical appearance of the characters. The slow decline of Dutch colonial power is represented by undermining the European concepts of superiority of race, ethics, and family values.

Chapter 5 gives a detailed analysis of the novel *Tjoet Nja Din* (1948) by Madelon Székely-Lulofs. This novel was — and is — not very popular in the Netherlands, and it has not received the attention that it deserves on grounds of quality. The Dutch writer ascribes her new way of looking at the colonies to her Hungarian husband, László Székely. He revealed to her the true nature of colonialism thanks to his position as an outsider, as she points out. I set out in my analysis to answer the question of the extent to which colonial and anti-colonial narrative strategies prevail in the book. I use the 'figures of discrimination' of Maaike Meijer, which she in turn borrows from Toni Morrison's study *Playing in the Dark*.[22] Székely-Lulofs's novel also raises the question of the very problematic relation of the Netherlands to its own colonies after the Second World War.

The sixth chapter focuses on the short story *De zwijnen van Kirkè* (*Circe's Swine*, 1905) by the Flemish symbolist author Karel Van de Woestijne. First, I show how literary convention manipulates later representations, then, making use of Lanser's feminist narratology, I try to prove that — contrary to Hans Vandevoorde's article — the female voice in a literary text does not in itself guarantee that it will prevail.[23] The condition for the prevalence of the female voice is that it should be heard not through a manifold mediation but from a subject position as the voice of a real, active agent. The representation of Kirkè is examined in the context of the Flemish *fin-de-siècle* and symbolism.

The last chapter is a comparative analysis of female development in Dutch prose over several centuries. *Beatrijs* (*The Tale of Beatrice*), a Dutch Virgin Mary miracle tale from the Middle Ages (probably the first half of the fourteenth century), can be seen as a story of female development. I analyse the text using categories of gender, plot, social and narrative subject- and object-positions and endings. It seems that *Beatrijs* initiates a special tradition of narratives of female development in which characteristic narrative patterns, such as a circular storyline, 'a voyage in', recur. Literary works are in dialogue with each other. Therefore later works of female development in Dutch literature, such as *Sara Burgerhart* (1782) by Betje Wolff and Aagje Deken, *Van de koele meren des doods* (*Deeps of Deliverance*, 1900) by Frederik van Eeden, *Eva* (1928) by Carry van Bruggen, and *Een schitterend gebrek* (*In Lucia's Eyes*, 2006) by Arthur Japin are analysed using the same categories as in *Beatrijs* in search of thematic and structural parallels and differences. In all these, the category of gender seems to be essential in its effect on other analytical categories. The chapter examines not only the 'echo' of *Beatrijs* in later literary works of female development but — by means of corresponding reading — it also tries to give a new perception of the heroine Beatrijs herself as seen from the perspective of modern readings of modern stories.[24]

My position as a non-Dutch scholar of Dutch literature provides a different accent from that of some Dutch colleagues in the texts under discussion. The difficulties that this position may bring about are sensitively described by Jane Fenoulhet.[25] My decision to concentrate on ideological biases in literary works has to do with the society in which I grew up in Central Europe. Although not a colony in the traditional and historical sense of the word, Hungary fell under Soviet authority for forty years, during which time the supremacy of an ideology and permanent clash of ideologies were most prominently present even in everyday life. After the fall of the Berlin Wall in 1989 the country became a site or — to use a post-colonial term — a contact zone where several more ideologies met and struggled, and by now it is tending to regress to authoritarian ideas, presumed already long abandoned. In addition, Hungarian literature functioned for a long time as a mouthpiece of manifest or inherent ideologies. The connection between literature and ideology has always been the subject of vivid discussions. Therefore my choice for looking at how ideology works in literature is almost predestined, but it is also a sign of my engagement with equal human rights, emancipation, minorities, migrants, liberal democracy, and anti-racism.

Notes to the Introduction

1. Antal Bókay, *Bevezetés az irodalomtudományba* (Budapest: Osiris, 2006), p. 280.
2. Judit Gera, *Van een afstand: Multatuli's Max Havelaar tegendraads gelezen* (Amsterdam: Veen, 2001); Gera, 'De stem van Kirke. Een feministische lezing van "De zwijnen van Kirkè"', *Tijdschrift voor Genderstudies*, 7.2 (2004), 15–26; Judit Gera, '(Anti-)Koloniale tekststrategieën in *Tjoet Nja Din*', *Madelon Lulofs. Acta Neerlandica*, 5 (2007/5), 145–68; Judit Gera and A. Agnes Sneller, *Inleiding literatuurgeschiedenis voor de internationale neerlandistiek* (Hilversum: Verloren, 2010); Judit Gera, 'The Meaning of Silence in Max Havelaar', in *150 Jahre Max Havelaar/150 Years Max Havelaar*, ed. by Jaap Grave, Olf Praamstra, and Hans Vandevoorde (Frankfurt am Main: Peter Lang, 2012), pp. 125–32; Judit Gera, '*De Stille kracht* van Couperus als roman van hybridisatie', *Acta Neerlandica. Bijdragen tot de Neerlandistiek Debrecen* (, 9 (2012), 87–96; Judit Gera, 'Beatrijs en haar latere zusters. Narratieve structuren van de vrouwelijke ontwikkelingsverhalen', in *Lage Lande Studies 6. Beatrijs de wereld in. Vertalingen van het Middelnederlandse verhaal*, ed. by Ton van Kalmthout, Orsolya Réthelyi, and Remco Sleiderink (Gent: Academia Press, 2013), pp. 369–84.
3. Terry Eagleton, *Ideology: An Introduction* (London and New York: Verso, 2007).
4. Ibid., p. 22.
5. Dutch society was organized in ideological pillars from the end of the nineteenth century to the end of the 1960s. These pillars had their own institutions. The consensual character of Dutch politics had been formed by political representatives of these pillars who strived for mutual consent and compromise in their political decisions.
6. Maaike Meijer, *De lust tot lezen. Nederlandse dichteressen en het literaire systeem* (Amsterdam: Sara/Van Gennep, 1988).
7. Judit Gera, 'Momenten van zelfreflectie. Maaike Meijer: De lust tot lezen. Nederlandse dichteressen en het literaire systeem', *Internationale Neerlandistiek*, 50.1 (2012), 82–84.
8. The fulfilment of this approach was the five-volume series *Cultuur en migratie in Nederland* (2003–05), which maps the function and importance of migration in high and popular culture. Among the editors we find the most important representatives of the new approach to culture and literature: Rosemarie Buikema, Hester Dibbets, Isabel Hoving, Maaike Meijer, Marlou Schrover, and Wim Willems.
9. Ernst van Alphen, *Bang voor schennis? Inleiding in de ideologiekritiek* (Utrecht: HES, 1987).
10. Edward Said, *Orientalism* (New York: Vintage Books, 1979).

11. Mieke Bal, *De theorie van vertellen en verhalen. Inleiding in de narratologie* (Muiderberg: Coutinho), 1990); Mieke Bal, *Narratology: Introduction to the Theory of Narrative* (Toronto: University of Toronto Press, 1997).
12. Luc Herman and Bart Vervaeck, *Vertelduivels. Handboek verhaalanalyse* (Brussels and Nijmegen: Vantilt, 1987).
13. Susan Lanser, 'Toward a Feminist Narratology', in *Feminisms: An Anthology of Literary Theory and Criticism*, ed. by R. R. Warhol and D. Price Herndl (New Brunswick, NJ: Rutgers University Press, 1991), pp. 674–93.
14. Gérard Genette, *Narrative Discourse: An Essay in Method*, trans. by Jane E. Lewin (Ithaca, NY: Cornell University Press, 1980).
15. Mieke Bal, 'Reading as Empowerment: Teaching the Bible from a Feminist Perspective', in *Teaching the Bible as Literature in Translation*, ed. by Barry N. Olhsen and Yael S. Feldman (New York: Modern Language Association of America 1989); Maaike Meijer, *In tekst gevat. Inleiding tot een kritiek van representatie* (Amsterdam: Amsterdam University Press, 1996).
16. Anna Balakian, 'The Unfamiliar Literatures', in Anna Balakian, *The Snowflake on the Belfry: Dogma and Disquietude in the Critical Arena* (Bloomington and Indianapolis: Indiana University Press, 1994), pp. 236–40.
17. Van Alphen, 1987.
18. Willem van den Berg, Henk Eijssens, Joost Kloek, and Peter van Zonneveld, 'Inleiding', in Nicolaas Beets, *Camera Obscura*, ed. by Willem van den Berg, Henk Eijssens, Joost Kloek, and Peter van Zonneveld (Amsterdam: Athenaeum–Polak & Van Gennep, 1998), pp. 13–63.
19. Jacquelin Bel, 'Mansfield Park versus de Camera Obscura. "De familie Kegge" als koloniaal verhaal', in *Literatuurwetenschap tussen betrokkenheid en distantie* , ed. by Liesbeth Korthals Altes and Dick Schram (Assen: Van Gorcum, 2000), pp. 375–86.
20. Gera 2001.
21. Pamela Pattynama, 'Secrets and Danger: Interracial Sexuality in Louis Couperus's *The Hidden Force* and the Dutch Colonial Culture around 1900', in *Domesticating the Empire: Race, Gender and Family Life in French and Dutch Colonialism*, ed. by Julia Clancy-Smith and Frances Gouda (Charlottesville and London: The University Press of Virginia, 1998), pp. 84–107.
22. Meijer 1996; Toni Morrison, *Playing in the Dark: Whiteness and the Literary Imagination* (Cambridge, MA, and London: Harvard University Press, 1992).
23. Hans Vandevoorde, 'De onmacht die hem sarrend sloeg. Over Karel Van de Woestijne', in *Brussel en het fin-de-siècle. 100 jaar Van Nu en Straks*, ed. by F. de Crits (Antwerpen and Baarn: Houtekiet, 1993), pp. 105–16.
24. Odile Heynders, *Corrspondenties. Gedichten lezen met gedichten* (Amsterdam: Amsterdam University Press, 2006).
25. Jane Fenoulhet, *Making the Personal Political: Dutch Women Writers 1919–1970* (London: Modern Humanities Research Association and Maney Publishing, 2007), p. 1.

CHAPTER 1

The Colonial Subject as Subjugator: A Post-Colonial Reading of Bontekoe's *Journaal*

The Outside Context

The Beginnings of Dutch Colonization (East Indies)

Confronting the Dutch colonial past has begun only recently in the Netherlands. Publications which discuss this particular and important segment of Dutch history from a new point of view are part of this process. Piet Emmer's monograph *De Nederlandse slavenhandel 1500–1850* (*The Dutch Slave Trade 1500–1850*) is about the history of the Dutch slave trade.[1] In his 2008 book *Meer verleden dan toekomst. Geschiedenis van verdwijnend Nederland* (*More Past than Future: History of the Vanishing Netherlands*) Rudolf Dekker analyses the models of history writing past and present. He introduces the main turning-points of Dutch history — that of Dutch colonization among them — in an innovative, critical light.[2]

In his book Dekker gives an overview of Dutch colonization in the East Indies beginning with the Portuguese discovery of the sea route to South-East Asia. Bartolomeo Diaz sailed in 1487 to South Africa, while Vasco da Gama sailed to India in 1497–98. Seamen from the Low Countries worked on Portuguese ships from the very beginning. Jan Huygen van Linschoten (1563–1611), a Dutch seaman, sailed to the East Indies, also in the service of the Portuguese. He wrote various detailed descriptions of his voyage, of which *Itinerario* (*Itinerary*, 1596) is the most important.[3] This work came in handy for ships on their way to the East Indies. It was not until the end of the sixteenth century that Dutch ships set off for East Indies.

Dutch interest in the archipelago of the East Indies had a pragmatic basis: the Dutch wanted to take the monopoly on the clove trade from the Portuguese, who had 'discovered' the clove islands Ternate and Tidore as early as 1512.[4] The Dutch were later also interested in other spices such as nutmeg and pepper. The price of these spices was very high at that time in Europe. After some decades the Dutch were selling clove for fourteen times more than its buy-in price. The use of Eastern spices was already widespread in the Middle Ages. They were used mainly for seasoning meat, making cakes and wines more tasty, and even for scents, but also against fleas, for curing the sick, and allegedly also as aphrodisiacs.

Beyond commercial reasons, politics also paid an important role: from 1580 Spain and Portugal formed a single empire, and so in the Eighty Years War (1568–1648) the Dutch did everything in order to weaken the economic and military power not only of the Spanish but also of the Portuguese. The third motive — a common element of every colonial project — was the so-called 'civilizing mission', in other words: missionary work. The 'civilized' Dutch considered the Muslim, Buddhist, and Hindu peoples of the East Indian archipelago barbarians. They aimed at converting them to Protestantism.

Several small companies, the so-called 'compagnies', came to life at the end of the sixteenth century in order to organize sailing to the East Indies. The first one was called Compagnie van Verre (Company of Distant Regions). The first voyages were not always successful. The literally 'Eerste Scheepvaart' (First Voyage), also organized by Compagnie van Verre, set sail at the beginning of April 1595 with four ships under the command of Cornelis de Houtman (1565–1599), who had the manuscript of Van Linschoten's work *Reys-Geschrift van de Navigatiën der Portugaloyers* (*Record of the Navigation of the Portuguese*) to hand. It was more than a year before they reached Bantam on Java. The town was already a booming commercial centre. Half of the crew died on the way, and one of the four ships was also lost. As mentioned before, mushroom organizations similar to the very first one started up and they all began competing with each other from the harbours of Amsterdam, Hoorn, Enkhuizen, Delft, Rotterdam, Middelburg, and Veere. The statesman Johan van Oldenbarnevelt (1547–1619) realized, however, that it was worth uniting the several small organizations into one effective joint-stock company. It was his initiative that resulted in the Vereenigde Oost-Indische Compagnie (United East India Company), the VOC, in 1602. The arms of the company were designed by the painter Jeronimus Becx II: on the left there is Poseidon, on the right his wife, Amphitrite, with a mirror in her hand. Between them in the middle of the shield is a ship at sea flying Dutch flags. Underneath is seen a variety of shells, while above there are arrows, edged weapons, and navigation instruments.

The VOC was directed by seventeen men, De Heeren XVII (The XVII Gentlemen). The most respected institution of the young Republic, the Staten-Generaal or Parliament, endowed the Company with sovereign rights. This meant that the VOC could manage and defend its factories. These rights also extended to its operations, so in the long run a private enterprise was granted powers of state. This state of affairs lasted until 1799, when the VOC became bankrupt.

At the time of the VOC the East Indies were not only what we now know as Indonesia, but also the whole territory to the east of the Cape of Good Hope and to the west of the Straits of Magellan. The most important of these were: Mocha, Malabar, Coromandel, Ceylon, Bengal, Malacca, Java, the Molucca Islands, Formosa and Dejima. Vietnam, China, Yemen, Persia, Cambodia, and Thailand were also commercial partners of the VOC.

There was a special relationship between Japan and the VOC. Only the Dutch were allowed to trade with Japan at that time. Their headquarters were on the island of Dejima. The propagation of Christianity was forbidden there, as was the presence of European women. Sexual contact was only possible with geishas appointed for this kind of task. Jacob Coeman's painting *The Batavian Senior Merchant Pieter Cnoll and his Family* (1665) (see cover illustration) in the Rijksmuseum in Amsterdam is a good illustration of this. The painter worked as an employee of the VOC. His task was to console the sick in the East Indies. This painting was done in Batavia, and gives a precise picture of the hybridization between the Dutch and the Japanese: in the foreground we see Pieter Cnoll in an elegant black garment. He also was an employee of the VOC, and as such controlled the trade of Batavia. His wife and his two daughters, also dressed elegantly and in European style, stand at his side. His wife was born in Japan; her father was a Dutch merchant, her mother a Japanese courtesan. Not only the wife but also the two daughters have somewhat oriental features. One daughter holds a betel box in her hand, the other a fan, both objects symbolic of Eastern culture. Behind the married couple in the foreground stand two dark-skinned slaves, a boy and a girl. Like the other figures in the painting the boy was a real historical person who later ran away from his master. He fought first on the side of the Dutch, later on the side of his own people. The painting holds a mirror to Dutch colonial careers and to the meeting of cultures in which pure Dutch identity becomes hybrid as a result of mixing with Asian peoples.

The Dutch also played an important role in the spread of scientific and technical innovations. The small island of Dejima, not far from the harbour of Nagasaki in Japan, was between 1641 and 1859 a Dutch trading post, the only contact between the Western world and Japan. The Dutch brought several books to Japan on medical science, astronomy, mathematics, geometry, geography, military science, biology, pharmacy, etc. These books were soon translated into Japanese. Japan became open to the world only in 1853.

At first the VOC managed the spice trade from the Molucca islands. Later on, however, Batavia (its original name was Jayakarta or Jacatra) on the island of Java became the centre of management under the leadership of governor-general Jan Pieterszoon Coen (1587–1629). He built a new fort there. In 1621 he occupied the Banda islands — the only place where nutmeg was cultivated. This spice was considered a great luxury at that time in Europe, so Coen wanted it to be grown as efficiently as possible. In order to achieve this, he actually exterminated the whole population of these islands. Soldiers and officers of the VOC began to cultivate nutmeg, employing slaves. Peonage and the slave trade — already forbidden under seventeenth-century Dutch law — ended only in 1860 in the Dutch East Indies thanks to the political activities of the parliamentarian Walter Robert van Hoëvell (1812–79). The Dutch were notoriously inhumane in the seventeenth century in these islands: they worked slaves to death not only in the fields but also around the house. The tiniest fault was punished harshly. Coen's personal story also contributed to the negative image of the Dutch: the illegitimate daughter of another high-ranking VOC bureaucrat was allegedly caught *in flagrante delicto* with an officer Coen had the girl flogged, but the officer was beheaded. When the girl's father was appointed as his successor Coen allegedly died of horror.[5]

The seed capital of the VOC amounted to 6.5 million guilders. This amount was raised by issuing shares. Among the investors we find merchants, minor entrepreneurs, and even craftsmen. A major role in financing the VOC was played by the rich burghers from Antwerp who had fled to the northern parts of the Netherlands, and also by Portuguese Jews. During the existence of the VOC 4,700 voyages were made between the Netherlands and Asia by 1,772 ships, of which 629 vanished or sank. In the eighteenth century the importing of spices was challenged by that of coffee, tea, porcelain, textile, and opium. English and French competition developed. The maintenance and working of the VOC cost more and more money, which could not be covered. For that reason the company accumulated a huge debt, and corruption predominated. New employees lacked experience in the field of commerce and could not achieve the same results as their seventeenth-century predecessors. Book-keeping was inadequate and the cash-flow was not transparent. Between 1780 and 1784 the fourth Dutch-English War took place, which meant that Dutch ships from Asia could no longer reach the Netherlands. In 1781 the Company was unable to pay a dividend. Even the support of Parliament was not enough to stop the ultimate demise of the VOC. It became bankrupt in 1799, and all its debts and properties were taken over by the state.

Logbook, travel writing, travel literature

Texts about colonialism can be divided into several genres. Marijke Barend-van Haeften[6] distinguishes three main categories: logbook, travel writing, and fictitious (imaginary, utopian) travel literature. In the following paragraphs I shall give a short summary of her article.

As far as logbooks were concerned, there were no individual or literary ambitions involved. Keeping a logbook was compulsory for captains and high-ranking officers on VOC ships to Asia. Barend-van Haeften emphasizes that more than one logbook would be kept on the same ship depending on the function of the crew members. The captain wrote a logbook different from that kept by sailors, merchants, bookkeepers, surgeons, or consolers of the sick. Each ship to Asia was equipped with four logbooks, which contained the same categories. Date, heading, distance, latitude, longitude, weather conditions, and wind direction were noted on the left-hand side, while special data, events, reports on trade transactions, rest stops, revolts or pirate attacks, illnesses and deaths on the right. These logbooks lacked personal style; they had a pragmatic aim: they served as instructions for later sailors and mapmakers. They counted as confidential and could be used only by VOC employees. They were not available to the general public.

This general public, however, Barend-van Haeften argues, became more and more interested in the exotic vicissitudes and adventures of the ships going to and fro. Printers, working at that time also as publishers, began real campaigns in search of travel reports written on ships to Asia. These 'book-makers' gradually left out the dull shipping data of the logbooks, and the word 'logbook' was no longer mentioned on the title page or in the paratexts. The presence of the author became more prominent, the events described more adventurous and provided with more and more editorial comment. So printed versions of logbooks were different from the manuscripts because publishers reworked them more or less with regard to a wider reading public.

Travelogues were usually written after, not during, the voyage and they were more often reworked for the public than logbooks. More emphasis was put on specialities such as descriptions of far-away landscapes and their strange inhabitants. So the logbook yielded place to the travelogue. Van Linschoten's above-mentioned *Itinerario* can be put into this category. The author wrote his work on his way to Goa when serving with the Portuguese as a bookkeeper between 1583 and 1588. He returned to Enkhuizen in 1592 and his work, which was considered a colonial encyclopaedia, was published in 1596. It was translated into several languages and was considered the most important Dutch travelogue because of the importance of the political, commercial, and shipping information it contained. Another important travelogue is *Reisen en de Oost-Indische Spiegel* (*Voyages and the Mirror of the East Indies*) from 1701 written by Nicolaas de Graaff, a surgeon, who made sixteen voyages around the world.

Travel literature was born when imagination and fiction gained more and more ground in order to entertain the reader. One branch of this genre is so-called imaginary or utopian literature, which is about the mores, politics, economy, and culture of far-away countries represented in an idealistic way and holding up a mirror to European countries. An outstanding example of the genre is the work of the Dutch surgeon from Zwolle, Hendrik Smeeks (1645–1721), entitled *Beschryvinge van het Magtig Koningryk Krinke Kesmes* (*Descriptions of the Powerful Kingdom of Krinke Kesmes*) of 1708. Travel literature differs from the other two genres due to the predominance of fiction. A general name for the three genres — logbook, travelogue, and travel literature — proposed by Barend-van Haeften is travel texts.

Marijke Barend-van Haeften also summarizes in her article how these genres have been regarded in Dutch literary history. It was the writer Conrad Busken Huet (1826–86) who included logbooks and travelogues as parts of the national literature. According to Busken Huet, these texts were not written as literature but in order to spread scientific information. He argues that together with the *Staten–Bijbel*[7] (*Bible of the Seven Provinces*) these texts also contributed to the development of the standard language in the seventeenth century. Following Busken Huet, the literary historian Gerrit Kalff (1856–1923) also considered logbooks and travel writings as literature and he mentions these accordingly in his famous seven-volume literary history written at the turn of the twentieth century. Since that time this has become a tradition.

These texts could be considered escapist literature in their own time. Not every logbook or travelogue complied with the quality requirements of seventeenth-century literary standards. One of these was 'utile et dulce', useful and pleasant. That is why the most popular texts were not always the most adventurous ones. The style of narrating and the didactic content were just as important as the excitement and the quantity of new information.

Bontekoe's *Journaal* from a Historical, Cultural, and Literary Perspective

Jan Jansz. Deutel (?–c. 1652) was a publisher, bookseller, and 'rederijker' (rhetorician), that is, a writer himself, in Hoorn. He saw fantasy in Bontekoe's *Journaal*: the description of the exploding ship (see below) ensured great sensation, and other exotic adventures, supplemented by some Christian propaganda, guaranteed success on the book market at the time. The erudite literary expert Deutel edited the text and published it, and in so doing had an enormous success. The role and figure of Deutel will be further discussed later.

Dutch literary scholars have often dealt with Bontekoe's *Journaal* in the twentieth and twenty-first centuries. The *Journaal* undoubtedly belongs to the Dutch literary canon. However, the relationship between the *Journaal* and colonization is not brought out in these studies. This text is one of the first of Dutch colonial literature and as such it is inseparable from colonial ideology. It not only reflects this ideology but also actively takes part in constructing and transmitting it to further generations. It inscribes itself in the web of colonial texts which reproduce and strengthen stereotypes and prejudices related to the East. Therefore I shall read this text accordingly, and focus on that very colonial ideology under which the text was born and of which the text itself is a constituent. Before I begin analysing the text in this critical way, I shall give a short overview of the most important Dutch studies on the *Journaal* from the twentieth and twenty-first centuries.

The study by Vibeke Roeper and Diederick Wildeman[8] describes the historical and economic context. The town of Hoorn, where Willem Ijbrantsz Bontekoe was born, flourished in the sixteenth and seventeenth centuries. The most developed branches of industry were shipping and shipbuilding. The transportation of Norwegian wood, corn from the Baltic, and French and Portuguese salt was made possible by these activities. Hoorn was the most important Dutch port of the time, full of shipping entrepreneurs, cargo ships, seamen, and sailors. Here were the offices of the West Indian Company, the Northern Company, and the East Indian Company. Captains mostly did not own the ships. They were owned by several persons who had shares in the ownership. Most of the shareholders were merchants who did not take part in the everyday practice of shipping. Steering, crew and equipment were the responsibility of the captain.

The author of the *Journaal*, Willem Ysbrantsz (see Fig. 1.1), was born in 1587. His father, Ijsbrandt Willemsz, worked in European shipping as a captain. His ship, of which he was in command around 1600, was called *Bontekoe*. Before long the whole family was spoken of by this name, as was Willem Ysbrantsz as well. After his father's death he took over command of the *Bontekoe*. Before his famous voyage to the East Indies he had already been sailing for ten years in European waters: he sailed to France for salt and rye, to the Baltic for grain, to Norway for wood. He even went as far as Archangel, where he bought furs. Even European voyages were not safe. When he sailed to Seville in 1617 Berber pirates attacked the *Bontekoe*. The ship was taken to Algeria and the crew were imprisoned. Captain Bontekoe and one of his brothers, who was also a member of the crew, were almost sold as slaves, but one of the pirates bought them out. His name was Soliman Reis, a Dutchman

The Colonial Subject as Subjugator 17

Fig. 1.1. 'WILLEM YSBRANTZ BONTEKOE VAN HOORN', portrait of the man, almost frontal, half shape, with globe, compasses and cramp, open sea in the background, author unknown, Paper, 13.8 x 17.5 cm, Collectie Westfries Museum

who had become a Muslim. He paid 750 silvers for the brothers. They returned to Hoorn but, of course, without their ship. This was Willem Ysbrantsz Bontekoe's last European voyage.

Bontekoe was thirty-one when he entered the service of the VOC. Hoorn was one of the VOC's chambers. Bontekoe was appointed captain of the *Nieuw Hoorn* and had a crew of 150 under his command. The captain of a ship going to the East Indies had to have a thorough knowledge of ocean navigation, and had to take an examination to prove it. Most people undertook the dangerous and unsafe journey, which lasted at least nine months, because compared to other paid work those in the service of the VOC were given a safe contract good for three or five years, together with full board and lodging. Those who did not die on the voyage were rich for the rest of their lives.

As Roeper and Wildeman argue, Bontekoe might also have had religious motives besides financial considerations in joining the VOC. As a member of the Remonstrant community he had to experience critical times. The liberal Remonstrants were opposed by the orthodox Calvinists or anti-Remonstrants. Their conflicts became so sharp that there was a danger of civil war. The Remonstrant community eventually became the losing party in the disputes and they were obliged to subject themselves to laws which discriminated against them.

It is notable that Roeper and Wildeman, while describing the beginnings of Dutch colonization, consider the presence of the Dutch in Asia as an obvious, almost an unquestionable, necessity. That is the case when they point out why it was a necessity to set up Dutch communities and administration in the Dutch East Indies. The reason was, so they say, that sailing to and fro was unprofitable. The authors emphasize that trading was carried on with the consent of the local potentates — and that was true of course, but the whole truth is that the VOC acquired its commercial monopoly by playing those very local potentates off against one another. Another strange thing is that Roeper and Wildeman consider Jacatra as a much less important seaport than the islands of Banda, Ambon, and Ternate. However, this town was the biggest harbour of the Sunda Monarchy in the twelfth century and the Portuguese built a fort there at the beginning of the sixteenth. On 22 June 1527 the leader of one of the nearby Northern Monarchies, Fatahillah, gave the name Jayakarta to the Hindu settlement which had originally been called Kalapa. The word 'Jayakarta' means 'victorious' and 'flourishing' in Javanese. The renaming of Jacatra as Batavia — forcing the town to become Dutch — also seems quite natural to the authors. So their description presents the situation as if the town of Jayakarta or Jacatra had been quite unimportant before the appearance of the Dutch on the one hand, and on the other hand they gloss over the responsibility of the Dutch for the bloody and violent aspects of the events which took place when they moved in, and for the basic asymmetry and injustice of the relationships. This rhetoric of the cultural-historical essay implicitly maintains colonial ideology, and reproduces colonial discourse by presenting events and processes as natural and necessary, while in fact they took place in accordance with colonial interests and conscious social decisions. In this way the authors legitimize the Dutch presence in the East Indies even at a later date, but they do not even discuss the legitimation of this presence in the colonies.

Quite surprising is also the way Karel Bostoen discusses Bontekoe's *Journaal* in the same volume.[9] He focuses on the aesthetic values of the *Journaal* and on the problem of authorship. The original *Journaal* was, of course, destroyed together with the ship when it blew up. When Bontekoe arrived at Batavia after a perilous voyage he was received by Coen, who wrote a report on Bontekoe's oral account of his adventures. Bontekoe wrote his travelogue around 1626 when he returned to Holland, but the manuscript about the period 1618–25 has been lost, although Deutel makes mention of it in his own somewhat rewritten edition dedicated to the leaders of the VOC. According to Bostoen, the dramatic style of the *Journaal* is probably due to the conversations between Bontekoe and Deutel about the voyage. As already mentioned, Deutel had written some literary works before editing the *Journaal*. In 1641 he wrote a moralizing poem *De Huwelyckx Weeg-schaal* (*The Scales of Marriage*) supplied with illustrations. His *Een kort tractaetje tegen de toovery* (*Short Tractate against Sorcery*) of 1638 was published posthumously in 1670. He was an active member of the chamber of rhetoric *De Rood' Angieren* (*Red Carnations*) in Hoorn. In the same year as he published Bontekoe's *Journaal* he won first prize in a competition held by the Hoorn chambers of rhetoric. Members of *De Rood' Angieren* wrote poems in praise of Bontekoe's *Journaal*, which contributed greatly to the success of the book. Karel Bostoen deduces the literary values of the work from this background of the chambers of rhetoric. Seventeenth-century Dutch prose was often written in the style of works from antiquity. It was Justus Lipsius (1547–1606), a humanist of the Low Countries, who published the works of Tacitus and Seneca with commentaries. Bostoen shows that Lipsius's style was characterized by short sentences, striking phrases, puns, and antitheses. The most important Dutch representative of this style was Pieter Cornelisz. Hooft (1581–1647). He used Lipsius's edition for his translation of Tacitus. According to Bostoen, Deutel probably possessed Hooft's main work, *Nederlandsche Historiën* (*Histories of the Netherlands*), written in the style of the ancient authors mentioned above and published in 1642. It was this work which might have influenced him in editing Bontekoe's *Journaal*. Another source of the style was, as Bostoen argues, Dutch baroque drama, such as *Aran en Titus* (*Aran and Titus*, 1641) by Jan Vos (1612–67). These dramas abounded in horrifying, bloody scenes, exciting adventures and blood-curdling disasters. So Bostoen recognizes the figure of Bontekoe in the hero-types of baroque drama, namely in those who show a combination of classical and Christian virtues. Bontekoe's wisdom is typical of the former while his pious faith illustrates the latter. Bostoen attributes the literary quality of the text to Deutel, who edited it following the literary fashion of the time. Bostoen, however, acknowledges the vividness of the adventures as an accomplishment of Bontekoe himself, whom he calls 'the hero of a blood-curdling drama'.

The problem of colonization itself does not play a role in Bostoen's analysis. He glosses over it by researching only the literary and stylistic elements of the text and its effects over the centuries. My thesis is that historical descriptions as well as the study of aesthetic values may adumbrate the delicate questions of colonization itself and redirect the reader's attention. Situating the text of the *Journaal* in the tradition of Roman history writing and literature, which are generally considered by Europeans as one of the sources of European culture, legitimates the colonial ideology of the text by raising it to a level at which it becomes immaculate.

That part of the recent *History of Dutch Literature* that discusses the period between 1560 and 1700 also, of course, deals with logbooks, among them Bontekoe's *Journaal*.[10] Besides the information mentioned above we also learn that Deutel, the editor of the book, was an Anabaptist. Therefore the history of Bontekoe in his edition became a model text of the type which was read by the contemporary Dutch as an apotheosis of the new, persevering, solid faith. Another point is that the *Journaal* appeared on the contemporary book market as a typical piece of entertaining literature, satisfying the insatiable curiosity of readers about foreign landscapes, spectacular events, disasters, strange animals, and cannibals. These authors do not consider the meeting of cultures as the most crucial point of the *Journaal*, but they do mention the dodo, an exotic bird which Bontekoe saw on the island of Mauritius.

In his article *De Indisch-Nederlandse literatuur uit de VOC-tijd* (*Dutch Indies Literature in the period of the VOC*) Bert Paasman counts the seventeenth and eighteenth centuries as belonging to the pre-colonial period.[11] This was opposed by Theo D'haen, the editor of the volume in which Paasman's article was published. In the 'Introduction', Theo D'haen points out that white Europeans legitimated their colonial adventures with a self-evident superiority which they sustained throughout five centuries.[12] He places the beginnings of European colonialism in the early sixteenth century, which means that Bontekoe's *Journaal* also belongs to the colonial period and its literature. Paasman is, however, right when he says that the importance of the texts written in the seventeenth and eighteenth centuries lies not so much in history writing, but much more in studies researching the changing representations of the East Indian colonies. Another substantial statement is that it was not Coen who gave a new name to Jacatra, but the leaders of the VOC, the so-called Seventeen. Paasman does not, however, mention that the name 'Batavia' was ideologically laden, as it was a reference to the Batavians, who were considered to have been the mythical forefathers of the Dutch. So the fact that it was not Coen but the Seventeen who renamed Jacatra as Batavia may be relevant for historians, but it does not alter the basically annexing, colonial gesture of the new naming. By not elaborating on this Paasman neglects the very aspects that he considers more important than history writing.

In his analysis of Bontekoe's *Journaal*, Paasman writes further about the silver coins and explosives which the ship was transporting to the East Indies. When the ship blew up 'ongeveer honderdvijftig opvarenden kwamen om, maar door Gods hulp werd de schipper gered [...] Bijna zoals in een middeleeuwse Marialegende wordt de vrome schipper gered' [about hundred and fifty sailors died, but with the help of God the captain was saved [...] Almost as in a medieval Maria-legend the pious captain was saved].[13] When Paasman, in describing the contents of the book, comes to the arrival of Bontekoe and his men at the coast of Sumatra, he mentions 'een nieuw gevaar' [a new danger] which 'dreigt van gevaarlijke inlanders' [the threat coming to them from dangerous natives].[14] Paasman summarizes the story, identifying himself with the narrator (Bontekoe) and without maintaining any distance. However, he attributes the religious message of the text to Deutel and not to Bontekoe: those who believe in God are saved by God. Paasman also elaborates on the lesser-known second part of the travelogue, in which Bontekoe transports coral limestones for the building of the Castle in Jacatra, supplies VOC stations with food, and takes spices from them. In 1622 Bontekoe took part in a Chinese expedition too, because the VOC wanted to play a bigger part in the silk trade between China and Japan. The Chinese undertaking failed. Bontekoe returned eventually to his fatherland aboard the *Hollandia* at the age of thirty-eight. The *Journaal* had already been reprinted in 1648 and it appeared in more than seventy editions before 1800. It has been translated into several languages, among others into Javanese, Sundanese, Malay, and Chinese.

In short: Paasman's study analysing Bontekoe's *Journaal* does not examine the representation of Dutch colonization of the East Indies either, while he himself says that the importance of researching these documents lies only in the study of representations. I have not yet found a thorough study in the secondary literature on Bontekoe's *Journaal* that identifies the work as a cultural document of Dutch colonization and provides a discourse analysis of the text. I shall try to do this in the next section in order to show the explicit colonial orientation of the text. This means that I interpret the *Journaal* as a textual contact zone 'where cultures meet, clash, and grapple with each other, often in contexts of highly asymmetrical relations of power, such as colonialism, slavery, or their aftermaths[...]'.[15]

Rhetorical Context and Plot

Bontekoe's 'Journaal' (1646)

As already mentioned, Bontekoe describes his voyages between 1618 and 1625 as a captain in the service of the VOC (see Fig. 1.2). He was employed on the second biggest ship ever built by the VOC chamber of Hoorn, named *Nieuw Hoorn*. The voyage began with a fleet of seven ships. After some months the *Nieuw Hoorn* lost sight of the other ships. There was an outbreak of scurvy, so Bontekoe looked for a possible place to rest and recuperate on the island of Réunion between Madagascar and Mauritius. After five months they sailed back to Madagascar in order to stock up their water and food supplies (see Fig. 1.3). Two months later their ship was in the neighbourhood of the Sunda Strait. One afternoon fire broke out on the ship and it blew up (see Fig. 1.4). Of the 206 crew seventy-two men escaped on the nine-metre longboat. Of these, sixty-five survived the tragedy. The unfortunate survivors even thought about eating their younger companions for lack of food. They tried to catch seagulls and flying fish. Eventually the Sunda Strait came in sight. Near Bantam the boat met a big VOC fleet. Bontekoe and the leader of the merchants, Heyn Rol, were brought to the governor-general, Jan Pietersz Coen. Coen gave Bontekoe command first of an old, poorly equipped ship; later on, however, he was appointed to the beautiful *Groningen*. After this, Bontekoe worked for five years in Coen's service. He made several voyages between Batavia and the nearby islands, and visited Sumatra and the Molucca islands very often. He took part in offensives against several Chinese villages, the aim of which was to develop a permanent

FIG. 1.2. The cover of the first Dutch edition of the *Journal* of Bontekoe. Paper, Leiden University Libraries 1365 G 62: 1

Fig. 1.3. The Dutchmen on the ship Santa Maria, at Madagascar.
Paper, Leiden University Libraries 1365 G 62: 1

Fig. 1.4. The explosion of the ship Nieuw Hoorn.
Paper, Leiden University Libraries 1365 G 62: 1

commercial station on the Chinese coast. The Dutch were first defeated by the Portuguese and later by the Chinese. The day came when Bontekoe felt homesick and he returned to Holland.

The *Journaal* became famous because of the description of the voyage from Holland to the East Indies. This was the result and also the cause of the same mapping impulse which Svetlana Alpers considers one of the most characteristic features of seventeenth-century Dutch culture.[16] In its original verbal function the *Journaal* could serve as a verbal map. It is questionable, however, whether a written document such as the *Journaal* 'can offer a detached or perhaps even a culturally unbiased view of what is to be known in the world', as Alpers puts it when writing about 'mapped history'.[17] Because the text is not only descriptive but also narrative, an impartial view is not possible. The point of view is not neutral but much too personal, strongly rooted in its cultural and social context. The reader is offered the perspective of the first-person narrator to identify with, and we see the world described in the *Journaal* through his subjugating eyes.

The *Journaal* became popular not only because of the sensational events surrounding the blowing up of the ship, in my view, but also because it could be read as propaganda for the material and intellectual wealth of the young Republic. What we should not forget, however, is that this economic, scientific, technical, navigational, cartographic, and religious propaganda was used not only to strengthen the good name of the Republic, but also in order to make colonization possible.

The *Journal* begins with the self-introduction of the narrator:

> In het jaar onzes Heren 1618, op 28 december, ben ik Willem Ysbrantsz. Bontekoe uit Hoorn, als schipper van Texel uitgevaren met het schip de Nieuw Hoorn, dat bemand was met 206 koppen en ongeveer 350 last mat. Er stond een oostenwind.[18]

> [In the year of Our Lord 1618, the 28th December, I, Williams Ysbrantsz Bontekoe of Hoorn, set sail from Texel, being captain of the ship named *New-Hoorn*, manned with 206 men, of size about 1,100 tons, the wind being East.][19]

This first sentence already informs us about the exact place and time of the events, the most important data of the ship, and the identity of the first-person narrator: a burgher brought up in the Netherlands whose occupation is closely connected to the colonies, that is, a captain of a ship in Hoorn. As I mentioned before, Hoorn was a town of great importance, because it had an office not only of the VOC but also of the Company of the West Indies, and the town was also the centre of the territories above the river IJ in the sixteenth and seventeenth centuries. It was the birthplace of Jan Pietersz Coen, the main figure of Dutch colonization, who was responsible for the mass murder of thousands on the island of Banda. The town of Hoorn can be considered as the metonym for Dutch colonial enterprise in the East Indies.

The 'I' in the text is a construct partly of Bontekoe and partly of Deutel. This double construct of 'I' was created in accordance with well-defined interests and embodies also the colonizing subject of the *Journaal*. His story (history), reading it back from the present day, cannot be considered a purely literary work independent of its contemporary political and social circumstances. Bontekoe is part of the colonial enterprise because of his strong roots in his sociocultural context. He acquires authorization, not only in the sense of becoming an author of a journal but also in a colonial sense: his task is to go out and colonize. The first — being an author — is rather a result of the second — going out to colonize.

He becomes captain of the *Nieuw Hoorn*, transporting gunpowder for Coen on behalf of the VOC. His aim was not scientific or cultural, nor even commercial in the first place, but military and subjugating. This consideration cannot be neglected in the analysis of the *Journaal*.

There are several aspects of Bontekoe's identity, and the textual representation of these aspects takes our mind off the subjugating character of the enterprise. One such aspect of his identity is his Christianity. He often alludes to this during his adventures. It is important to know that his religious denomination is also a new identity: the Eighty Years War was fought partly for the legitimation of this new denominational identity, namely Protestantism. In the East Indies Bontekoe used the triumph over the Spaniards, who had persecuted Protestantism, in order to prove the hard-won superiority of his denomination. Bontekoe's gaze is determined by his Dutch and Protestant identity, and it is this very gaze with which he looks at the East Indian archipelago and its indigenous people. This position creates one of the most important binary oppositions of the work, that is, the opposition between Christianity and 'paganism'. How does this show in the rhetoric of the text? Anaphoric constructions are conspicuous at certain points. At the beginning of the *Journaal* we read:

> De 29e van die maand zijn wij de Hoofden gepasseerd.
> De 30e kregen wij 's avonds Portsmouth in zicht, nog steeds bij een oostenwind; de 31e passeerden wij Plymouth.
> Op 1 januari 1619 voeren we Lands End voorbij, nog steeds met dezelfde wind, waarna we in zee staken, koers zuidwest ten zuiden.
> Op 2 januari ruimde de wind naar het zuidoosten en hielden we bij een stijve bries een zuid-zuidwesterlijke koers aan.
> Op 3 januari ruimde de wind naar het zuiden; terwijl het stevig woei voeren we westzuidwest.
> De 4e ruimde de wind naar zuidwest en wakkerde zo aan, dat wij de marszeilen moesten innemen. 's Nachts begon het zelfs zo hard te waaien dat wij ook de fok innamen. Met nog maar één zeil bij weken we steeds meer naar het westen uit.[20]

> [The 29th day we passed the Heads.
> The 30th day, in the evening, we sighted Portland, the wind still easterly. The 31st day we passed Plymouth.
> The 1st January 1619 we passed England's End, the wind being the same, and set our course out to sea, S.W. by S.
> The 2nd day the wind veered to S.E.; set our course to S.S.W.
> The 3rd day the wind changed to South with a stiff breeze; set our course to W.S.W.
> The 4th day the wind came S.W. with increasing force, so that we were compelled to take in our topsails During the night the wind blew so hard that we took in the foresail and lay to westward with one sail.][21]

This anaphoric rhetoric of the text reminds one of certain passages in the Dutch translation of the Bible, for example the description of the Exodus of the Israelites from Egypt:

> Zij reisden dan van Raméses; in de eerste maand, op den vijftienden dag der eerste maand, des anderen daags van het pascha, togen de kinderen Israëls uit door een hoge hand, voor de oogen van alle Egyptenaren;
> Als de Egyptenaars begroeven degenen, welke de HEERE onder hen geslagen had, alle eerstgeborenen; ook had de HEERE gerichten geoefend aan hun goden.
> Als de kinderen Israëls van Raméses verreisd waren, zo legerden zij zich te Sukkoth.
> En zij verreisden van Sukkoth, en legerden zich in Etham, hetwelk aan het einde der woestijn is.
> En zij verreisden van Etham, en keerden weder naar Pi-hachirôth, dat tegenover Baäl-Sefon is, en zij legerden zich voor Migdol.
> En zij verreisden van Hachirôth, en gingen over, door het midden van de zee, naar de woestijn, en zij gingen drie dagreizen in de woestijn Etham, en legerden zich in Mara.[22]

> [And they departed from Rameses in the first month, on the fifteenth day of the first month; on the morrow after the passover the children of Israel went out with an high hand in the sight of all the Egyptians.
> For the Egyptians buried all their firstborn, which the LORD had smitten among them: upon their gods also the LORD executed judgments.
> And the children of Israel removed from Rameses, and pitched in Succoth.
> And they departed from Succoth, and pitched in Etham, which is in the edge of the wilderness.
> And they removed from Etham, and turned again unto Pihahiroth, which is before Baalzephon: and they pitched before Migdol.
> And they departed from before Pihahiroth, and passed through the midst of the sea into the wilderness, and went three days' journey in the wilderness of Etham, and pitched in Marah ...][23]

The quotation from the Dutch text is about the dislocation essential to the colonial enterprise travelling from Europe to the East and vice versa. Dislocation is important not only in a geographic sense but also in an intellectual and cultural sense. Bontekoe and his companions take a whole culture and infrastructure with them on their ship, transporting this culture and infrastructure into another context. Their ship is actually a small floating piece of the Netherlands. It contains almost every achievement of Western civilization up to that time. There is a high degree of division of labour on the ship; one can find all kinds of occupations — bakers, welfare officers, sail-makers, smiths, ropers, and several other representatives of different professions. There was a special function, such as the reader of psalms in order to console the sick. Beyond that the ship was a storehouse of technical instruments such as a compass, a square, different charts, calipers, and several other things. A telling circumstance is that the crew of the ship had such a detailed knowledge of these instruments that they could cope even after the ship had blown up, and were even able to reproduce them:

> De barbier was ook wel bij ons aan boord, maar hij had geen medicamenten.
> Hij kauwde echter wat brood en legde het kauwsel op de wonden, waarmee

ik door Gods genade genas. [...] We bepaalden onze koers aan de hand van de sterren, want we wisten wel ongeveer waar die behoorden op te komen en onder te gaan. De koers uitzetten deden we dus 's nachts. [...] Op 21, 22, en 23 november maakten we een graad-boog, om op de hoogte mee te nemen: we tekenden een kwadrant op de plecht, en brachten op een stok met dwarslat de graadverdeling aan. We hadden de kistenmaker Teunis Sybrantsz. uit Hoorn aan boord, en die had een passer. Hij beschikte ook over enige kennis om een graadverdeling te maken, zodat we met elkaar dus een graadboog vervaardigden en instelden, waarmee we de zon schoten. Bovendien sneed ik op het achterdek een zeekaart uit, waarop ik Sumatra aangaf, alsmede Java en Straat Sunda tussen beide eilanden in.[24]

[The barber we had with us in the boat, but he had no medicaments; so he chewed some bread and laid it therewith on the wounds, by which (by God's favour) I was cured. [...] We then began to set our course by the stars, for we knew well enough where the stars should rise and set; so we set our course in the night time. [...] The 21st, 22nd and 23rd November we put together a sextant to take our height; we cast a quadrant on the quarter deck and drew a stick with a cross piece therefrom. We had the coffin maker, Teunis Sybrantsz, of Hoorn, in the boat, and he had a pair of compasses. He had also some knowledge of drawing a stick so that together in that way we made and shaped a sextant, with which we shot the sun. I also cut a sea-chart on the board aft and laid the island of Sumatra therein, with the island of Java and the Strait of Sunda that runs in between the two islands.][25]

These instruments were in fact the embodiments and the textual representation of the power derived from the wide, modern, scientific, technical, and practical knowledge of seventeenth-century Holland. The first quotation from the *Journaal* contains the rhetoric of monotonous repetitions, and with good reason: the additive inventory of the wind and the geographical directions and the technical means of navigating are given greater emphasis by repeating them, and they also play a crucial role in orientation both in the literal and in the metaphorical sense of the word. We should recall the religious origin of the word 'orientation', which contains 'orient' (i.e. 'east') in it. The word means actually 'facing east'. Churches were usually constructed with their main altar at the eastern end, literally and spiritually orienting believers to the east, meaning Jerusalem, the common geographic place of Judaism, Islam, and Christianity.[26]

There are several Dutch portraits and still lifes where representations of knowledge are displayed in a similar additive way as in the *Journaal*. Examples are the painting by Jan van der Heyden, dated *c.* 1712, in the Museum of Fine Arts in Budapest, *Stilleven met rariteiten* (*Still Life with Rarities*), or the painting by Thomas de Keyzer, *Portret van Constantijn Huygens en zijn secretaris* (*Portrait of Constantijn Huygens and his Clerk*), dating from 1627, in The National Gallery, London.

I consider the biblical rhetoric of the long march of the Jews from Egypt as a textual prefiguration of the description of Bontekoe's long voyage from Holland to the East Indies. This biblical colouring, which might have been obvious to the contemporary reader, gives a mythical magic to the voyage, legitimizing the colonial enterprise, as it were. This mixture of biblical faith and modern science offered to its burghers by the Dutch Republic proved to be a basic instrument of power against the newly discovered world. Both faith and knowledge represent obvious interests here. A telling example of this fusion of professional expertise and Christian faith is the following comparison: 'Wij verheugden ons zeer, want onze mast stond er weer zo fraai bij dat het een lust was om te zien — hij was nu bijna zo dik als een kerkpilaar[27] [we all mightily rejoiced, for there our mast stood again so fine it was a pleasure to see. It was nearly as thick as a pillar of a church].[28] The picture cited compares the equipment of the ship to the architecture of a church. As Bontekoe himself admits, the comparison of the mast to the pillar of a church originates from the writing of the earlier mentioned voyager, Jan Huygen van Linschoten. At a later point in the journal Bontekoe refers to him explicitly when he is describing the Chinese river Zhangzhou and the landscape around it:

> Deze rivier is onmiskenbaar, want zoals Jan Huygen van Linschoten schrijft: op de ene hoek aan de noordoostzijde liggen twee heuvels, waarvan er één net een kerkpilaar is, en aan de zuidwesthoek van de rivier ziet men leeg duinlandschap, met een weinig landinwaarts een toren of althans iets wat daarop lijkt.[29]
>
> [This river is easily recognizable, for such as Jan Huygen van Linschoten doth relate: at the corner on the N.E. side are two hills, one of which is like the pillar of a church, and the S.W. side of the river is low, sandy ground, and a little to the inside of the S.W. corner can be seen a tower or what has the likeness thereof.][30]

Bontekoe's text contributes thus to the dynamic semantic space of previous texts by taking over and repeating words and figures of speech containing what, from his point of view, are basic messages, thereby intensifying their meaning. Van Linschoten's texts are descriptions of observations and information indeed, and Bontekoe goes out sailing relying on these. His story appears as part of a cognitive and cultural tradition. This leads gradually to a grammar of colonization. This grammar consists of names, modes of name-giving, and other symbolic acts. Changing the name of Jacatra to Batavia is an example of deculturation when an original, indigenous culture is violently replaced by a foreign dominant culture.[31] Deculturation begins very often with new name-giving, deleting and overwriting old names. There is a close relationship between place, history, and language.

The blowing up of the ship itself is a narrative turning point, both a divide from and a link to Europe and non-Europe, home and not-home, 'we' and 'they'. As mentioned earlier, the cultural representations of the Orient contributed to the dichotomy between Europeans and non-Europeans. Thinking in binary oppositions is partly due just to these texts: if Europe is civilized, the Orient is barbarian, if true faith is a specific trait of Europeans, non-Europeans are heathens, if Europe has qualities attributed to men, such as domination, knowledge, culture, the colony is given characteristics attributed to women, such as being subjugated, emotional, and natural. In this respect it is interesting to examine what kind of an image of the indigenous people of the East Indies is constructed by Dutch seamen in the *Journaal*. On meeting them for the first time at the bay of St. Lucia, the Dutch do not understand the language of the inhabitants:

> Toen zagen we een paar mensen het strand op komen; een van onze maats sprong overboord en voegde zich bij hen, maar hij kon ze niet verstaan. Ze

> wezen met hun handen naar het zuiden, alsof ze zeggen wilden dat daar wel een plaats was om te meren.³²
>
> [we saw many people come on the shore and one of our men sprang overboard and got them, but he could not understand them, they waved their hands downwards as it were to say that there was a place to land.]³³

There is no immediate linguistic contact between the indigenous and the Dutch. As a consequence the Dutch have only preconceptions about what the indigenous are up to. In spite of the fact that this quotation is rather about the helpfulness than any animosity of the natives, they are sometimes called 'animals' or 'fools', or 'barbarians'. There are many remarks on the colour of their skin which the Dutch see as yellowish-black:

> We bekeken dit volk met verbazing. We boden hun wijn aan in een zilveren schaal, maar in plaats van die normaal op te drinken, staken ze hun hoofd of gezicht in de schaal en dronken ze net zoals dieren uit een emmer. En toen ze de wijn in 't lijf hadden gingen ze tekeer als gekken. Dit volk was geheel naakt, op een lendendoekje na dat de schaamdelen bedekte, en ze waren geelachtig zwart van kleur.³⁴
>
> [We did much marvel at these people. We gave them wine to drink from a silver bowl, yet they had not the sense to know how to drink therefrom, but stuck their head or face in the basin and drank as does a beast from a bucket, and when the wine was in them they did bawl like as if they were mad. These people were stark naked save for a cloth round their middle to hide their private parts; they were in colour a yellowish black.]³⁵

This is a typical example of the rhetoric of difference. The distinguishing characteristics attached to the indigenous identify the Dutch implicitly as 'men', 'normal', 'civilized', and 'educated'. The difference of the indigenous is repeatedly emphasized, for example at the following meeting:

> Wij konden geen blijken van godskennis of godsdienst bij deze mensen bespeuren, maar op sommige plaatsen hadden ze buitenshuis wel ossenhoofden op staken opgericht, en we zagen ze er wel eens voor neervallen om te aanbidden; het leken vreemde lieden, zonder gevoel voor de ware God.³⁶
>
> [We found in them no sign of any knowledge of God or any religion, but they had in some places outside their houses the heads of oxen fixed on poles, before which (it seemed to us) they fell down and worshipped; this appeared mighty strange and without sense of the true God.]³⁷

The text displays the puzzlement of the Dutch observer about those who apparently are not acquainted with Christianity. 'True' God means culture, the well-known, the homely, while the ritual worship of 'heads of oxen fixed on poles' is nature, the unknown, the strange.³⁸ This is an illustration of the colonizing character of the hierarchic gaze. Later in the text we find similar figures of speech such as 'thank God' or 'with the help of God' or 'by the grace of God', which, by way of repetition and the Christian implications, legitimize colonial practices.

When the sailors are tossing in the boat after the explosion, they suddenly feel so hungry that they almost think of eating each other. This is a moment when the European stereotype about cannibalism and indigenous people is reversed: the power of hunger makes cannibals of the civilized Dutch. In this dramatic moment Bontekoe begins to pray to God again not to let things come to that. God seems to help him to discourage his mates from doing such a thing: 'Ik zei: "Mannen, laat ons dat niet doen; God zal wel uitkomst geven, volgens onze dagelijkse berekeningen kunnen we immers niet ver meer van land zijn."'[39] [Men, let us not do this thing. God will deliver us, for we cannot be far from land, as shown by our daily measurements].[40] In addition to solid faith in God, once again a specific knowledge of latitude and longitude, the positions of the stars, and other daily calculations is needed here in order to save the sailors and for them to reach their destination. Curiously enough, after the explosion a psalm book remains intact, from which they sing psalms if needed. There appears another biblical hint: Bontekoe becomes so disappointed and hopeless at a certain point that he has to withdraw from his mates, and he climbs a nearby mountain to pray to stay alive and find the right way. Contemporary readers could easily recognize in his figure Moses, who led his people out of the desert to Canaan.

When they make landfall they are afraid of the people living there, although they had had only positive experiences with the indigenous thus far. It is their own fear they project onto the East Indians:

> [...] verschenen de inlanders, met de bedoeling om ons daar allemaal dood te slaan, zoals aanstonds zal blijken. [...] We namen daarom brandende takken in de hand en trokken daarmee tegen hen op in het donker; [...] Ze vluchtten weg van ons, het bos in, en wij keerden terug naar onze vuren.[41]

> [[...] the inhabitants of the land came with intent to slay us all, as I shall hereafter describe. [...] taking up burning faggots in our hands, we set off towards them in the dark; [...] They took flight away from us, behind the woods, and we returned again to our fires [...]].[42]

'Hereafter' it turns out that the indigenous do not intend to kill them at all; quite the contrary, they give the Dutch rice and chicken for free. Prejudices about 'wild natives' and 'civilized Europeans' are defied by the text itself.

One of the characteristics of European discourse about the 'other' is that the narrator describes the 'other' as a member of a group while the Dutch are represented always as individuals, with name and history. There is only one exception to this in the text, a Chinese man who mediates between the Dutch and another Chinese person. He does have a name: Cipzuan. They meet in the contact zone, where they exchange data with one another, and the 'other' may have a name because he is the one who mediates between Europeans and non-Europeans. The contact zone also gains importance when colonizers become dependent on natives. This is when colonizers need food or familiarity with the terrain.

Natives are much less aggressive in the whole narrative than the Dutch. The latter mix trade with military violence. Musketeers go out hunting, plundering, stealing bulls, pigs, chickens, setting villages on fire, confiscating boats, and killing their occupants. It is Jan Pietersz Coen, the governor-general, who gives orders to carry out similar military actions. The narrator tells us: 'De 18e kregen we opdracht om met acht zeilen, te weten drie schepen en vijf jachten, naar de Zhangzhou en de Chinese kust te gaan, om te zien of wij hen met dreiging van onze vijandschap en geweld niet tot handel konden bewegen'.⁴³ [The 18th day we, namely eight sail, three ships and five sloops, were ordered to go to the river Chinchu and the coast of China to see if through fear of our enmity and force we could move them to traffic with us [...]].⁴⁴ Christian piety and European culture are apparently not an obstacle to this kind of violence. Coen's motto is: 'Dispereert niet, ontziet uw vijanden niet, want God is met ons' [Do not despair, do not fear your enemies, because God is with us]. Bontekoe takes this mentality over without any problem. The two greatest achievements of the young Republic, namely, the Protestant faith and trading combined with scientific knowledge, are put at the service of colonial violence.

There is also an example of cultural exchange in the *Journaal*. One of these concerns music:

> Als we aan land gingen namen we meestal een speelman mee die op de viool speelde. De bevolking van het eiland verwonderde zich daar uitermate over, ze waren zo nieuwsgierig dat ze niet wisten hoe ze het hadden — ze gingen eromheen zitten en staan, knipten met hun vingers, dansten en sprongen, en waren vrolijk en verheugd.⁴⁵

> [Going on shore we took often a musician with us who played on the fiddle, the which did much astonish the people of the country, indeed it was a thing so new to them that they could make nothing of it; they sat and stood around, snapped their fingers, danced and capered and rejoiced right merrily.]⁴⁶

Non-verbal art forms such as music know no borders; they can cheer up people and entertain them regardless of the colour of their skins or the languages they speak. It also happens when Bontekoe is sitting between two natives in a boat and he is suddenly seized by fear:

> Daar zat ik dus, als een schaap tussen twee wolven, en alleen God weet hoe het mij in mijn angsten te moede was. [...] Het scheen daarop alsof ik een inwendige aanzegging kreeg te zingen, wat ik in weerwil van mijn angst ook deed; ik zong dat het schalde door de bomen en de struiken aan weerszijden van de rivier, en toen zij zagen en hoorden hoe ik in gezang uitbrak begonnen ze te lachen, met de mond zo wijd open dat je ze recht in de keel keek [...].⁴⁷

> [There I sat like a sheep between two wolves, in a thousand fears, God knows what I felt. [...] And it seemed that a voice within me said I should sing, which I did although I was in such distress; and I sang so that the trees and woods were filled with the sound, for the river on both sides was grown with high trees. And when they saw and heard that I thus began to sing they began to laugh and gaped till you could see down their throats [...].]⁴⁸

Apart from the first thought of how music can bring people of different cultures together, it should be remarked that in both cases it is the white Europeans who make music: they are the active party, while the natives again play the passive role of reception and being influenced by the music of the Dutch.

There are some passages where Bontekoe plays the role not only of the Dutch colonizer but also of a man of feeling. True, he is the only individual in the story, we hear no natives speaking directly. Their voice is always conveyed by the white European. The following quotation, however, is a nice example of the urge to tell, to speak about the colonial adventure, creating the beginnings of a long process, that of colonial discourse:

> Ik had mij voorgenomen om met de eerste gelegenheid naar Holland terug te keren — iedere vogel is graag daar waar hij is uitgebroed, zegt het spreekwoord, en ik wist nu uit eigen ervaring hoe waar dat was. Immers, welke prachtige landen, kusten of rijken men ook bezeilt en aanschouwt, welke omstandigheden, voordelen en vermakelijkheden men ook geniet, het zou alleen maar pijn doen als we niet meer de hoop konden koesteren dat alles één te kunnen navertellen in ons vaderland; want het is alleen deze hoop die ons reizen tot 'reizen' maakt; zonder die hoop zou er niet veel verschil zijn tussen reizen en ballingschap.[49]

> [I was now resolved at the first opportunity to go to Holland, finding the truth of the proverb the which is proved by experience: every bird returns gladly to the place where he was nested; for whatever splendid countries, coasts and kingdoms a man may sail to and look over; whatever conditions, profit or pleasures he may enjoy, would be but poor entertainment were we not supported by the hope of once upon a time relating our adventures at home; for in that very hope do we call our journeyings 'travels', otherwise such hopeless wanderings would be no better to a man than exile.][50]

The reader should be alert to just these human traits, which gloss over the colonial character of the whole. It is Bontekoe who is focalizing and this is always a challenge for the reader to identify. That is why it is so important to read texts in context and to distance oneself from the temptation of identification with the focalizing narrator. There are rare self-reflexive moments when Bontekoe criticizes Christians as opposed to the Chinese: '[...] — voorwaar een blijk van grote deugd, beschamend voor veel christenen die, zodra ze uit het nauw zijn, zich dikwijls weinig meer om hun beloftes bekommeren.'[51] [Verily a great virtue, putting to shame many Christians, who once they are out of the trap often think little of their promises].[52] This is perhaps the first glimpse of a critique of the home culture which will, at some point, appear later on in Dutch literature, as, for example, in *Reinhart, of natuur en godsdienst* (*Reinhart, or nature and religion*) of 1791–92 by Elisabeth Maria Post, and in Multatuli's *Max Havelaar* (1860).

The Afterlife of the *Journaal*: the Presence of the Colonial Past in Modern Holland

It is quite clear that in Bontekoe's journal it is through the narrator's filter that the Orient is represented. His value judgements are also defined by his own culture, of course. Contemporary Dutch readers identified themselves with Bontekoe and the Dutch. So it happened that after publishing the book Bontekoe himself immediately became a hero and was seen as such in later times too.

An example is the work of Everhardus Johannes Potgieter (1808–75), who in 1840, inspired by the *Journaal*, wrote a long epic poem about the story of Bontekoe, concentrating on the songs which Bontekoe sang in the company of the two natives in order to save his life.[53] Potgieter was a representative of early Dutch romanticism. He was one of those writers who promoted the high culture of seventeenth-century Holland as an example to the society of his own time. It is a well-known fact that the great painters of this Golden Age were also 'discovered' in the nineteenth century. So Potgieter's long epic poem also served to awaken and strengthen national literature by adapting an exemplary seventeenth-century story. The poem has here and there parts written in prose, while in the poetic verses of different lengths he uses sometimes pair rhymes, sometimes crossing rhymes or embracing ones. All these serve only as an introduction to the songs which, according to Potgieter's imagination, were sung by Bontekoe in his fear in the boat, and which he had to thank for staying alive. As with Scheherezade, telling a story or singing a song acquires a performative function: that of saving life. The two natives obviously enjoy the songs and Bontekoe thinks he will be not killed while he keeps singing them. Potgieter 'rewrites' Bontekoe's songs by reaching back to Dutch songs of the seventeenth century, both to their thematic and to their formal characteristics. Both these and the songs by Potgieter were written to already existing melodies. Like his favourite seventeenth-century poet, P. C. Hooft, Potgieter notes together with the title the melody to which the songs should be sung. The songs are not linked to each other thematically but they are, of course, of the same culture. One of them is about the meeting of Neptune and a Dutch seaman during the war against the Spaniards, another recalls a tavern scene, still another represents skating lovers in the style of seventeenth-century genre paintings. It is no accident either that one of the songs is about Prince Maurits of Orange's sailing car and the journey he made in it in Scheveningen. In the prose introduction Potgieter names the source of this story as J. P. Van Cappelle's *Bijdragen tot de Geschiedenis der Wetenschappen en Letteren in Nederland* [Contributions to the History of Science and Literature in the Netherlands] of 1821. This in turn refers to a work of the seventeenth-century Dutch philosopher Hugo de Groot. According to this, the vehicle was constructed to the design of the Flemish mathematician Simon Stevin, who was of Dutch origin. It was equipped with sails, and could move on land helped by the wind just as perfectly as a sailing ship on water. On the occasion of the journey described there was a distinguished international company of twenty-eight members in the land yacht, among others the brother of the Danish king, the French ambassador, and Hugo de Groot himself. The machine was among the most modern inventions of the time, and as such was the embodiment of Dutch national pride, the culmination of early modern European civilization. After the blowing up of their ship, Bontekoe and his mates also re-create their lives on the basis of Dutch scientific knowledge preserved in their heads. When he sings, the natives, of course, cannot understand what he is singing about, but the power of his singing in Potgieter's poem comes from that very social, scientific, cultural, and artistic background from which he sprang and of which he was a son. It was this creative, progressive character of the seventeenth century that Potgieter found so exemplary for nineteenth-century Holland, which he thought was decadent.

In 1924 another author, Johan Fabricius (1899–1981), rewrote the story for the youth in the form of a novel entitled *De scheepjongens van Bontekoe* [Bontekoe's cabin-boys]. Bontekoe is no longer the main character any more, but his cabin-boys are, with their exciting adventures. The book is still very popular, and in 2007 it was even filmed.

Bontekoe's cabin-boys were immortalized in the form of sculptures by Jan van Druten. The three boys, dressed in seventeenth-century clothes, were unveiled in 1968. They are still to be seen on the embankment in Hoorn in their relaxed posture, life-size. They hardly emerge from their environment but they make Hoorn a place of cultural memory (*lieu de mémoire*). Even the bloody-handed son of Hoorn, governor-general Coen, was given a sculpture in 1893. It still stands on the main square of the town. He also stands at one of the corners on the famous bourse building in Amsterdam built by the famous architect Berlage in 1903. The tunnel under the Noordzeekanaal was named after Coen in 1966. The first two words of his motto, '*Dispereert niet*' [*Do not despair*], were not only the title of prime minister Hendricus Colijn's (1869–1944) speech given in 1937 on the occasion of the 350th anniversary of Coen's birth, but also were those with which Queen Wilhelmina ended her speech to the Dutch people on radio Oranje on 12 May 1940. Only in recent years have there been popular attempts to remove the sculpture, or at least to alter the plaque at its foot to reveal the darker side of Coen's character too. Jan Jacob Slauerhoff (1898–1936), the great Dutch poet, wrote a critical drama about him with the title *Jan Pietersz. Coen*. In the Netherlands, which we usually think of as a liberal, tolerant country, this play was prohibited by politicians until 1948. Even since then it has not been staged very often. Coen is alive in Dutch cultural memory as a romantic hero rather than a colonizer subjugating other peoples.

The text of the *Journaal* was translated into modern Dutch in 1989 by Lennaert Nijgh. In 2001 one of the most outstanding writers of the Netherlands, Thomas Rosenboom, made another modern Dutch translation provided with contemporary illustrations and notes to help better understanding of the context. The introduction (written by Vibeke Roeper[54]) still lacks any criticism of the representation of Dutch colonialism.

My post-colonial analysis of the text has revealed relationships different from those of any other approach, be it historical (Roeper en Wildeman), aesthetic (Bostoen), or literary historical (Barend-van Haeften). I consider the *Journaal* as a contact zone between different cultures which are not symmetrical: the European clearly subjugates the non-European, using Christian piety as a narrative device to conceal military and colonial intentions. Preconceptions and fear of the 'other' define the image of natives formed by the Dutch. Using the technical knowledge of the young Republic gives the Dutch power over the indigenous people of the East Indies. The *Journaal* is part of a long textual tradition of Dutch travel writing which continues and re-establishes colonial discourse.

In what follows I look at a story in which the Dutch colonist is not leaving for the colonies, but is returning, to re-establish himself and his family in nineteenth-century Holland. I shall examine how far-away colonies determine and influence life in Holland and what kind of textual strategies make the colonial presence possible.

Notes to Chapter 1

1. Piet Emmer, *De Nederlandse slavenhandel 1500–1850* (Amsterdam and Antwerp: De Arbeiderspers, 2000). The next paragraphs are partly drawn from this book.
2. Rudolf Dekker, *Meer verleden dan toekomst. Geschiedenis van verdwijnend Nederland* (Amsterdam: Bert Bakker, 2008), pp. 233–50. Other parts of the summary rely on the tenth chapter of this book.
3. Jan Huygen van Linschoten, *Itinerario, voyage ofte schipvaert naer Oost ofte Portugaels Indien* (Den Haag: Martinus Nijhoff, 1955).
4. Rob Nieuwenhuys, Bert Paasman, Peter van Zonneveld, *De geschiedenis van de Indisch–Nederlandse ietterkunde. Oost-Indisch Magazijn* (Amsterdam: Bulkboek, 1990), pp. 9–10. My summary of the Dutch colonial enterprise derives largely from this book.
5. Dekker, p. 234.
6. Marijke Barend-van Haeften, 'Van scheepsjournaal tot reisverhaal: een kennismaking met zeventiende-eeuwse reisteksten', *Literatuur*, 7 (1990), 222–28.
7. This is the name of the standard, classical Dutch translation of the Bible from 1637. The commission for the translation was given by the Dordrecht Synod in 1618 and it was financed by the Staten–Generaal, the Dutch Parliament.
8. Vibeke Roeper and Diederick Wilderman, 'Schipper Bontekoe', in *Bontekoe. De schipper, het journaal, de scheepjongens*, ed. by K. Bostoen and others (Amsterdam: Scheepvaartmuseum; Zutphen: Walburg Pers, 1996), pp. 9–34.
9. Karel Bostoen, 'Held in een bloedstollend drama', in *Bontekoe. De schipper, het journaal, de scheepjongens* ed. by K. Bostoen and others (Amsterdam and Zutphen: Walburg Pers, 1996), pp. 41–52.
10. Karel Porteman and Mieke B. Smits-Veld, *Een nieuw vaderland voor de muzen. Geschiedenis van de Nederlandse literatuur 1650–1700* (Amsterdam: Bert Bakker, 2008), pp. 419, 635.
11. Bert Paasman, 'De Indisch-Nederlandse literatuur uit de VOC-tijd', in *Europa buitengaats. Koloniale en postkoloniale literaturen in Europese talen*, ed. by Theo D'haen (Amsterdam: Bert Bakker, 2002), pp. 33–97 (pp. 33, 35).
12. Theo D'Haen (ed.), *Europa buitengaats. Koloniale en postkoloniale literaturen in Europese talen* (Amsterdam: Bert Bakker, 2002), p. 17.
13. Paasman, pp. 69–70.
14. Ibid., p.70.
15. Mary Louise Pratt, 'Arts of the Contact Zone', *Profession*, 91 (1991), pp. 33–40 (p. 34).
16. Svetlana Alpers, *The Art of Describing: Dutch Art in the Seventeenth Century* (University of Chicago Press 1984), pp. 119–68.
17. Ibid., p. 163.
18. For Dutch quotations I use the modern translation of Thomas Rosenboom of *Het Journaal van Bontekoe* (Amsterdam, Athenaeum–Polak & Van Gennep, 2001), p.25.
19. For English quotations I use the English translation of the *Memorable Description of the East Indian Voyage: 1618–25*, trans. by C. B. Bodde-Hodgkinson and Pieter Geyl, with an Introduction and Notes by Pieter Geyl (New York: Robert M. McBride & Company 1929), p. 19.
20. *Het Journaal*, p. 25.
21. *Memorable Description*, p. 19.
22. *Staten-Bijbel*, Numeri 33: 3,4,5,6,7,8.
23. *The King James Bible*, Numbers 33: 3,4,5,6,7,8.
24. *Het Journaal*, pp. 45–46.
25. *Memorable Description*, p. 46.
26. See further about orientation Robert T. Tally, *Spatiality: The New Critical Idiom* (London: Routledge, 2013), p. 20.
27. *Het Journaal*, p. 28.
28. *Memorable Description*, p. 23.
29. *Het Journaal*, p. 76.
30. *Memorable Description*, p. 89.

31. Daniel P. Kunene, 'Deculturation — The African Writer's Response', *Africa Today*, 15. 4 (1968), 19–24.
32. *Het Journaal*, p. 30.
33. *Memorable Description*, p. 27.
34. *Het Journaal*, p. 30.
35. *Memorable Description*, p. 35.
36. *Het Journaal*, pp. 37–38.
37. *Memorable Description*, pp. 35–36.
38. We cannot help thinking here of Joseph Conrad's *Heart of Darkness* (1902), where Kurtz surrounds himself with similar objects, a prominent example of his acculturation seen by Marlow as a horrifying estrangement from European culture.
39. *Het Journaal*, p. 49.
40. *Memorable Description*, p. 52.
41. *Het Journaal*, p. 53.
42. *Memorable Description*, p. 58.
43. *Het Journaal*, p. 78.
44. *Memorable Description*, p. 100.
45. *Het Journaal*, p.37.
46. *Memorable Description*, p. 36
47. *Het Journaal*, p. 57.
48. *Memorable Description*, p. 62.
49. *Het Journaal*, p. 104.
50. *Memorable Description*, p. 128.
51. *Het Journaal*, p. 89.
52. *Memorable Description*, p. 108.
53. Everhardus Johannes Potgieter, 'Liedekens van Bontekoe', in *De Werken, Deel 12. Verspreide en nagelaten poëzy. Deel 2.* (Haarlem: H. D. Tjeenk Willink, 1840/1896), pp. 1–52.
54. Vibeke Roeper, 'Inleiding', in *Het Journaal van Bontekoe* (Amsterdam: Athenaeum–Polak & Van Gennep, 2001), pp. 7–21.

CHAPTER 2

The Parvenu as Subjugator: Colonial Connotations of the Short Novel *De familie Kegge* by Nicolaas Beets

The Outside Context

The beginnings of Dutch Colonization in the West Indies

The other Dutch colonial company of importance beside the VOC was the West-Indische Compagnie (West India Company, WIC for short), founded in 1621. In its organization it was quite similar to the East India Company. There was, however, one conspicuous difference, namely, that it did not have sovereign rights. In the event of wanting to start wars, it was obliged to ask permission from the Staten-Generaal (Parliament). The WIC had authorization covering West Africa, America, and the islands in the Pacific Ocean between America and the eastern point of New Guyana. The most important territories under the control of the WIC were Nieuw-Nederland (there were bloody fights here between 1643 and 1645 with the Indians), Curaçao, Brazil, and Surinam. Nieuw-Nederland became later the State of New York, and also New Jersey, Delaware, and Connecticut. The city of New York was called Nieuw-Amsterdam in 1625, while Harlem and Brooklyn were named after the Dutch towns Haarlem and Breukelen. In 1664 these territories were occupied by the British, who in 1667 offered the Dutch Surinam in exchange together with several Caribbean islands such as Curaçao, Tobago, Essequibo, and Berbice in Guyana. Other territories also offered to the Dutch included Nieuw-Holland, that is, the east coast of Brasil, which was recaptured by the Portuguese in 1654. In West Africa the Gold Coast near Elmina (in Ghana), Sao Tomé, and Angola belonged to the commercial network of the Dutch.

Like the VOC, the WIC also functioned as a shareholder group. It had five chambers which provided for the equipment of the ships. The five were located in Amsterdam, Middelburg, Hoorn, Rotterdam, and Groningen. The Directorate had seventy-nine members, of which nineteen formed the Executive Committee, the so-called Nineteen. Like the VOC, the WIC was also involved with the leading social groups of the towns, the ruling families.

The most important products that the WIC imported to Europe were sugar and tobacco. The WIC became notorious, however, for hijacking foreign ships and for the slave trade. The route taken was in the form of a geographical triangle: first they set off with cargoes bound for Africa, where they exchanged them for slaves whom they transported to America, before returning to the Netherlands. The most profitable undertaking was the slave trade, so that we cannot consider the WIC as a purely commercial company. Their activity had a strongly military and political character as well.

Frijhoff and Spies describe the process from the initial repudiation of slavery by the Calvinist Dutch burghers to its eventual acceptance.[1] The initial repudiation, they argue, was based on one of the fundamental tenets of Calvinism, namely the idea of natural freedom which was absolutely opposed to any form of slavery. The work of the German theologian Zacharias Ursinus, co-author of the *Heidelberg Catechism*, was translated into Dutch in 1602 by the pastor and Bible-translator Festus Hommius under the title *Schat-boek der Christelycke Leere* (*Treasure-Book of Christian Doctrine*). This work, referring to Exodus, repudiated every form of 'stealing a man',[2] the more so because this activity was attributed to the Papists — that is to say, to the Portuguese and the Spanish — who really had begun the systematic transatlantic slave trade earlier. Within the borders of the young Dutch Republic it was strictly forbidden. There was also general agreement on the prohibition on keeping Christians in slavery irrespective of whether they were Protestants or Catholics, and so slaves who were permitted to be christened had to be freed.

Slavery became a profitable economic tool when single-crop farming and planter agriculture were implemented in the East Indies. The organized Dutch transatlantic slave trade began when the Dutch governor of Brazil, Johannes Maurits van Nassau, occupied Fort Elmina in 1637; this had previously been under Portuguese control, and was a depot for indigenous slaves. Ten years later the Dutch had shipped thousands of slaves from Africa to America.

The conscience of the Calvinists was slowly salved by other texts. To these belonged commercial handbooks of religious undertone such as *'t Geestelyck roer van 't Coopmans Schip* (*The Spiritual Wheel of the Merchant's Ship*) of 1638 or the *Practyce van de Christelijcke hooft-deugden* (*The Practice of the Main Christian Virtues*) of 1640. Both were written by the Zierikzee preacher Godfried Udemans. According to Udemans, slavery could be acceptable if slaves were acquired in a just war or if someone inherited slaves from his parents. The slave trade was held also to be permissible if slaves were given the right to be christened and to humane treatment in the long run. The 'long run', however, became longer and longer because black people were not considered ready to receive Christianity. As Frijhoff and Spies explain, the basis for legitimation of the difference between white and black was found again in the Bible, this time with reference to Genesis 9:18–27. The conviction spread in the Middle Ages that the three sons of Noah were the founding fathers of the three continents known at the time: Japheth of Europe, Shem of Asia, and Ham of Africa. The descendants of Ham, who had been cursed by his father Noah, were in a subjugated position in Christian thinking, and so making them slaves was legitimized in Christian eyes. Both the initial repudiation and the later acceptance of slavery referred thus to earlier texts on the subject. What Edward Said argued, influenced by Michel Foucault's assertion that Orientalism was a discourse, held partly true for colonialism. Therefore, colonialism cannot be studied without taking into consideration that it was established, upheld, and recreated by a discursive network of texts and other representations.[3]

Under the influence of the Enlightenment the abolition of slavery and the slave trade were on the agenda in the Netherlands too, though much later than in England, and the demand for abolition was also much less strong than in England. In 1793 a certain Pieter Paulus, jurist and politician, wrote an essay under the title 'Verhandeling over de vrage: In welken zin kunnen de menschen gezegd worden gelijk te zijn? En welke de regten en pligten die daaruit voortvloeien?' (Treatise on the Question: In what sense can people be said to be equal? And what are the rights and obligations ensuing from this?). He attempted to draft the political programme of the Batavian Revolution on the lines of the French Revolution, and in it condemned both slavery and the slave trade on the grounds of natural rights and the ideas of Christianity.[4] Meanwhile slave revolts broke out in the colonies in the West Indies, among others in 1795 in Curaçao. In the National Council of the Batavian Republic, which was founded on the French model, a long discussion on the constitution took place. The question of abolition was raised again but without success. After the passing of the English Abolition of the Slave Trade Act in 1807 the United Kingdom of the Netherlands also joined in the elimination of the slave trade in 1814, but the institution of slavery was maintained in the Dutch colonies. In England the actual abolition of slavery took place in 1834. In the Netherlands it happened much later. The process was strongly influenced by Harriet Beecher Stowe's novel *Uncle Tom's Cabin or Life among the Lowly*, the Dutch translation of which was published in 1853, a year after the American publication. In the same year a tract against the institution of slavery appeared, written by Julian Wolbers. The strongest impact, however, was made by the two volumes written by the liberal member of parliament Baron Van Hoëvell, consisting of essays, pamphlets, descriptions of landscapes and journeys, and fiction. The title was *Slaven en vrijen onder de Nederlandsche wet* (*Slaves and Freemen under Dutch Jurisdiction*) and it was published in 1855. Van Hoëvell had worked as a chaplain in the Dutch Indian colonies until 1848, and was also editor of one of the most important journals there, *Tijdschrift voor Nederlandsch-Indië* (*Journal for the Dutch Indies*). After returning to the Netherlands he became one of the most radical critics of the colonial system and slavery as a Lower House politician. Slavery was eventually abolished in the Dutch East Indies in 1859 and in the Dutch West Indies in 1863.[5]

Definition of Dutch Literature of the West Indies

The literature dealing with the West Indies written in Dutch is an important element of Dutch literature even though it comprises fewer works than there are about the East Indies. According to Michiel van Kempen, one of the best informed experts on Dutch-language literature about the West Indies, the number of colonial works about Surinam in the library of the University of Amsterdam is roughly 170.[6] Van Kempen defines colonial literature as literature written by colonizers who wrote about a reality basically new and strange to them. It was a literature of those who were considered strangers themselves in the Dutch West Indies. Van Kempen says that this definition is unambiguous from two points of view: on the one hand, colonial literature is defined from the perspective of the author, and this is also the perspective from which the work has been written. On the other hand, the audience addressed is that of the Dutch community. Non-colonial texts on the West Indies belong at the same time to the literature of the colonized country. These are Indian myths and the oral tales of different folk groups. The diary and notes written by Johannes King (c. 1830–98) in the Sranan language too form part of Surinamese colonial literature.[7] Colonial authors wrote primarily for their own country, the Netherlands.

Van Kempen calls attention to a problem in his definition. Works of native Surinamese authors who did not or do not live in Surinam are not considered as belonging to Surinamese literature. They are often accused of writing from a Dutch perspective. The perspective of those writers continuously living outside Surinam is not, of course, automatically Dutch, or if so it is not identical with the view of the ex-colonizers. A good example is Astrid Roemer (born 1947), the Surinamese author who lives sometimes in Surinam, sometimes in the Netherlands. She writes in Dutch but not from a Dutch perspective. Van Kempen considers the literature of the Surinamese living in the diaspora as having special status.

The author whose work I am going to analyse had never been to any of the Dutch West Indian colonies. This, however, does not mean that the world of the West Indies and its influence are not present in his works. From this point of view it is irrelevant whether or not Nicolaas Beets's *Familie Kegge* (1851) answers the definition of colonial literature. It does not do so insofar as Beets himself was never confronted personally with the colonial world, and had no personal experience of why this world was new and strange compared to the one that he knew so well. As far as the perspective and the audience addressed are concerned, it does fit into the definition: it was written from a Dutch perspective for a Dutch reading public and the theme is partly about the Dutch West Indies. The Dutch perspective, however, is not automatically a colonial one. The novella *Familie Kegge* has been examined more than once from the point of view of how it registers, mirrors, and perpetuates those cultural reflexes which are implanted by the colonizing power into its citizens.[8]

Familie Kegge was published in *Camera Obscura* in 1851 (see Fig. 2.2). The volume itself appeared for the first time in 1839 and each new edition was enlarged during the lifetime of its author: each time Beets wrote new texts for this collection of prose works, *Kegge* was published for the first time only in the third edition. *Camera Obscura* has also been published several times since the death of its author in 1903. The latest, a critical edition, dates from 1998.

This work has a distinguished place in the Dutch literary canon, perhaps even among the first ten masterpieces. The literary canon consists of those novels, short stories, poems, and dramas which literary critics, university professors, and journalists evaluate as 'evergreen' masterpieces on the ground of their 'evergreen' aesthetical and ethical values. Readers more often than not accept the judgement

FIG. 2.1. Portrait of Nicolaas Beets by Johannes Philippus Lange, after William Grebner, published by Johannes Immerzeel, 1820–41, Steel-engraving, 13.5 cm × 10.5 cm, Digitale Bibliotheek voor de Nederlandse Letteren

of the above-mentioned intellectual elite and consider the selected works also as masterpieces. This is the case with Nicolaas Beets and his *Camera Obscura*. Several monographs, essays, and books have been published about both the author and his main opus. The summary of the author's life and work I give below draws on the long 'Inleiding' (Introduction) to the critical edition of *Camera Obscura*.[9]

Nicolaas Beets (1814–1903)

Nicolaas Beets was born the son of a pharmacist (see Fig. 2.1). This is important because in his literary work he showed the life of the social group to which his father belonged: the everyday life of the petty bourgeoisie. His first years at school were strongly influenced by his teacher Pieter Johannes Prinsen (1777–1854), a follower of the famous Swiss pedagogue Pestalozzi (1746–1827) and a great enthusiast for his ideas. According to these thinkers, knowledge is based upon experience and observation. After these follows naming of things and only in the end is judgement possible. These ideas can also be found in the stories in *Camera Obscura* because they are all descriptions of people, habits, towns, and society, based on observation.

After the so-called elementary Dutch School, Beets continued his studies at the French School, where not only French but also English was taught. This counted as an exception at that time in the Netherlands. The *gymnasium* was called the Latin School, and there Beets studied Latin and Greek. His knowledge of English and English literature was also developed by his friend John Ingram Lockhart, who was a member of the British parliament. They read together the works of Lord Byron and Walter Scott, and these authors had an enormous influence on Beets's first period. He wrote his first prose work, *Proeve eener hulde aan Sir Walter Scott* (*An Essay in Honour of Sir Walter Scott*), on the occasion of Scott's death in 1832. Another of Beets's literary ideals was Willem Bilderdijk (1756–1831), a Dutch poet and representative of the Dutch conservative and Protestant Romantic movement, the Réveil (Awakening).

When Beets studied theology at Leiden University between 1833 and 1839, he was a man of wide erudition, and some of his poems and prose had already been published in literary journals and almanacs. *Camera Obscura* was also born during these university years. Since the foundation of Leiden University in 1575 the city of Leiden had given a greater degree of freedom to its students than to its citizens. Dutch society in the 1830s was strictly defined by its social classes and groups. There was no passage from one to another, except for students. They formed a distinct group and scorned and despised all the other groups, which they knew through and through.

After the 1830 Belgian revolution the Leiden students took part enthusiastically in the Tiendaagse veldtocht (The Ten-Day Battle) in 1831 in order to prevent the secession of Belgium from the Netherlands. By this they tried to show their unconditional loyalty to, and love for, their country. They took not only their swords but also their pens to display their national feelings. That is how the special type of the student-author evolved. Many students in Leiden — especially students of theology — also had literary ambitions which were fed both by the political situation and by their position in Dutch society. Not yet settled, they had a critical attitude to the petit bourgeois society around them. During their university years they were both outsiders and insiders of their world. This position made them critical of the way of life of the lower middle-class inhabitants of Leiden. However, it was a mild, ironical criticism mixed with sympathetic feelings. Not only Beets belonged to this type, but so did one of his best friends, Klikspaan (pseudonym of Johannes Kneppelhout), together with J. P. Hasebroek, L. R. Beynen, and Bernard Gewin. In 1833 they founded the so-called Rederijkerskamer voor Uiterlijke Welsprekendheid (Chamber of Rhetoric for the Performing Arts) which was also called De Romantische Club (The Romantic Club).[10] As the name tells us, the main aim was to perform the poems of their favourite poets as brilliantly as possible. To these favourites belonged the above-mentioned Willem Bilderdijk, Goethe, Byron, and Victor Hugo. The members of the society wrote poems and prose works too, under the influence of European Romanticism. Beets not only translated the works of Byron but also wrote long epic poems in Byronic style.[11]

In 1836, however, he became disaffected with his Romantic period, met his future wife, and threw himself into his studies and the literary life of Leiden. He grew more and more popular, and *Camera Obscura* was published in 1839 (see Fig. 2.2). In 1840 he married and embarked on his theological career. He was first employed in Heemstede, later in Utrecht. He took his profession very seriously, did a lot for the development of Christian education, and took a definite position against slavery.[12] After the death of his first wife, who had presented him with nine children, he married her younger sister, who delivered him a further six. He wrote a lot but never succeeded in surpassing the success of *Camera Obscura*. In 1875 he was appointed a professor at Utrecht University, where he taught Church History. He was respected everywhere, and a whole literary circle formed around his person. He became a balanced, moderate, and satisfied citizen of the very same society which, as a young man, he had criticized and mocked in so vitriolic a fashion.

Camera Obscura, a Classic Work of Dutch Realist Prose

The 'Introduction' to the critical edition is again a good example of what I described in the previous chapter: setting a literary work in its contemporary literary tradition and analysing it on its purely aesthetic merits can cover some other disturbing aspects of the same work such as its eventual colonial connotations.

The authors of the 'Introduction' begin with the description of the volume. *Camera Obscura* is a collection of shorter and longer prose works in which Beets records the everyday life of the Dutch petty bourgeois in the first half of the nineteenth century. Interiors, detailed descriptions of cityscapes, habits, typical figures, and types line up in the work. The authors quote the French art critic and novelist Champfleury (1820–89), who in his 1857 book *Le réalisme* mentions Nicolaas Beets under his pen name Hildebrand on a level with other great realists such as Dickens, Thackeray, Gogol, or Turgenev.[13] By putting him in the Pantheon of contemporary writers he endows him with an identity card which ensures admission to a well-defined interpretative field.

Fig. 2.2. The title page of the fifth edition of the *Camera Obscura* by Karel Frederik Blombléd, 1857, Leiden University Libraries 1001 C 20 001

The authors go on introducing Beets by enumerating the foreign literary influences on his work. This method is often employed when authors and the achievements of the so-called 'less-known cultures' are compared to representatives of 'well-known cultures' in order to contextualize, legitimize, emancipate, and introduce them. As the American scholar Anna Balakian puts it:

> The Comparatist who is familiar with the so-called major literatures as well as with one of the more unfamiliar ones has more credibility when he or she passes a value judgement on the unfamiliar in relation to the familiar. I see this activity as one of the significant roles of the comparative dimension of literary criticism.[14]

So the authors of the 'Introduction' mention the American Washington Irving and his *The Sketch Book of Geoffrey Crayon, Gent.* (1820–21), containing the famous story of Rip van Winkle and several other essays and descriptions. This volume expanded over the years in the same way as Beets's *Camera*. Geoffrey Crayon was also a pen name used by Irving just as Beets used his own pen name Hildebrand. Irving introduces an eighteenth-century spectator called Crayon, who reports on the reality of his own time, just as Beets does via his protagonist, Hildebrand. Both Crayon and Hildebrand play a double role: as outsiders they criticize people, habits, and ways of life in their immediate environment while they themselves are also characters in their own stories. Another influence, according to the authors of the 'Introduction', could be Bulwer-Lytton (1803–73) and his volume *The Student* (1835), subtitled *Tales and Essays*. Beets knew this work, the Dutch translation of which was published in 1836. Another inspiration could be, the authors argue, *Sketches by Boz* (1836) by the young Charles Dickens (1812–70). Boz is again a figure similar to Crayon and Hildebrand: he shows everyday life by describing the smallest details. The subtitle of Dickens's work — *Scenes, Tales, Characters* — is again a reference to the diversity of the genres. Attention to the lower social groups and sympathy with the poor was a relevant new feature in contemporary European literature. Beets has these in his *De familie Stastok* (*The Stastok Family*), where impoverishment and empathy play an important role. In other stories Beets does not tackle these problems because in the years 1831–40 Dutch society was not yet as industrialized as that of Britain, so that the concomitant social phenomena were less prominent.

The editors of Beets's *Camera Obscura* illustrate a similar way of describing and observing everyday life by aligning two quotations. One is from the story 'London Recreations' in *Sketches by Boz*.

> The heat is intense this afternoon, and the people, of whom there are additional parties arriving every moment, look as warm as the tables which have been recently painted and have the appearance of being red-hot. What dust and noise! Men and women — boys and girls — sweethearts and married people — babies in arms and children in chaises — pipes and shrimps — cigars and periwinkles — tea and tobacco. Gentlemen, in alarming waistcoats, and steel watch-guards, promenading about, three abreast, with surprising dignity (or as the gentleman in the next box facetiously observes, 'cutting it uncommon fat!') — ladies, with great, long, white pocket-handkerchiefs like small tablecloths in their hands, chasing one another on the grass in the most playful and interesting manner, with the view of attracting the attention of the aforesaid

gentlemen — husbands in perspective ordering bottles of ginger-beer for the objects of their affections, with a lavish disregard of expense; and the said objects washing down huge quantities of 'shrimps' and 'winkles', with an equal disregard for their own bodily health and subsequent comfort — boys, with great silk hats just balanced on the top of their heads, smoking cigars, and trying to look as if they liked them — gentlemen in pink shirts and blue waistcoats, occasionally upsetting either themselves, or somebody else, with their own canes.[15]

The other quotation is taken from Beets's 'Een onaangenaam mensch in den Haarlemmerhout' (An Unpleasant Man from the Haarlemmerhout) in *Camera Obscura* (see Fig. 2.3).

> Zo zal de natuuronderzoeker, die des zondagsmorgens de kerk verzuimt of naar de vroegpreek is geweest (wat ik liever onderstellen wil) en om tien uur, half elf, in De Hout komt, op het Plein of bij de Koekamp (de naam is niet welluidend), enige zwermen feestvierende vogels van de Haarlemmerdijk inhalen, per schuit van zevenen uit Amsterdam vertrokken. De mannetjes zijn blauw of zwart getekend en hebben sliknatte, fijngekrulde bakkebaarden. Ze zijn voorzien van lange Goudse pijpen, waaruit ze òf roken, òf die ze losjes bij de kop tussen de vingers houden en zo, met de steel naar beneden, onverschillig laten slingeren. Merk de regenschermen. De wijfjes zijn wit. Zij houden haar opperkleed op, zo dikwijls ze over een droppel water stappen, en dragen 't geheel opgespeld als er wezenlijk plassen liggen van de regen van zaterdag. Zij eten gezadig uit haar zak; sommigen in de zwerm hebben daarenboven nog een toegeknoopte kinderluur met mondkost bij zich. Men ontmoet ze meestal in koppels van negenen: twee mannetjes op zeven wijfjes. Ze dwalen een heel end ver, somtijds wel tot Heemstede of de Glip af, maar strijken 's namiddags, onder een kruik bier en een bosje scharren, aan de Groene Valk of in de Aalbessenboom neder, om met de laatste schuit naar Amsterdam te vertrekken, terwijl intussen de toegeknoopte kinderluur van knapzak tot een korfje is omgeschapen, om 'blommen' in thuis te brengen, die drie weken lang in een aarden melkkan zonder oor, in een klein winkeltje, of op de bovenste trap van een kelder, hier zonder licht, en daar onder de frisse adem van een stinkend riool, het geluk en de rijkdom zullen uitmaken van iemand die garen en band verkoopt en tevens besteedster is, of van iemand die turf en hout slijt en tegelijk uit werken gaat.[16]

> [So the naturalist who neglects going to church on Sunday morning, or perhaps he attends the early sermon (which I will assume), and comes around ten or half past ten to De Hout or the Square or the Koekamp [Cowcamp] (the name does not sound very nice), will catch up with the celebrating birds of the Haarlemmerdijk, but for all this he must have taken the seven o'clock boat from Amsterdam. The men are clothed in blue or black and have pomaded and curly whiskers. They are equipped with long Gouda pipes which either they smoke or they hold the bowl of the pipe casually between their fingers and so, with the stem to the ground, they walk around unconcernedly. Look at the umbrellas! The women wear white clothes. They hold their outer garments up each time they step across a drop of water and they pin them up entirely if there are considerable pools left from the rain on Saturday. They eat satisfiedly from their bags; some of the swarm have their snacks in knotted napkins. You meet them usually in groups of nine: two gentlemen for seven ladies. They walk

Fig. 2.3. *Een onaangenaam mensch in den Haarlemmerhout* by Ch. Rochussen, Digitale Bibliotheek voor de Nederlandse Letteren

great distances, sometimes even to Heemstede or Glip, but in the afternoon they arrive under the weight of a pint of beer and a packet of flatfish at the Green Falcon or at the Aalbessenboom in order to take the last boat back to Amsterdam, while the knotted napkins change from bags of food into flower baskets so that some flowers can be taken home, 'flowers' which will stay fresh for three weeks in a milk-jug without handles and which will bring happiness and will care for the wealth of someone who, in a small shop or at the top of a stairway leading to a cellar, here without any light and there in the ripe odour of a stinking gutter, tries to sell thread and bandage but who at the same time also hires out maids, or for someone else who sells turf and lumber but who at the same time also goes out to work somewhere else.]

Both quotations show the outsider position of the observers and the irony with which they look at the world around them. As if the narrators came from another planet, they give an almost ethological description of the behaviour of their fellow-creatures. Both quotations describe groups, not individuals. Another parallel between the two is that they thematize the characteristics of a new way of life: spending free time together with others. This was really a new phenomenon in the first part of the nineteenth century when industrialization began to become more prevalent and people fled the city for nature in order to have fun in a public space.

The editors of the critical edition point out another related work from English literature, namely Laurence Sterne (1713–68). He was one of Beets's favourite authors. In his diary Beets mentions *The Life and Opinions of Tristram Shandy* (1759–67), and he also gives evidence of having read *A Sentimental Journey through France and Italy* (1768). At a certain point he reports that on 7 January 1835 he missed the diligence from Haarlem to Amsterdam and while waiting for the next one took *Tristram Shandy* out of his pocket in order to kill time. When the vehicle came, being unable to read because of the jostling he began to examine his companions, again remembering Sterne, who categorized the travellers. This was done, however, as we learn from the 'Introduction', not in *Tristram Shandy* but in *A Sentimental Journey*, where Sterne made eleven categories for his travelling companions. Inspired by Sterne, so the editors argue, Beets also put down in his diary the kind of companions that he had. At a later time he notes: 'Gebruikt, voor de familie Stastok Aanvang' (Used for the beginning of The Stastok Family). This is how *De familie Stastok* begins:

> In het kleine stadje D — werd op een donderdag in de maand oktober, des namiddags omtrent één uur, de steile ijzeren trede neergelaten van een gele diligence, rijdende over D van C tot E vice versa, en uit dezelfde daalde, tot grote bemoddering van degene die hem onmiddellijk volgde, en die niemand anders was dan zijn eigen cloak, uw onderdanige dienaar Hildebrand. Hij had gereisd met een bleke dame, die het roken had verboden en gedurig de kronkelbochten van haar boa had zitten te verschikken, dan eens had gezucht, dan eens ingesluimerd was, dan eens eau de cologne genomen, dan weer eens geslapen had, en aldoor lelijk was geweest. Op dezelfde bank met deze had een jong juffertje gezeten, in een blauwe geruite mantel niet gedoken, het denkbeeld is te ruim, maar gestoken; een mantel, die, naar een langvergeten mode vatbaar was om van achteren te worden ingehaald door een klein lapje van dezelfde stof, in de vorm van een souspied, op twee paarlemoeren

knoopjes uitgespannen; dezelfde juffer had een strohoed op met blauw gaas lint met bruine strepen, in grote lissen met een stevig soutien opgemaakt, en een hardgeel sjaaltje om de hals. Zij was zeer bang voor de bleke dame naast haar, en bleef op een schuwe afstand; soms had zij de goede wil haar in 't verschikken van haar boa te hulp te komen, en eenmaal had zij er werkelijk een dikachtig roodvingerig handje, met een ring, die bijzonder veel op tin geleek, voor ontbloot; maar de bleke dame had haar aangeblikt, en toen had zij haar neus genoten, volgens een in de omgang zeer deugdelijk stelsel, maar 't welk de neus alle mispassen, voorbarigheden en malle figuren misgelden moet. Dit was het personeel van de achterste bank geweest. Op de volgende had een jodin gezeten, als een oosterse edelsteen gevat tussen twee christenen; zij verborg onder een groen nopjesgoed manteltje een klein kind, dat al haar trots uitmaakte omdat het niet schreeuwde, zelfs niet toen zij het omstreeks halfweg een schone luier aandeed. Het kind nu was zeer klein, en had een zeer grote dot in de mond. Van de christenen, waartussen zij gevat was, had de een een grote rondglazige zilveren bril, een zilveren sigaarkoker, een zilver potlood, een zilver horloge, benevens zilveren broek- en schoengespen, waaruit ik opmaakte dat hij zilversmid was; en de andere een koperen doekspeld, een koperen tabaksdoos, een een koperen guirlande op zijn buik, waaruit ik besloot dat hij niet minder dan een banketbakkers' meesterknecht zijn moest.[17]

[In the tiny town of D, in the month of October, around one o'clock in the afternoon, a steep iron ladder was let down from a yellow diligence that ran via D from C to E and back, and from the same there descended, to the great thumping of the one following him — being none other than his own cloak — your humble servant Hildebrand. He had travelled in the company of a pale lady who had forbidden smoking and now and then moved her boa, sometimes sighing, sometimes dozing, then suddenly took eau de cologne, being ugly all the time. On the same seat there was a young lady not bundled in a blue checked cloak — the image would be too broad — but stuck in it; an old fashioned cloak it was, with a little bit of a belt on the back made of the same material as the cloak, similar to a strap stretched between two mother-of-pearl buttons; the same young lady had on her head a straw hat decorated with a blue tulle ribbon with brown strips and a flamboyant yellow shawl tied loosely around her neck. She was awfully afraid of the pale lady sitting beside her, and she maintained a discreet distance from her; sometimes she showed her good will and helped the lady to rearrange her boa, and once she even took the gloves off her pudgy, red-fingered hands in service of this aim; on one of her fingers there was a ring which seemed to be made of tin; the pale lady, however, only glanced at her and blew her nose according to the good manners of those times, in accordance with which the nose must be punished by all sorts of twisted forms and distortions. This was the company seated in the back. In the front there sat a Jewish woman, like an Eastern gem framed by two Christians; under her fluffy green coat she held a baby of whom she was very proud because it did not cry, not even when about halfway she changed its nappy. The child was very small and it had an enormous dummy in its mouth. One of the Christians framing the Jewish woman wore big, round, silver-framed spectacles and had a silver cigarette case, a silver pencil, a silver watch and silver clasps on his trousers and on his belt, from which I drew the conclusion that this man could not but be a silversmith; the other had a copper tobacco case and a copper scarf-pin on his belly, from which I drew the conclusion that this man could not be less than a confectioner's apprentice.]

Humour, the description of the many small details, and the sketching of the different human types make Beets's writing recognizable in an international literary context of realists such as Dickens and Sterne.

Sterne could have played a role in the title of the volume, as the editors point out. The narrator of *Tristram Shandy* enumerates different methods for representing the characters of the protagonists. The fifth method goes like this: 'Others [...] will make a drawing of you in the Camera; — that is most unfair of all, because, there you are sure to be represented in some of your most ridiculous attitudes.'[18] The camera obscura had already been popular in seventeenth-century Holland, and according to some art historians it is even possible that the photo-like genre and landscape paintings were made with the help of this instrument.[19] So it no longer counted as a novelty when Beets's *Camera* was first published. There was another technique which did count as a novelty at the time: this was Daguerre's photography. According to the motto of the volume, however, Beets did not wish to take photographs but:

> De schaduwen en schimmen van Nadenken, Herinnering en Verbeelding vallen in de ziel als in een Camera Obscura, en sommige zo treffend en aardig, dat men lust gevoelt ze na te tekenen en, met ze wat bij te werken, op te kleuren, en te groeperen, er kleine schilderijen van te maken, die dan ook al naar de grote Tentoonstellingen kunnen gezonden worden, waar een klein hoekje goed genoeg voor hen is. Men moet er evenwel geen portretten op zoeken; want niet alleen staat er honderdmaal een neus van Herinnering op een gezicht van Verbeelding, maar ook is de uitdrukking des gelaats zoo weinig bepaald, dat een zelfde tronie dikwijls op wel vijftig onderscheiden mensen gelijkt.[20]

> [Shadows and phantasms of Pondering, Recollection, and Fantasy fall into the soul as into a Camera Obscura and some of them fall so precisely and nicely that one feels like making drawings of them and with such elaboration, colouring, and structuring that you can even make small paintings of them which can be sent to the great Exhibitions, where a small corner will be enough for them. But one should not expect portraits among them; because not only does a nose of Recollection stand a hundred times on a face of Fantasy, but also the expression of a face is so poorly defined that the same facial expression is often very similar to at least fifty different people.]

The quotation shows excellently Beets's endeavour to depict types rather than individuals on the one hand, and on the other his ambition to intervene consciously and artistically in reality.

Jonathan Crary makes several interesting statements about the cultural history of looking at things in his book *Techniques of the Observer: On Vision and Modernity in the 19th Century* (1992).[21] Our way of looking at things changed radically, he argues, not in the second half of the nineteenth century with the upcoming impressionists as has usually been considered until now, but in the first half of the century. It was a change which replaced the mimetic with the representational paradigm. Crary also makes a distinction between *spectator* and *observer*, whereby the former is passive — an outsider, as it were — while the latter is active, merging with the observed world.

Beets's protagonist Hildebrand, who figures in several stories, is the author's alter ego, and rather an observer than a spectator. Although he keeps his outsider's — and therefore impeccable — position, he is at the same time one of the types that he himself observes, one of the people from the surrounding, drifting, strolling, whirling mass. The almost grotesque perception of this world makes Beets a forerunner of Dutch realist prose as it flourished in the later nineteenth and twentieth centuries.

Rhetorical Context and Plot
The Colonial Connotations of 'De familie Kegge'

The Dutch literary scholar Jacquelin Bel, inspired by Edward Said's book *Culture and Imperialism* (1994), compares *De familie Kegge* to Jane Austen's *Mansfield Park* (1814).[22] Both are classics in their own literature, argues Bel; they both come from the first half of the nineteenth century, they are both written in a humorous style, and different social strata and classes play an important role in each. The Dutch work, like the English novel, is about a European family which grew rich in the West Indies as a result of the colonial activities of the father. As Said pointed out, *Mansfield Park* can be interpreted in its colonial context in spite of the fact that the English Caribbean colony and Sir Thomas Bertram's journey to and fro are mentioned only tangentially: Mansfield Park is made possible, as it were, by the colony of Antigua. The colonial context designates a new interpretative field: the empire, the centre, points in its every aspect to the colonial periphery. Bel points out that while the Dutch work presents Kegge returning from the colony in a very critical way — he is ridiculed all the time as a parvenu — Sir Thomas's reputation remains stable in spite of his plantations in the West Indies. The criticism of Kegge is, according to Bel, criticism of colonization itself. This kind of representation forms the beginning of Dutch colonial literature in which Dutch colonies are represented from a certain distance and with a critical touch. It can be seen in the later colonial novels of Multatuli, Couperus, Daum, and Madelon Székely-Lulofs. Bel argues that it is precisely this critical attitude of the Dutch writers which shows the difference between Dutch and English colonial literature.

The story of *De familie Kegge* has been mostly interpreted in the Netherlands as a realistic work showing the petty bourgeois Dutch parvenu as simply a ridiculous idiot from the beginning of the nineteenth century. There were some exceptions in the 1970s where the colonial context was touched upon.[23] The editors of the 1998 critical edition place the whole oeuvre strictly in the context of the author's biography, his time, and the influence of world literature. With this critical edition they make the impression of having said the last word about Beets's oeuvre. Criticizing this attitude, Bel correctly points out that more recent times place literary works in new perspectives offering ever newer interpretative alternatives. This seems to be true, because the 1998 edition never touches on the colonial connotations of *De familie Kegge*. The critical edition is again a good example of traditional analysis which accentuates the aesthetic values of a work which otherwise also contains delicate ideological considerations.

The following analysis had been written before I read Bel's exciting interpretation.

By close reading and post-colonial based criticism I set out to show how the colonial connotations of the text are essential to its very structure.

At the beginning of the story, the protagonist Hildebrand is nursing his sick college friend, William Kegge. William soon dies. After his death Hildebrand informs William's family in Demerara (today Guyana), a colony ceded by the Dutch to the British in 1816. Two years after the death of their son William the enriched Kegge family repatriates to the Netherlands. The father of the deceased William, Jan Adam Kegge, invites Hildebrand to his house for a longish stay. This gives Hildebrand the possibility to become acquainted with the whole family. The *paterfamilias*, Adam Kegge, is a real parvenu: he has all the material wealth needed to belong to patrician circles. What he lacks is education and culture; he has not been socialized as a patrician. Nevertheless, his greatest wish is to enter the highest social circles. His daughter, Henriette, has the same ambitions and is courted by the shallow but self-conscious and no less pretentious Van der Hoogen. Kegge's niece, Saartje de Groot, lives in a poor family where Hildebrand is also invited to take part in the arrangements for St Nicholas's Eve (5 December), a very important Dutch family feast. At the end of the evening Hildebrand walks Suzette Noiret home. She is a very lovely girl with a pure heart, whose old, sick mother lives in a so-called 'hofje' (a kind of retirement home for elderly women). Suzette is very attached to her and spends all her time nursing her.

Hildebrand becomes closely acquainted with the members of the Kegge family, so much so that he even meddles actively in the lives of certain characters. In the end the reader is informed how everybody has fared.

Of the eleven chapters of the story the first — 'Een treurige inleiding' (A Sad Introduction) — begins with a rhetorical question: is there anybody who does not know the illness called tropical fever? This tropical fever is actually the same as typhus, but typhus is not mentioned as such in the story. Typhus is an illness which attacks the bowels in the first place and which is endemic in countries where hygiene is bad. The opening scene of the story takes the reader immediately to a strange place, far from the Netherlands. This place acquires concrete form only at a later point in the text: it is Demerara. Demerara was, with Essequibo, a Dutch colony until 1815. Later the Dutch ceded it to the British, but a lot of Dutch people stayed there even after that. There is a dichotomy of sickness and health in the text. Sickness is bound to the colony, to the non-European space, while health, cleanliness, and hygiene are linked to the Netherlands and Europe. There was a general fear of becoming dirty in nineteenth-century Europe and dirt and cleanliness were used metaphorically in all kinds of discourse, as Arnold Labrie points out. He writes:

> De microbe was het onzichtbare gevaar dat de grenzen van het lichaam bedreigde. Het lichaam kon daarbij gemakkelijk dienen als projectiescherm voor politieke en sociale angsten. Ook de natie werd immers voortdurend bedreigd door een invasie van vreemde elementen.[24]

> [The microbe was an invisible danger which threatened the borders of the body. The body could therefore easily serve as the screen for political and social fears. Also the nation was being continuously threatened by the invasion of foreign elements.]

The series of rhetorical questions goes on: who has not seen among his or her loved ones somebody dying of this disease? The question makes the reader draw the conclusion that there is at least one such a case in each Dutch family or among acquaintances. This implies that from each Dutch family or from the circle of anyone's acquaintances at least one person actually has been to the colonies. Of course, it must be taken into consideration that typhus is a highly infectious disease. It is interesting to see how the description of the disease reflects the relations between power and subjugation: 'Wie heeft haar nimmer bijgewoond, die verschrikkelijke worsteling der zenuwen en vaten, waar deze zich onderling het gezag betwisten, totdat de lijder — meestal, helaas — onder die kampstrijd bezwijken moet' [Who has never experienced that horrible wrestling between the nerves and veins during which each participant tests the power of the other until the subject suffering from the disease — unfortunately, in most cases — must himself become the victim of this combat].[25]

The beginning of the story refers at the same time to Dutch and non-Dutch circumstances. Hildebrand, who functions as witness and is at the same time the narrator in the first person of the story, is also one of the characters — and thus an extra- and intradiegetic narrator — and goes on to tell the reader that he has seen several such cases and at some time in the past has even had the disease himself. Given his position in the text, however, it is not probable that he himself has been to the colonies; otherwise there would be references to this in the text. The disease from the colonies is infectious, so nobody can feel safe, even those who have never been outside the good, old, and especially secure Netherlands. The disease is not only a somatic symptom in the text but also a metaphor of intellectual infection, everything that the 'colonial' is.

Soon after this part William Kegge — born in Demerara, friend and neighbour of the narrator in Leiden — is introduced: 'In het begin van het derde jaar van mijn verblijf te Leiden, was er een jong mens, uit Demerary geboortig, in mijn buurt komen wonen' [At the beginning of my third year in Leiden, there came a young man, born in Demerara, to stay in my neighbourhood].[26] Leiden is one of the most historic Dutch towns; its university was founded by William of Orange in 1575. When it is mentioned in the same sentence as the South American Demerara, there appear the dynamic spaces of the tensions of the plot. As mentioned before, William is suffering from typhus and he dies right at the beginning of the story. Although he is a member of a Dutch family, the use of the English version of his name in the text is an allusion to English colonial connections and to English cultural influences: Demerara was by turns under Dutch and English rule. When William's landlady visits Hildebrand she gives a report on William's nightly sufferings. She thinks it is a dangerous thing for William to sleep with the windows open, because foreigners are not used to this. This is another reference to William's strangeness and to the fact that cool Dutch weather may be destructive for someone who is used to a warmer climate. Dutch weather and the climate of the colonies are further tesserae of the narrative structure of the story based on dichotomies. The next scene is about William's funeral. The deceased William's guardian asks Hildebrand to write a letter about the sad case to William's family in Demerara. When the family returns to the Netherlands two years later, Jan Adam Kegge, the father of the deceased

William, invites Hildebrand to visit the Kegge family in their new Leiden home by sending him a letter and a box of Havana cigars.

The first four pages of the work are already full of colonial references: typhus, the warm South American climate, and the box of Havana cigars form the appropriate beginning for the further development of the colonial context of the plot.

When the Kegge family repatriates to the Netherlands they catch another 'illness', namely the illness of being a parvenu, a word borrowed from the French, 'parvenir' — meaning 'to reach', 'to arrive' — of which 'parvenu' is a past participle. Notions connected to meanings such as travelling, arriving, reaching — that is dislocation from non-Europe to Europe, from life to death, from ignorance to the realms of knowledge, from a lower class to a higher one — are among the basic elements of several colonial narratives.

The chapter entitled as 'Kennismaking met mensen en dieren' (Getting Acquainted with People and Animals) also strengthens the system of cultural blending. Hildebrand ironically calls the gift of Havana cigars 'the altar of incense'. This may refer to the rituals of the Old Testament in which people burnt aromatic material while praying and singing. This wording of the gift as 'an altar of incense' can be again placed within the coordinate system of nature versus culture, biblical mythology versus modernity. The moment that Jan Adam Kegge appears on the scene with his 'tanned skin' the reader is again reminded of the warmer climate outside the Netherlands. Thus the virtual journey is continued. Having introduced Kegge, the text goes on showing similar persons and all these make the impression of a collection of waxworks or fossils. It is not only Kegge's skin which has been tanned to a fossil but also his mind: his snobbishness connects him to a dead, stiffened world, not to real life. It is no accident that the first thing Kegge wants to do on arriving at Leiden is to visit the Museum of Natural History, which had been founded in 1820, and the Museum of Antiquities: in the former you could see extinct animals, in the latter unborn embryos. Kegge would further like to see the Chinese and Japanese collections of the physician and natural scientist Dr Franz von Siebold and the portraits of deceased professors in the senate room of the university. The presence of the different kinds of collections is a *mise en abyme* of the work itself. Just as the volume of *Camera Obscura* presents a collection and a list of the fossil types of the Dutch burghers of the early nineteenth century, the novella *De familie Kegge* presents also the passion for collecting and possessing hidden in the cloak of science.

A further station on the 'colonial journey' comes when Kegge draws attention to himself in a restaurant by sprinkling more Cayenne pepper on his food than was usual for the Dutch. Kegge always has the ivory shaker containing the Guyanan spice with him. Before Hildebrand's visit the family sends him a pot of exotic jam made in the West Indies as another gift. Hildebrand's world, which consists of Scaliger, Walter Scott, Bulwer, the Dutch chambers of rhetoric, and Leiden University, is invaded brutally by the colonial elements of the West Indies. With the repatriation of Kegge two cultures meet, each being a stranger to the other. The name Kegge, which means 'wedge', refers to the position of this character between two cultures.

When Hildebrand visits the Kegge family, the 'journey' continues: this time it is a Dutch home where different objects from the colonies can be seen. Chinese porcelain figures, aromatic vials, shells, cigar boxes, silver wall clocks, mirrors, paintings, small tables, stuffed birds and a stuffed tiger shot by Kegge on a sugar plantation, a tiger-skin rug, a living cockatoo, a jewel box made of goat-skin. These exotic objects are blended with pieces of Dutch interiors also well-known from Dutch paintings: a piano, books and music, a fireplace made of Carrara marble, and the life-size portraits of the owners and their children. The Kegge family house is the contact zone of different cultures, Europe and the West Indies, the space of transculturation: Scotch whisky, English pickles, Spanish greyhounds, and illustrated books of travel mingle with Indian arrows and a lot of exotic accessories, non-European drinks and food. The composition of the characters is no less diverse: Henriette, the eldest daughter, is twenty years old and she is biologically 'perfectly developed in accordance with the tropical human race', 'her mother is much browner than her daughter, [...] and much less beautiful from a European point of view'. The grandmother is even browner than Kegge's wife, she does not speak much and if she does, it is in broken Dutch. The blackest person is, however, the servant brought by the family from the plantations, who does not even have a name in the story. Thus the hybrid composition of the family unfolds. In the female line the grandmother is the daughter of an Englishman and an indigenous black mother. Later she had married an English planter, Willliam Marrison. Their daughter is Kegge's wife. The 1665 painting by Pieter Cnoll mentioned in the first chapter comes to life again. In addition to the broad spectrum of shades in between white and black, there is also a relation between the colour of skin and the quantity of speaking in the text: the darker the colour of one's skin, the less one speaks in the story. There is an illustrative scene when the Kegge family carriage tears down the streets of Leiden:

> In een koffiehuis kwamen drie of vier heren, met horizontaal opgeheven pijpen in de mond, over het horretje kijken, en alles toonde ontzag voor de fraaie schimmels, het mooie rijtuig, de deftige koetsier, en de zwarte lakei achterop, die met onbeweeglijke plechtigheid zat rond te kijken en iedereen eerbied inboezemde, behalve de boven alle vooroordelen verheven straatjongen, die hem nariep: 'Mooie jongen, pas op, hoor! Dat de zon je niet verbrandt!'[27]
>
> [In a café there came three or four gentlemen, with their pipes horizontally lifted in their mouths, to peep through the net curtains and everything showed respect for the beautiful white horses, the fabulous coach, the elegant coachman and the black servant in the back, who was looking around with motionless dignity and everybody became very respectful under his influence except a street boy who was above all prejudice and who shouted at him: 'Pretty boy, take care, I say! Don't get yourself sunburnt!']

Back to the Kegge family. When their several children are introduced, those who died at an early age are also mentioned. One of them 'had been poisoned by a bestial Negro woman', says Kegge. Although this statement is never repeated afterwards, the tragedy in the background, an unsolved crime, implies deep conflicts.[28] Father Kegge seems to be not very moved by the deaths of some of his children: one more or less does not make any difference. Kegge also calls himself a parvenu in the positive sense of 'the newly arrived': there is more freedom and a more libertarian way of life in his rich house under the influence of the colonial lifestyle, and this is quite different from the European mode of the 'aristocrats and pretentious knights':

> Je moet maar denken: wij in de West zijn familiaar. In Europa is men vrij wat stijver. Je hebt hier adellijke heren en grote hanzen; daar behoor ik niet toe; warachtig niet; ik ben niet van adel; ik ben geen grote hans; ik ben een parvenu, zo je wilt.[29]
>
> [Don't forget: we are very familiar in the West. People in Europe are much more stiff. You have here aristocrats and pretentious knights; I don't belong to them; really not; I am not from an aristocratic family; I am not a pretentious knight; I am a parvenu, if you like.]

During the story, however, he mentions these 'aristocrats and pretentious knights' so often that his greatest wish is evidently to belong to them.

When Hildebrand sits alone with the eldest daughter of the family, Henriette, it turns out that the girl herself is the same kind of parvenu as her father: she complains that the higher circles stay closed to them there in the Netherlands, while families who would be happy to be friends with them, the Kegges, are not good enough for them. After this we read a long, ironic comment by Hildebrand: the repatriates — either from the East or from the West — may have tons of gold, but material wealth is not enough to gain admission to the patrician circles. This is followed by rhetorical questions from Hildebrand: why cannot these people feel good in the social class into which they have been born? In higher circles they would only let themselves down, and that in its turn would only cause angst and awkward situations. Hildebrand calls this 'a silly ambition'; he does not understand why these rising people cannot rid themselves of this trait. Hildebrand's philosophy is that everyone should stay in the social class into which they have been born; mobility between the different social strata is not desirable. This static social philosophy was generally approved of in the early-nineteenth-century Netherlands. As Van Bork points out in his article, Isaäc Da Costa (1798–1860), the conservative poet and historian of the period, who belonged to the orthodox Protestant Romantic Réveil Movement, wrote with good reason in his 1863 poem '1648 en 1838' [1648 and 1838]: 'God wilde 't onderscheid van gaven, rijkdom, rangen' [God willed differences of talents, wealth, and ranks]. Beets was admittedly a great admirer of Da Costa, at least for a certain period of his life. His *alter ego* Hildebrand points out:

> Moet dan, mejuffrouw! omdat uw vader met ettelijke tonnen gouds uit Oost of West terugkwam, en de achtbaarste patriciër, die beste edelman naar de ogen steekt door uiterlijke praalvertoning, die achtbare patriciër, die doorluchtige edelman al de uwen terstond de hand reiken, en u tot gade voor zijn zoon begeren? Weet gij dan niet, dat indien de kringen, welke gij zo verlangend zijt binnen te treden, zich voor u openden, gij in gestadige angst zoudt verkeren voor een toespeling op uws vaders afkomst, een hatelijkheid op uw aangewaaide rang? Zou het niet veel beter zijn, indien gij u rustig aansloot aan de stand waartoe gij behoort, die even goed is als een hogere, en waarin gij zoudt worden geëerd en ontzien?[30]

[Is this respectable patrician, this superb nobleman, then obliged, Miss, to give his hand immediately to your caste? and to wish you to be the bride of his son merely because your father has returned with several tons of gold from the West or the East, and so can compete with the most honourable patrician, the most outstanding nobleman, as far as outward glitter is concerned? Don't you know then that if those circles to which you have such a desire to belong really opened to you, you would have to live in constant anxiety amidst innuendos concerning your father's pedigree, and that it would be a hateful circumstance in your newly won rank? Would it not be much better if you joined the stratum of society where you belong, which is just as good as a higher circle, and wherein you would be respected and honoured?]

Somewhat later Hildebrand compares the parvenu to bats which are accepted neither by birds nor by mice. This is in fact an ethology of the parvenu. During a conversation with Henriette, it turns out that the girl had had slaves at her service at every moment of her life:

In de loop van ons gesprek verhaalde Henriette mij wonderen van het huis en de paarden en de slaven, die de familie in de West had; een slaaf voor de zakdoek, een slaaf voor de waaier, een slaaf voor het kerkboek, een slaaf voor de flacon![31]

[During our conversation Henriette told me about the wonders of the house, the horses and the slaves that the family had had in the West; a slave for the handkerchief, a slave for the fan, a slave for the prayer book, a slave for the flask!]

Hildebrand's sarcasm and his criticism of the family is prominent in the way he reports on the conversation with Henriette, who put horses and slaves on the same level, repeating the word 'slave' four times in one sentence in relation to ridiculous, everyday actions. However, Henriette wanted to break out from her middle-class lifestyle and she criticized Dutch society in her turn when she mentioned how people peered from behind curtains to see what others were doing, how horrified they were when they saw a lady on horseback, let alone when she appeared in public with a man. Like her father, she too had some affinity for freedom; in her case it was even a gender-sensitive freedom, which was not of European origin. Hildebrand acknowledges that he has heard this kind of complaint earlier, from others, but he cannot really sympathize with it. He is not disturbed by Dutch inequalities: his agenda includes keeping the borders between classes, strata and sexes rather than crossing them. His criticism of the parvenu is actually of a conservative nature; he does not accept social dynamism in respect either of social strata or of gender roles. He — that is Beets — however, critically shows the wealthy parvenu in his colonial context and by doing so is one of the first in Dutch literature to criticize colonialism.

It is no accident that the chapter 'Grootmoeder' (Grandmother) is placed in the middle of the story. This central position shows the grandmother's importance. As mentioned before, she is the daughter of an English father and a West Indian indigenous mother and she has the darkest skin in the family. All these circumstances, her great age and her fidelity to her deceased grandson make her lonely and isolated in the family. The narrator meets her in the library: the place of knowledge as opposed to the shallow, false value system of the family. Her only company is her dog and she is reading an English language Bible, to be precise, 'The Epistle of Paul to the Romans': 'For we are saved by hope: but hope that is seen is not hope: for what a man seeth, why doth he yet hope for? But if we hope for that we see not, then do we with patience wait for it.'[32] The quotation describes the same value system which is embodied by the grandmother: it is about personal longing to be away from the present situation and about invisible values, the wealth of the inner world. Thus it is this grandmother who is depicted as the most precious, most amiable member of the Kegge family, the one with the darkest skin, and the one who has the greatest difficulty in striking roots in Dutch soil.

There are other chapters beside the first two and that about the grandmother which touch on the colonial theme. De Maete, the suitor of Suzette Noiret, is under the influence of his untrustworthy friend, Bout. That is why De Maete forges a plan to go to the West Indies to make a fortune so that he can marry Suzette after a year spent working in the colony. As it turns out, this is all deliberately and viciously arranged by Bout in order to get De Maete away so that his no less false friend Van der Hoogen can seduce Suzette. Bout reckons that by the time De Maete comes home again Suzette will be so compromised that the proposed marriage will come to nothing. As a consequence of Hildebrand's investigations, it is these malicious intentions that come to nothing. Mayor Van Nagel, a real gentleman, gives De Maete a position at his office which ensures him the necessary financial circumstances so that he can marry Suzette without going to the colonies. In the end Hildebrand draws the conclusion: good or bad qualities are not related to social class, the point is that nobody should wish to belong to a social class other than that into which they have been born. Even Jan Adam Kegge is cured of his 'disease'. The wicked get their punishment, the good are rewarded. At the end of the last chapter the circle is closed: the grandmother takes care that Hildebrand inherits her deceased grandson's ring and handkerchief after she herself dies. She encloses an English language letter in the small package: 'Gedenk aan de lieve William en aan zijn Grootmoeder, E. Marrison' [Remember dear William and his Grandmother, E. Marrison].[33]

Beets inserts minor stories into the main story which work as counterpoints. One such minor story contrasts Henriette's ostentatious wealth with the simple, puritan way of life of her niece Saartje and her family. Saartje's father is a baker who is baking cakes for St Nicholas's Eve, the most precious Dutch feast. Family members and friends come together to wrap gifts in tinfoil. The company reflects the types already shown by Beets in his 1841 volume *De Nederlanden* (*The Netherlands*): there is a tailor, a grocer, a bricklayer, a butcher, and the daughter of a widow living in an old people's home. This is the social stratum which has the greatest sympathy from the narrator and also from Beets: ordinary people who earn their living by honest toil and do not want to seem either more or less than what they really are. It is the same social stratum between the upper rich and the poor from which Beets himself came.

Suzette Noiret, the main character of another minor storyline, belongs to the group of characters who come from a lower social class. She is a descendant of the French Huguenots who once fled to the Netherlands. Van der Hoogen is a social climber and a pretentious womanizer. He courts not only Henriette but also Suzette. One day Hildebrand witnesses his making advances to her in the street and decides to reveal his despicable conduct and by so doing to save both young ladies from the rogue.

This episode not only criticizes the dependence of women on men, but also the social circles to which Van der Hoogen belongs. By way of digression I would like to point out a literary device of Beets's that is so typical of nineteenth-century realism: showing the details of the tangible world is a means of characterization of human beings. There are several detailed descriptions of interiors through which we can draw conclusions with respect to the human traits of the characters who live there. The following example is a metonymy of Van der Hoogen:

> De kamer was niet bijzonder charmant; zij was slecht gestoffeerd en alles behalve net. Een gemakkelijke leuningstoel was het beste meubel. Aan de muur hingen een paar prenten met Robert Macaire, en enige vrouwenbeelden van de hand van kunstenaars, die zich bijzonder op het naakt schenen te hebben toegelegd. Boven de schoorsteen een schermmasker, schermhandschoenen en floretten, en de staart van een fazantehaan, die Van der Hoogen moest verbeelden eenmaal geschoten of gegeten te hebben. In de rand van de spiegel staken een menigte invitatiekaarten, waaronder sommige van reeds zeer oude datum. Op tafel stond een grote flacon met reukwater en lag een deeltje van Paul de Kock opgeslagen. Er brandde een vuur in de haard, dat echter in het laatste half uur slecht scheen onderhouden te zijn. Een onaangeroerd ontbijt stond op, en van de kook geraakte theewater onder de tafel.[34]

> [The room was not very charmant; the upholstery was tattered and the whole was far from being neat. A comfortable armchair was the best piece of furniture. On the wall there hung prints depicting Robert Macaire, and some portraits of women made by artists who must have specialized in nudes in particular. Above the fireplace there were a fencing mask, fencing gloves and swords, and the tail of a cock pheasant which Van der Hoogen must have thought that he had once shot or eaten. At the edge of the mirror and the mirror itself lots of invitation cards were stuck, some of them of very old date. On the table stood a big bottle of perfume, and a volume by Paul de Kock lay open. There was a fire burning in the fireplace, but it seemed not to have been attended to in the last half-hour. There was an untouched breakfast on and cold tea water in a kettle under the table.]

The word 'charmant' is ironic: it is Van der Hoogen's favourite word, which he uses of everything and everybody. Robert Macaire was a notorious brigand, familiar from French plays. One of the popular novels on Bohemian habits by the French author of Dutch origin, Paul de Kock (1793–1871), the nudes on the wall, the weapons, the trophy of a pheasant's tail, the old invitation cards, the perfume bottle and the mess in the room, all allude to the Bohemian, superficial way of life and the weak character of the occupant of the room, Van der Hoogen, just as the Kegge family's interior is a metonymy of their colonial background.

Van der Hoogen's sexual aggression towards Suzette Noiret is related through a special word of Beets's to the subjugation of black slaves. Van der Hoogen refers to Suzette at a certain point as 'the small black beauty'. 'Black' is here, of course, a reference to the colour of Suzette's hair, or perhaps to her name, Noiret. The word 'black' stands in the Dutch text in the diminutive form: *zwartje*. That is the paternalist Dutch appellation for black slaves from the colonies. The Kegges' servant brought from Demerara is such a *zwartje*. This word forms a semantic link between the position of Suzette, the sexually assaulted young woman, and the colonial subjugation of the black servant. Parallels between the subjugation of women and colonized people will be touched upon in more detail in the next chapter.

This train of thought is confirmed by the speaking names of other characters: Van der Hoogen has in his name the Dutch word *hoog*, which means 'high' in English and can imply 'arrogant', while De Maete involves the Dutch word *maat* which means 'moderate' and he is really a virtuous young man living very moderately. As mentioned before, Kegge means 'wedge' which also depicts his position between different cultures and social classes.

Beets pillories every social relationship in which one party can subjugate another: the macho seducer against the unprotected woman, the empty formal prescriptions of the Church against the deep, devout faith of individuals, the parvenu who made his fortune by exploiting others against the cordial, simple, working lower middle class, the middle-aged, white Dutch man's brutality against the dark-skinned old lady's rich emotions. One of the morals of the story is that one has no need to go to the colonies to amass the fortune which is expected for a responsible marriage. But the criticism of the Kegge family is related to the criticism of other social strata and relations. The colonial background is only one of these. As mentioned before, the story also shows Kegge's somewhat more libertarian mind, and in the end both he and his daughter become 'tamed down'. The social stratum above the Kegges is compromised by the characters of Van der Hoogen and his friend. Van Nagel and his daughter, who belong to the same high social stratum, are, however, depicted as ideal embodiments of civil values. Social strata and their representatives are judged according to how much they fit into the ideal value system of a civil society where these layers have rigid borders. This ideal value system implies a modest fortune earned by work, intimate and true religious devotion and family ties, and acceptance of hierarchy inside the family. The suggestion is that there are examples of good and bad in each social stratum, people may even change but should always remain inside their own social group. You cannot cross social borders without being changed for the worse. This moral implies, of course, the notion that colonial subordination too can never be changed and should be interpreted as due to providence.

After writing *De familie Kegge* in 1840 and after inserting the story in *Camera Obscura* in 1851, Beets gave a lecture entitled 'De Bevrijding der Slaven' [The Emancipation of Slaves] for the Nederlandsche Maatschappij tot bevordering van de Afschaffing der Slavernij [Dutch Society for Supporting the Abolition of Slavery]. In his speech he called for the emancipation of slaves in the West Indies in the name of philanthropy, culture, and Christianity. These European values, he pointed out, served as incontestable arguments against the exploitation of man by man.

While working on *De familie Kegge* he must have already been occupied by the question of abolition. The short novel can be considered as a literary precursor of the lecture.

Whether Beets was really opposed to colonization itself is another question. Neither the short novel nor the lecture gives grounds for such a conclusion. Beets advocates the equality of men and condemns disproportionate wealth earned without actual work, but he does not criticize the institution of colonization, and he argues for keeping the borders between social groups. Nevertheless, the sophisticated and critical depiction of colonial people, their social relationships, and the interrelations between Dutch society and the colonies — to paraphrase Said's words: Leiden was made possible by the colony Demerara — makes Beets's work one of the most important links in the critical chain of Dutch colonial literature.

Notes to Chapter 2

1. Willem Frijhoff and Marijke Spies, *1650. Bevochten eendracht* (Den Haag: Sdu Uitgevers, 1999), pp. 110–12. A good part of this introduction is based on their chapter on slavery in this book.
2. *The Standard King James Bible*, Exodus 21:16, 'And he that stealeth a man, and selleth him, or if he be found in his hand, he shall surely be put to death.'
3. Edward Said, *Orientalism* (New York: Vintage Books, 1979), p. 3.
4. Wim van den Doel, *Zo ver de wereld strekt. De geschiedenis van Nederland overzee vanaf 1800* (Amsterdam: Bert Bakker, 2011), pp. 25–29.
5. Wim van den Doel, pp. 8–86.
6. Michiel van Kempen, '"Van grouwelijcke monsters en kinderen gods". De Nederlands-koloniale literatuur over Suriname', in *Europa buitengaats. Koloniale en postkoloniale literaturen in Europese talen*, ed. by Theo D'Haen (Amsterdam: Bert Bakker, 2002), pp. 160–98 (p. 160).
7. Michiel van Kempen, *Een geschiedenis van de Surinaamse literatuur* (Paramaribo: Okopipi, 2002), pp. 249–54.
8. Jacqueline Bel, 'Mansfield Park versus de Camera Obscura. "De familie Kegge" als koloniaal verhaal', in *Literatuurwetenschap tussen betrokkenheid en distantie*, ed. by Lisbeth Korthals-Altes and Dick Schram (Assen: Van Gorcum, 2000), pp. 375–86.
9. Willem van den Berg, Henk Eijssens, Joost Kloek, and Peter van Zonneveld, 'Inleiding', in *Nicolaas Beets, Camera Obscura*, ed. by Willem van den Berg, Henk Eijssens, Joost Kloek, and Peter van Zonneveld (Amsterdam: Athenaeum-Polak & Van Gennep, 1998), pp. 13–63.
10. Peter van Zonneveld, *De Romantische Club: Leidse student-auteurs 1830–1840* (Leiden: Athanae Batavae, 1993).
11. 'José, een Spaansch verhaal' (1834), 'Kuser' (1835), and 'Guy de Vlaming' (1837).
12. Nicolaas Beets, *De bevrijding der slaven. Redevoering gehouden in openbare vergaderingen van de Nederlandsche Maatschappy ter bevordering van de afschaffing der slaverny* (Haarlem: Bohn, 1856).
13. Champfleury, *Le realisme* (Paris: M. Lévy frères, 1857).
14. Anna Balakian, 'The Unfamiliar Literatures', in *The Snowflake on the Belfry: Dogma and Disquietude in the Critical Arena* (Bloomington and Indianapolis: Indiana University Press, 1994), pp. 236–40 (p. 239).
15. Charles Dickens, *Sketches by Boz* (London: John Macrone, 1837), pp. 127–28.
16. Nicolaas Beets, *Camera Obscura en verspreide stukken* (Utrecht and Antwerp: Veen, 1982), p. 44.
17. Ibid., pp. 56–57.
18. Laurence Sterne, *The Life and Opinions of Tristram Shandy* (Harmondsworth: Penguin Books Ltd, 1983), p. 98.
19. Svetlana Alpers, *The Art of Describing: Dutch Art in the Seventeenth Century* (Chicago: The University of Chicago Press, 1983), passim.
20. Nicolaas Beets, *Camera Obscura en verspreide stukken* (Utrecht and Antwerp: Veen, 1982), p. 8.
21. Jonathan Crary, *Techniques of the Observer: On Vision and Modernity in the 19th Century* (Cambridge, MA: The MIT Press, 1992).
22. Jacqueline Bel, 'Mansfield Park versus de Camera Obscura. "De familie Kegge" als koloniaal verhaal', in *Literatuurwetenschap tussen betrokkenheid en distantie*, ed. by Liesbeth Korthals-Altes and Dick Schram (Assen: Van Gorcum, 2000), pp. 375–86.

23. G. J. van Bork, 'Enkele sociale aspecten van de "Familie Kegge"', *Spectator*, 4 (1974–75), 284–88, and P. van 't Veer, 'De biografie van J. A. Kegge (1796–1854)', *Hollands Maandblad*, 15.312 (1973), 39–42.
24. Arnold Labrie, 'Romantische politiek. Moderniteit en het ideaal van de zuivere gemeenschap', in *De zieke natie*, ed. by Liesbet Nys, Henk de Smaele, Jo Tollebeek, and Kaat Wils (Groningen: Historische Uitgeverij, 2002), pp. 58–73 (p. 70).
25. Beets, p. 157.
26. Ibid., p. 158.
27. Ibid., p. 181.
28. A similar crime is one of the main motifs in Couperus's novel of 1906 *Van oude mensen, de dingen die voorbijgaan*. G. J. van Bork in his 1974–75 article mentioned above holds it possible that the child really became a victim of a slave's revenge. Kegge worked as a supervisor, and family members of such supervisors were often murdered in revenge by subordinate slaves.
29. Beets, p. 166.
30. Ibid., p. 171.
31. Ibid., p. 172.
32. *The Standard King James Bible*, Romans 8:24, 25.
33. Beets, 1982, p. 238.
34. Ibid., p. 221.

CHAPTER 3

Speaking and Silence of the 'Other': Parallels of Colonial and Female Subjugation in Multatuli's Novel *Max Havelaar*

The Outside Context

Dutch Colonialism in the first half of the Nineteenth Century (The Dutch East Indies)

The VOC enterprise increasingly made losses, among other reasons because of British and Chinese competition. The definitive crash was caused, according to historian Rudolf Dekker, not by corruption inside the VOC or by malfeasance but by lack of capital which made it impossible to access new markets and products (such as Chinese tea, for example).[1] The British drove the Dutch even out of the Indian textile industry. By 1799 the decline could no longer be arrested and the bankrupt enterprise was taken over by the Batavian Republic. This meant the new era of modern colonization in the Netherlands.

During the Napoleonic Wars, territories under Dutch hegemony had been occupied by England. The East Indies were restored when peace was re-established between 1816 and 1819. This was partly due to the recognition that England needed a strong Netherlands assuring her position against France. A strong state was to be achieved by colonial possessions, according to contemporary conceptions. In 1824 England and the Netherlands signed an agreement about all this. Dutch colonial possessions in Asia were called the Dutch East Indies, and their status changed so that they belonged from then on under the jurisdiction of the Dutch state. Like the VOC, the Dutch state also aspired to a monopoly in the commerce and transportation of colonial goods. In 1824 the Nederlandsche Handel-Maatschappij [Dutch Trade Company] was established. This company worked as an agent of commerce and transport: it received coffee and tea on consignment and sold them on in the Netherlands. This operation resulted in the so-called Dutch Indian profits, out of which the Nederlandsche Handel-Maatschappij (NHM) received a prodigious agent's percentage.

After 1830, agricultural production in the Dutch East Indies was regulated by the so-called *cultuurstelsel* [agriculture-system]. This meant that one-fifth of cultivable land had to be planted with the crops ordered by the Dutch government which were considered most profitable in Europe, such as coffee and sugar. This system opened the door for large-scale exploitation of the native population. The planting of obligatory crops operated to the detriment of rice production, which often resulted in food-shortages in the East Indies.

This agricultural system was later criticized both from an economic and from an ethical point of view. Liberals wanted to stop it, but they did not want to lose the profits that it produced. After the abandonment of the agricultural system free entrepreneurs travelled from the Netherlands to the Dutch East Indies. Although they could not own land, they could rent it. While in 1852 there were fewer than 20,000 Europeans in the Dutch East Indies (not counting soldiers) by 1905 their number had risen to 95,000.

Colonial possessions had a special importance for the Netherlands not only economically but also in so far as European prestige was concerned. This still did not go as far as in England: while Queen Victoria became Empress of India, William III did not become Emperor of the Dutch East Indies.

Nevertheless, how could such a small country as the Netherlands keep such a huge territory as the East Indies in its power? Primarily by military means. There were wars almost throughout the whole nineteenth century: first the Palembang war (1819–21), then the Java war (1825–30). In 1832 the Koninklijk Nederlandsch Indisch Leger [KNIL, The Royal Dutch Indian Army] was formed. Between 1846 and 1849 there came the Bali war, and in 1873 the Aceh war broke out.

Some Trends in the Reception of *Max Havelaar* in the Netherlands in the Twentieth and Twenty-first Centuries

Dutch literary criticism in the 1930s was shaped by the journal *Forum* (1932–35) and by its 'founding fathers', Menno ter Braak (1902–40) and Edgar du Perron (1899–1940). According to them, the most important evaluative criterion of literary works was the integrity and authenticity of the author's personality: his humanistic, ethical commitment should be clearly inscribed in his work. Modernism which focused upon formal aspects of literary works was rejected.[2] Multatuli was the standard icon for this circle: as the members of the circle argued, there was a strength and an emanation of such a strong authorial personality in Multatuli's work, especially in his *Max Havelaar*. Multatuli committed himself to the same humanistic value system which was depicted in his work (see Fig. 3.1). Therefore Multatuli was reckoned a standard of measurement: each writer was compared to him and evaluated according to his relation to Multatuli.

In the 1960s *New Criticism* also became popular in the Netherlands. It gave rise to structuralism, in which the text and its close reading were central to analysis. The journal *Merlyn* (Merlin, 1962–66) became the most prominent forum of this trend in the Netherlands. Several text-centred analyses of *Max Havelaar* saw the light at that time. The first was probably that by Jaap Oversteegen, one of the founders of *Merlyn*.[3] The main idea of his essay is that the structure, despite the many detours, forms a closed, coherent fictional world, of which the most important message is the

Fig. 3.1. Portrait of Multatuli by August Allebé, 1874, lithograph Collectie Documentatie Nederlandse Letterkunde

'affair': the injustice of Dutch exploitation of the Javanese and Havelaar's justice in fighting against the establishment. Droogstoppel, the grotesque philistine, becomes a monster by the end of the novel, while Havelaar, Multatuli's alter ego, is an unambiguous positive hero. In analysing the structure, Oversteegen does not pay attention to the details and their ideological implications. The scene where Havelaar helps the 'Indian lady', the indigenous nanny, out of the carriage forms, according to Oversteegen, the best part of Havelaar's character and personality. Parallels between the frame and the main story are mentioned, but only from a structural point of view. The main function of these stories, argues Oversteegen, is to prepare the non-fictional pamphlet at the end which closes the fictional part of the novel.

Oversteegen's essay is followed by Sötemann's dissertation, first published in 1966.[4] Like Oversteegen, Sötemann too evades questions outside the novel such as biographical implications, who was right, and how the 'affair' ran its course.[5] He analyses only the structure of the novel, which he too considers a coherent whole despite the diversity and seemingly disorderly character of the work.

Yet another trend in the analysis of the novel is when scholars situate the work in its contemporary context, and the 'affair' depicted in the novel is examined in relation to real events and to contemporary colonial circumstances. In these biographical approaches Multatuli's real struggles in the contemporary political arena are focused upon.[6]

In her book, Saskia Pieterse mentions beside these trends those which analyse *Max Havelaar* from a post-colonial point of view.[7] She finds it important to emphasize that the authors of all these are literary scholars outside the Netherlands.[8] Their common feature is that they question the unquestionable status of this novel in the Dutch literary canon, that they find Multatuli's criticism of contemporary colonial circumstances problematic, and that they critically analyse the position of women and indigenous people in the novel.

Another group is that which regards the novel as the forerunner of post-colonial critical theories.[9] According to the 'post-colonial group' (to which I belong), Pieterse argues, Multatuli is a representative of European dominance despite all his commitments to the colonized, while the second group emphasizes his anti-imperialist way of thought.

In my essay published in the Netherlands in 2001 I tried to demonstrate that in Multatuli's novel there unfolds an ambivalent value system: he is at the same time Eurocentric and not Eurocentric, paternalistic and not paternalistic. Among other things I argue:

> Vanuit een ideologiekritische vraagstelling is het evenwel belangrijker dat het boek het probleem van het koloniale systeem thematiseert en er vraagtekens bij stelt. Het brengt bij lezers een denkproces op gang dat de wezenlijke onbillijkheid van kolonisatie helpt onthullen. De schrijver weet heel vaak een eurocentrische kijk te vermijden. Hij weet dat macht tot een verkeerde beoordeling en representatie kan leiden. [...] Kijken we naar de tekst van de roman en naar de door Multatuli zelf later toegevoegde noten, dan kunnen we tot geen andere conclusie komen dan dat de roman anti-kolonialistisch en kolonialistisch tegelijk is. Belangrijk is dat we niet vooringenomen door de klassieke literatuurkritiek noch door de uitdaging van

de deconstructivistische praktijken naar het boek kijken. De kolonialistische visie sluit de anti-kolonialistische denkwijze niet uit, en omgekeerd. Het boek blijft ambivalent.[10]

[From an ideology-critical point of view, however, it is more important that the book focuses upon the colonial system and puts question marks to it. It triggers a thinking process in readers which helps them to recognize the basic injustice of colonization. The author often succeeds in avoiding Eurocentrism. He is conscious of the fact that power leads to distorted value judgements and mistaken representations. [...] If we examine the text of the novel and the notes which were added later by Multatuli we cannot but draw the conclusion that the novel is anti-colonial and colonial at the same time. It is essential that neither traditional literary criticism nor the challenges of deconstructivism should make us prejudiced while analysing this book. Colonial conceptions do not obviously exclude anti-colonial thoughts and vice versa. The book maintains its ambivalence.]

This quotation proves that I do not consider Multatuli's novel Eurocentric and colonial on the whole. In what follows I introduce the method that I used for the analysis. After that comes the analysis itself.

'*Max Havelaar* na 150 jaar'[11] [*Max Havelaar* after 150 Years] — an example of a mainstream discourse on the novel today

The Multatuli Genootschap [Multatuli Society] in the Netherlands requested teachers of modern Dutch literature at universities outside the Netherlands to give a lecture at their home university on Multatuli's *Max Havelaar* on the 150th anniversary of its first edition in 1860 (see Fig. 3.2). An indication of the thoroughness and tact of the Society is the fact that they attached a 'ready-made' lecture written by (an) anonymous author(s) in case the speakers concerned might run out of material. The text — also because of its anonymity — is an outstanding example of the discourse inside the Netherlands concerning both the colonial past and the novel itself. This discourse has begun to change in recent years under the influence of post-colonial studies, and it has produced several critical approaches.

Discourse is a special form of language which is regulated and determined by situational rules and the given context. The working of power also forms a constituent of this notion of discourse. One of Foucault's relevant questions is: 'Who has the right to use a particular discourse, what benefits accrue to them from using it, how is its usage policed, and where does it derives its authority from?'[12] It was also Foucault who introduced the notion of discursive formation. This means a set of systemic statements, a system produced by a certain discursive practice. This concrete discursive practice indicates a regulation system working at a certain moment of history, very often common to several societies at the same time. These rules arise organically; they are not intentional, objective. They are not simply laws or social regulations. They are rather rules which determine the production of utterances, what can and what cannot be said at a certain moment, or what can be said at all. For analysing history and society Foucault suggests non-linearity and dispersion instead of causality. He argues that changes in the most diverse social

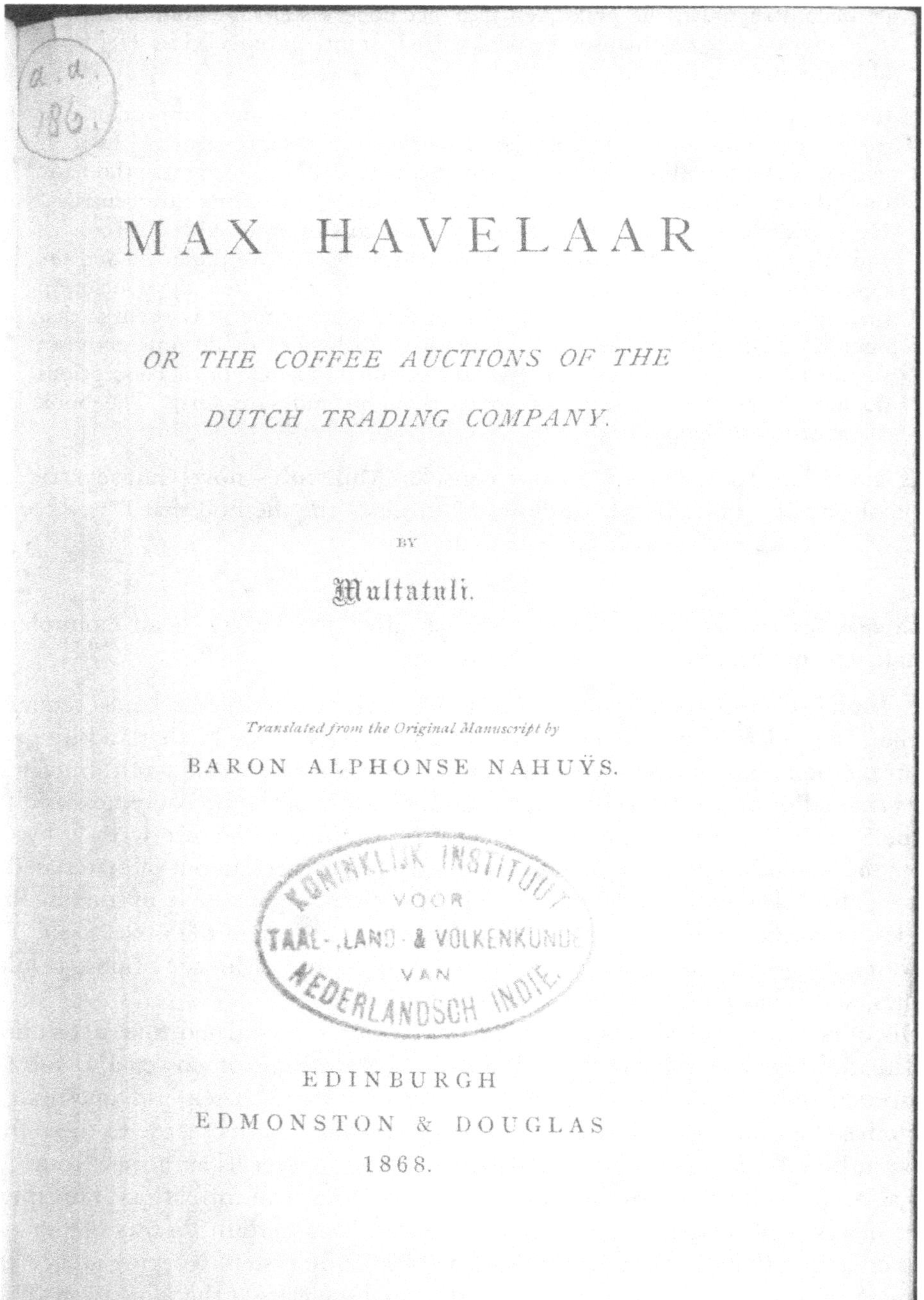

MAX HAVELAAR

OR THE COFFEE AUCTIONS OF THE

DUTCH TRADING COMPANY.

BY

Multatuli.

Translated from the Original Manuscript by
BARON ALPHONSE NAHUŸS.

EDINBURGH
EDMONSTON & DOUGLAS
1868.

[*All rights reserved*]

FIG. 3.2. Cover of the 1868 English edition of the *Max Havelaar*.
Leiden University Libraries, M aa 186 001

fields are connected by discursive links. Changes are not the result of one mind or a special intention, but of a discursive practice becoming more and more visible, coming about in the course of time. Discursive formations emerge slowly and in an uncertain way, objectively.[13]

The text of the pre-written Dutch lecture is, I argue, a discursive formation dictated by an invisible power. The interest of this invisible power is again to fend off new approaches and new readings by accentuating the aesthetic values of the novel; we have seen this same mechanism in previous chapters.

The following text-fragments are the English translation from the first part of the pre-written Dutch lecture, which I provide with my critical comments. In these comments I shed light on how, and to what extent, this is a discursive formation.

Some fragments of the Dutch lecture critically commented on

> In mei 1860 verscheen bij de Amsterdamse uitgever Joost de Ruyter een tweedelig boek met een echt negentiende-eeuwse, maar ook wel wat misleidende titel: *Max Havelaar, of de koffie-veilingen der Nederlandsche Handel-Maatschappij, door Multatuli*. Van deze schrijver 'met zijn larmoyante pseudoniem', zoals Menno ter Braak het bijna tachtig later zou omschrijven, had in die tijd nog niemand gehoord, behoudens een paar lezers van het radicale vrijdenkersblaadje *De dageraad*, waarin Multatuli het jaar daarvoor zijn debuut had gemaakt.

> [In May 1860 the Amsterdam publisher Joost de Ruyter brought out a two-volume book with a real nineteenth-century, somewhat misleading, title: *Max Havelaar, or the Coffee Auctions of the Dutch Trading Company, by Multatuli*. At the time, nobody had heard of this writer 'with his sentimental pen-name', as Menno ter Braak would describe it some eighty years later, except some of the readers of the radical and liberal journal *Dageraad* (*The Dawn*), in which Multatuli had debuted a year before.]

Menno ter Braak was one of the most renowned Dutch literary authorities in the 1930s. His influence lasted almost to the end of the century; his taste and judgements were unquestioned. Mentioning his name at the very beginning of the text seems to be inevitable as he wrote a lot about Multatuli's novel.[14] However, this is a reference to a literary authority — for most Dutch readers incontestable — which helps to continue a tradition of schematic, uncritical, non-innovative reading of the book. In the meantime, feminist literary criticism has begun to analyse Menno ter Braak's sexist, misogynist judgements, which has started a critical re-evaluation of him.[15]

> Achter het pseudoniem — dat betekent: ik heb veel geleden — iets wat je in de negentiende eeuw nog niet hoefde uit te leggen aan de kleine groep boekenkopers en lezers — , ging een bestuursambtenaar schuil, die enkele jaren tevoren zijn ontslag had genomen. Zijn naam was Eduard Douwes Dekker. In 1838 had Douwes Dekker, toen achttien jaar oud, besloten naar Nederlands-Oost-Indië te gaan. Er waren allerlei redenen voor hem om dit te doen: een mislukte schoolopleiding, even weinig succesvolle pogingen om bij handelskantoren te werken, en bovenal: een vader die als scheepskapitein met zekere regelmaat naar de Oost voer. Toch was het een ingrijpend en avontuurlijk besluit, om vele redenen. Nederlands-Indië was een 'nieuwe' kolonie.

[Behind his pen-name — which means 'I have suffered a lot' and which did not have to be explained to the small group of book buyers and readers at that time — there hid a clerk who had quit his job some years before. His real name was Eduard Douwes Dekker. In 1838 the eighteen-year-old Douwes Dekker decided to go to the Dutch East Indies. He had several reasons for this: unsuccessful school years, similarly unsuccessful endeavours to find permanent work with trading companies, and most of all his father, who as a ship's captain sailed more or less regularly over to the East. The decision had an elemental power and an adventurous nature for various reasons. The Dutch East Indies was a 'new' colony.]

The Dutch East Indies was not a new colony, only its name was new. The VOC, founded in 1602, had functioned as a private enterprise, but it already followed a pre-imperialist colonial practice. After the bankruptcy of the VOC in 1799 the colonies — up till then in private ownership and known by the name of East Indies — acquired the name Dutch East Indies and became state property. So the difference lies not in having new colonies, as the text deceptively suggests, but in the renaming of old colonies and the new power structure hidden behind the new names, that is, the nationalization of colonies once in private ownership.

> De Verenigde Oost-Indische Compagnie was er weliswaar ruim tweehonderd jaar actief geweest, wat had geleid tot een grote Nederlandse invloed, ook politiek.
>
> [True, the VOC had been active for more than two hundred years, and this led to a great Dutch influence in politics too.]

The activities of the VOC led not only to important Dutch influence but also to the immense wealth of the Dutch — unique in seventeenth century Europe — and also to East Indian cultural influence on Holland. Accentuation of Dutch influence fits into a colonial discursive practice in which European power plays an active role, whereas colonial culture is cast in a passive, receptive position. The truth, however, is that the East Indies, later the Dutch East Indies, penetrated several fields of Dutch culture from gastronomy to fine arts.

> Maar het waren de Engelsen die in de Napoleontische tijd Java en delen van de andere eilanden hadden veroverd en verenigd. In 1816 werden deze gebieden overgedragen aan Nederland, en daarmee was dit kleine Europese land, amper hersteld van de Franse overheersing, opeens een koloniale mogendheid van formaat geworden.
>
> [However, it was the English who occupied and united Java and parts of other islands in Napoleonic times. In 1816 these territories were ceded to the Netherlands and by this the small European country, just recovered from French rule, suddenly became a colonial power of great importance.]

The English did not renounce but gave back these territories to the Dutch. The Dutch became not suddenly but once again a colonial power of great importance.

> Maar het had ook meteen te kampen met de onrust die bij zo'n nieuw verworven — we zouden tegenwoordig zeggen: bezet gebied — hoort.
>
> [But it also had to engage in the unrest which belongs to such a newly acquired — today we would call it: occupied — territory.]

Once again: it was not newly acquired but recovered territory, which had already been colonized in the seventeenth century. And yes, 'unrest', in other words, the protests of local people, goes with the situation inevitably when intruders want to appropriate a territory for their own benefit.

> Maar er waren in 1838 meer gevaren voor de jonge Indischman. De vaart naar Indië was bijvoorbeeld lang: net als in de eeuwen van de VOC zeilde — zeilde, ja, want het tijdperk van de stoomschepen moest nog aanbreken — zeilde men dus met een wijde boog om Afrika heen, gebruikmakend van zeestromingen en passaatwinden. Het Suez-kanaal zou pas een jaar of dertig later worden geopend. De reis, die zo'n drie maanden duurde (soms zelfs langer), was zwaar en riskant. Onderweg overleden altijd wel een paar reizigers, en een enkele keer verging zelfs het gehele schip. In Indië zelf waren het vooral de tropische ziektes die de Europeanen bedreigden, de zogeheten moeraskoorts voorop, die aan de slechte lucht ter plaatse werd toegeschreven. (Vandaar de naam mal aria.)

> [However, there were several dangers for a young man shipping out to the East Indies. It was a long journey: as in the centuries of the VOC one sailed — yes, sailed, because the age of steam had not yet dawned — one sailed in a broad curve around Africa, making use of maritime currents and trade winds. The Suez Canal would be opened only about thirty years later. The journey took about three months (sometimes even longer) and was difficult and risky. There were always passengers who died on the way, and in some cases even the whole ship capsized and sank. In the East Indies there were tropical diseases which threatened Europeans, especially the so-called swamp-fever, which was attributed to bad air in the region. (The name *malaria* means literally 'bad air'.)]

This formulation makes it sound as if this disease threatened Europeans, otherwise blameless from a hygienic point of view, exclusively in the Dutch East Indies. However, malaria was also endemic in the Netherlands until 1920, and after the Second World War there were still 10,000 cases registered each year. The Netherlands was one of the last countries to be declared malaria-free by the WHO in 1970. Connecting disease to colonies enhances negative stereotypes of the East which show the Orient as a reservoir of mysticism and incomprehensible dangers. Furthermore, all this picks up and maintains a European discourse of cleanliness in the nineteenth century, which beside the concrete, biological notion also used cleanliness in a metaphorical sense. It considered the mingling of 'races', and also the mere presence of non-European ethnics in Europe, to be a threat to cleanliness — *mutatis mutandis* to the cleanliness of Western European civilization.[16]

> Maar ook voor wie de reis en de tropische ziektes zou overleven, gold: het afscheid van de familie en vrienden in Nederland was vaak een afscheid voor altijd. 'Even' overkomen naar Europa was er niet bij; de telefoon moest nog worden uitgevonden, en zelfs de telegrafie bestond nog niet.

> [But also for those who survived the voyage and the tropical diseases, the farewell from family and friends in the Netherlands was very often a farewell forever. To go over to Europe 'just for a while' was out of the question; the telephone had not yet been invented at the time, nor did the telegraph exist.]

This text gives the impression that Dutch people who went to the Dutch East

Indies — even risking their lives, sacrificing their comfort, being deprived of their home in the Netherlands — deserve commiseration. These technical innovations of modernity, which were not yet available at the time of Dekker's voyage, are put into the context of colonization as if their availability or absence could only be interpreted in terms of whether they made the process of colonization easier and more comfortable for Dutch colonizers.

> *Max Havelaar* verscheen, zoals gezegd, in het voorjaar van 1860, en deed, in de woorden van het liberale Tweede-Kamerlid W.R. van Hoëvell, 'een rilling door het land gaan'. Hoewel niemand van Multatuli had gehoord, werd het boek in alle kranten besproken, en meestal lovend. 'Ik wil gelezen worden,' schreef Multatuli in het beroemde slot van zijn boek, en hij wérd gelezen. Het was niet de eerste keer dat de misstanden in Nederlands-Indië aan de kaak werden gesteld — dezelfde Van Hoëvell was hem daarin voorgegaan — , maar het was wel de eerste maal dat het op zo'n overtuigende wijze werd gedaan. Want, daarover waren vriend en vijand het eens, hier was een geniaal schrijver opgestaan.
>
> [As already mentioned, *Max Havelaar* was published in the spring of 1860 and, in the words of the liberal member of the lower chamber W. R. van Hoëvell, 'it gave the whole country the creeps'. Although nobody had previously heard of Multatuli, the book was reviewed in all the newspapers and mostly in a laudatory way. 'I want to be read', Multatuli wrote in the famous ending of his novel, and read he certainly was. It was not the first time that the abuse of authority in the Dutch East Indies had been criticized — the same Van Hoëvell was his predecessor in this respect — but it was the first time that it had been done in such a convincing way. Both friend and antagonist agreed that a brilliant writer had appeared on the scene.]

This remark also needs some correction. Right after the publication of the novel, but also at later times, there were serious or less serious negative criticisms of the book, so not everybody agreed that the writer was a genius.[17] This comment, of course, does not mean that I identify with the contemporary negative criticisms. My analysis is based upon a totally different point of departure and it has other objectives. The quoted text, however, illustrates the power of discourse which can, by using undifferentiated and schematic sentences, manipulate our image of the contemporary reception of the book.

Those were the fragments of the pre-written lecture by which I wanted to illustrate the Dutch discursive formation. On the basis of my comments one can draw more conclusions: (1) The beginnings of Dutch colonization are still put in the nineteenth century, 'forgetting' the long history of colonization from the end of the sixteenth century. (2) Dutch participants in the colonizing process are represented as victims while the real, indigenous victims of colonization are not mentioned at all. (3) Situating Douwes Dekker in the tradition of French Enlightenment and modelling him as an unquestionable figure of the canon of modern Dutch literature positions him as the unambiguous representative of the European humanistic tradition and avoids the complex analysis of his figure and of his works which they really deserve. (4) The responsibility of the Netherlands in the past is not mentioned, partly because of this idealistic presentation of Multatuli's activities and literary achievements. If the ambivalent character of his activities and literary achievements were to be taken as the point of departure, responsibility for the colonial project should also be examined.

Max Havelaar as the Literary Manifestation of Orientalism

I argue that Multatuli's novel is a literary manifestation of Orientalism. As already mentioned, Said defines Orientalism as a way of thinking based on biased constructions of difference between 'East' and 'West'. Orientalism is built on a subtle system of power relations and it is much more related to the European world than to the Orient. Said considers Orientalism an interaction between authors and the great political systems under which they write. From this point of view it is irrelevant whether a literary work is really a precise and faithful depiction of a certain (assumed) original reality. The 'East' is, in this case, a European invention, a construction. The eye of the European orientalist — whether natural scientist, writer, poet, painter, ethnographer or historian — re-creates, reinterprets the East. Said argues that writing about the East is nothing other than controlling it, monopolizing it, annexing it.

Post-colonial reading is in this sense reading and re-reading texts of colonial or colonized cultures in such a way as to call attention to the pervasive and inevitable presence of colonialism in them. This kind of reading demonstrates how the text contradicts its own unvoiced preoccupations and how hidden colonizing ideologies and processes can be exposed. Taking Said's suggestions into consideration, I shall do the same with Multatuli's novel *Max Havelaar* by examining the so-called surface of the text: by looking at and concentrating on details, descriptions of landscape, minor characters, I shall look for colonizing reflexes in the text.

Analogies between Post-Colonial and Gender Approaches

Both post-colonial and gender criticism are engaged with subjects forced into subjugated positions: they examine the origin, nature, and positions of revolt against subjugation. The American scholar Kimberlé Crenshaw coined the concept of 'intersectionality' in the 1980s.[18] According to her theory, gender and race are closely related when it comes to discrimination issues. The notion of colonization therefore refers not only to the subjugation of non-European countries and peoples by European powers, but also to the exploitation of powerless people by people who have power, for example that of women by men, children by parents, the elderly by the young. Categories of class, race, gender and age permeate each other and are interlocked. One of the characteristics of colonizing discourse is that only European subjects are individualized. Non-Europeans are presented as representatives of a race or social group. In *Max Havelaar,* therefore, we read often about 'the Javanese', 'the indigenous child', 'the Eastern people', or about 'Eastern languages'. Their problems are not depicted from the inside, even in chapter 17, where the protagonists are two indigenous characters and are also endowed with personal names; still they are only depicted as types, focalized by a white European man. Having names is in this case only a formal feature; Saïdjah and Adinda are not real characters, they are only illustrations.

Individualization or the substitution of a subject with a group also often works in a similar way in male–female relations. We never learn the forename of Batavus Droogstoppel's wife, or of Max Havelaar's wife; Tine, too has very few individualized traits: she represents an idealized image of woman in nineteenth-century European patriarchal society, that is, the image of the submissive wife and self-sacrificing mother. Patriarchal and imperialist systems deploy parallel forms of domination against those whom they consider subjugated. In both systems discourse plays a crucial role: that is why language and representation are the focus of gender and post-colonial criticism. Language is not only the result, the consequence or the mirror of patriarchal and imperialist practices; it is also their re-creator and conservator. At the same time, language may also serve as the means of revolt against these practices. My analysis tries to develop analogies between post-colonial and gender approaches.[19] I would like to demonstrate that Dekker, as a male writer in nineteenth-century Holland, presents 'only' a somewhat more enlightened version of the colonial attitudes of his society. The word 'only' is put between quotation marks because this achievement counts as exceptional at this time and it should not be decried. At the same time, I call attention to the female voices in the novel, which in their own way resist the main theme of the work and provide the necessary counterpoints.

My ideology-critical reading of *Max Havelaar* actualizes only one possible meaning in the playing field of all possible meanings. The meaning that I actualize here does not exclude other interpretations. I re-read *Max Havelaar* as a confrontation between nineteenth-century Dutch colonial and today's anti-colonial ideologies. The legitimation of such a re-reading is underpinned by one of the most brilliant structuralist scholars of Multatuli, Sötemann himself:

> Ten slotte vestig ik nog de aandacht op de ethische, en in het algemeen de levensbeschouwelijke categorieën, die evenzeer aan verandering onderhevig zijn. Ter illustratie: men denke aan de gewijzigde opvattingen ten aanzien van waarde en betekenis der seksualiteit, niet alleen in de loop van de laatste eeuw, maar zelfs sinds de Tweede Wereldoorlog.[20]

> [Finally, I draw attention to the ethical and ideological categories in general, which are also apt to change. By way of illustration: let us think about the modified conceptions concerning the value and meaning of sexuality, not only during the last century, but even since the Second World War.]

Since Sötemann, trends of post-cultural criticism such as New Historicism, cultural materialism, post-colonial and gender criticism have legitimized these re-readings. My analysis makes use of the results of the trends mentioned above. The novel has been written under certain social, political, and cultural influences and today too readers read it in a certain social, political, and cultural context. The clash of nineteenth-century value systems and those of today is inevitable. I do not assume any coherent ideologies either in the novel itself or in the influence that it exerts. The novel makes several different readings possible. My reading considers it as the resultant and the re-creator of power, subject positions, subservient, and controlling relationships. This leads to two conflicting conclusions. Whereas the author and the main character, Max Havelaar, give explanations of their own positions in the novel and try to justify their own interest- and power-constructions, revolt against these very same constructions is also depicted.

Rhetorical Context and Plot

An Ideology-Critical Approach to 'Max Havelaar'

Eduard Douwes Dekker, alias Multatuli, wrote his novel about his own experiences while he was staying as an assistant resident in Lebak for three months (see Fig. 3.3). The work was meant as a self-justification against the accusations he received about his supposed abuses. He wanted to be read: that is why he wrote a novel, not a pamphlet or some other non-fictional genre.

Multatuli creates two worlds, two life spheres in his novel: one in the frame and one in the main story. In the frame story the reader is confronted with the Netherlands in the first half of the nineteenth century with the coffee-broker, Droogstoppel, as the main character. He represents the genuine philistine who sees everything through the looking-glass of his own egotistical interests. One day he meets an old schoolmate of his, whose name he has forgotten. Therefore he names him — on the grounds of his most conspicuous piece of clothing — the Scarf-man. This Scarf-man is not as well off as Droogstoppel. He lives in straitened circumstances, and can maintain his wife and children only with great difficulty. He asks Droogstoppel to rework his 'parcel', which contains hundreds of essays, stories, poems, pamphlets, and studies, so that it can be published as a book. Droogstoppel accepts the request because he thinks it possible that the book can boost the coffee trade. But because the 'parcel' seems to be a chaotic muddle of papers, he passes it on to his German assistant, Stern, for further elaboration. Stern sets about the task, and his work becomes the main plot of the novel, that is, the Scarf-man's material edited by Stern. In these chapters Max Havelaar is the main character who is sent as deputy governor to Rangkas-Betung. After long descriptions of his arrival in Pandeglang and the social situation there, Max Havelaar himself reappears only at the beginning of the seventh chapter.

After the Havelaar chapters, in which the reader could clearly be convinced of the corrupt conditions in the Dutch East Indies and the role played by indigenous leaders and Dutch authorities in creating and maintaining them, Multatuli at last takes up his pen and orders his actors to leave the stage. He turns straight to King Willem III with a warning to change these miserable conditions:

> Want u draag ik myn boek op, Willem den derden, Koning, Groothertog, Prins ... meer dan Prins, Groothertog en Koning ... *Keizer* van het prachtige Ryk van *Insulinde* dat zich daar slingert om den evenaar, als een gordel van smaragd ...
>
> Aan U durf ik met vertrouwen vragen of het uw keizerlyke wil is: Dat Havelaar wordt bespat met de modder van Slymeringen en Droogstoppels?
>
> En dat daarginds Uw meer dan dertig millioenen onderdanen worden *mishandeld en uitgezogen in Uwen naam?*[21]

Fig. 3.3. Multatuli's house in Java, Rangkas-Bitoeng. Multatuli Museum Amsterdam

[For I dedicate my book to You, Willem the Third, King, Grand Duke, Prince ... more than Prince, Grand Duke and King ... EMPEROR of the glorious realm of the INSULINDE, that coils yonder round the Equator like a girdle of emerald ...

You I dare ask with confidence whether it is Your Imperial Will: that the Havelaars be spattered with the mud of *Slymerings* and *Droogstoppels*?

And that yonder Your more than *thirty million* subjects be MALTREATED AND EXPLOITED IN YOUR NAME?][22]

Literary scholars have identified the frame story with Droogstoppel and the main story with Max Havelaar, postulating these as two oppositional worlds, although they have also paid attention to correspondences between the two.[23] According to the classical interpretation, the frame story represents the Netherlands and its citizens as the colonial power while the main story represents the Dutch East Indies as the victim of the colonizing system, with Havelaar as the defender of the colonized. Because the book demands a more righteous life for the Dutch East Indies, the work is situated in the great, humanistic tradition of the European novel. Multatuli was, however, not an enemy to the colonizing system. He was a representative of contemporary Dutch society and this society was imperialistic — that is, a colonizing empire. Eduard Douwes Dekker wrote his novel, among other reasons, lest the Netherlands should lose its 'East Indian domains'. As Piet Emmer correctly remarks, the novel argued not for less, but for more colonialism.[24] The book was written against the old type of colonization, under which the indigenous leaders had made corruption possible and the simple Javanese peasants were exploited, while the corrupt Dutch administration remained uninterested in these problems. In the long run, Western norms of 'good governance' led to much greater profits than earlier forms of colonialism, under which the total exploitation of the profit-producing Javanese peasant and the corruptness of the Javanese oligarchy were both tolerated. If we accept Emmer's historical analysis, then we must find clear indications of this 'more-colonialism' in the novel. In my analysis I shall look for answers to the following questions:

(1). One of my hypotheses is that the structure of the novel is not only oppositional but also analogous. Is it possible to consider Max Havelaar to be a kind of extension of Droogstoppel? They are both colonizers: the former is a 'good', the latter a 'bad' one.

(2). There is a subversive hidden force working against both Droogstoppel and Havelaar, a kind of opposition, but this is hardly visible or audible. Opposition is embodied in silence, in the negation of speech. It is the silence of two symmetrical characters at two symmetrical points of the novel, that of Si Upi Keteh and Marie Droogstoppel. Can we consider them as two aspects of the same subversive identity? What roles do female characters play in the novel? What analogies can be discovered between the colonization of a less powerful land by a more powerful one and the subjugation of women by men?

Instead of Opposition an Analogy: Havelaar as the extension of Droogstoppel[25]

The depiction of Droogstoppel, the dapper philistine, and Havelaar, the romantic hero, is partly developed by the social constellation of the early nineteenth century. The period following the French Revolution is ambivalent: while cherishing the dream of 'freedom, brotherhood, equality' but experiencing the failure of their fulfilment in reality, people drew back to their private lives where they became — in Marx's terms — *bourgeois* instead of *citoyen*. The *bourgeois* is the embodiment of the philistine, who only has egotistic interests, while the *citoyen* represents the pursuit of the above-mentioned three values of the French Revolution. The ideal of the romantic hero struggling for noble purposes, however, had not vanished totally. It lived on as a desire. The reduplication of the burgher in this way was realized in literature in the duality of romanticism and realism. Romanticism and romantic irony form another duality at the time. Illustrative examples of the idealized good hero as opposed to his devilish alter ego can be found in the works of E. T. A. Hoffmann, F. M. Dostoevsky, and R. L. Stevenson.[26]

The dichotomy of the *citoyen* and the *bourgeois* can be also interpreted as ambivalence, not as an opposition but as a twofold projection of one and the same personality. As already mentioned, Dutch discourse consisted not only of people supporting the colonizing project, but also of people who criticized it. These two existed side by side. Accordingly, Havelaar embodies the discourse supporting colonialism and the discourse criticizing it at the same time. The shameless and manifest colonizer Droogstoppel and the enlightened, latent colonizer Havelaar constitute the same colonizing discourse of the same society.

Colonialism as a practice bears the same duality: like the *citoyen*, it considers its main task a civilizing mission. The *bourgeois* aspect of colonization is that there are exploiting, subjugating, and excluding mechanisms at work. These latter elements appear in Droogstoppel manifestly; therefore in accordance with the critical discourse of the time he is depicted as a grotesque, satirical anti-hero. Havelaar is, on the surface, the romantic hero of the civilizing mission. Their interrelation, however, can be seen in their parallel world-views and value judgements. Some features of Droogstoppel can also be discovered in Havelaar. For example, the reader discovers that Droogstoppel is not a great fan of the arts: their fictional character does not fit into his utilitarian turn of mind. He is only able to consider fictionality as lying, and lying must be rejected on moral grounds. Here is a famous passage on this subject:

> Ik heb niets tegen verzen op-zichzelf! Wil men de woorden in 't gelied zetten, goed! Maar zeg niets wat niet waar is. 'De lucht is guur en 't is vier uur.' Dit laat ik gelden, als het werkelyk guur en vier uur is. Maar als 't kwartier voor drieën is, kan ik, die myn woorden niet in gelid zet, zeggen: 'de lucht is guur, en 't is kwartier voor drieën.' De verzenmaker is door de guurheid van den eersten regel aan een vol uur gebonden. Het moet voor hem juist vier, vyf, twee, één uur wezen, of de lucht mag niet guur zyn. Daar gaat hy dan aan 't knoeien! Of het weér moet veranderd, óf de tyd. Eén van beiden is dan gelogen.[27]

[Mind you, I've no objections to verses in themselves. If you want to form fours, it's all right with me! But don't say anything that isn't true. *'The air is raw, the clock strikes four.'* I'll let that pass, if it really *is* raw, and if it really *is* four o'clock. But if it's a quarter to three, then I, who don't range my words in lines, will say: *'The air is raw and it is a quarter to three.'* But the versifier is bound to four o'clock by the rawness of the first line. For him, it has to be exactly four o'clock, or else the weather mustn't be raw. And so he starts tampering with the truth. Either the weather has to be changed, or the time. And in that case, one of the two is false.][28]

Droogstoppel's insensitivity towards art is just one of the characteristics of the colonizing Dutch philistine so negatively represented in the novel. Well, Max Havelaar, the romantic hero with his poetic soul, the so-called antidote to Droogstoppel, says the following about painting:

— Maar nu neem ik een schildery dat 't onthoofden van Maria Stuart voorstelt. [...] je gaat voor de schildery zitten, om goed en lang te genieten — we genieten nu eenmaal by 't aanschouwen van iets akeligs — en welken indruk meent ge dat zy op je maakt?
— Wèl, schrik, angst, medelyden, ontroering ... [...] We hebben gesteld dat de schildery volmaakt is, ik moet dus daarvan geheel denzelfden indruk hebben als van de werkelykheid.'
— Neen! Binnen twee minuten voel je pyn in je rechterarm, uit sympathie met den beul die zoo lang dat zwaar stuk staal onbewegelyk omhoog moet houden.
— Sympathie met den beul?
— Ja! evenlydendheid, gelykvoeligheid, weetje? En tevens met de vrouw die daar zoo lang in ongemakkelyke houding, en waarschynlik in onaangename stemming, voor dat blok ligt. Je hebt nog altyd medelyden met haar, maar ditmaal niet, omdat ze onthoofd moet worden, maar omdat men haar zoo lang laat wachten vóór ze onthoofd wordt, en als je nog iets zeggen of roepen zoudt, in 't eind — gestel dat je aandrift voelt je met de zaak te bemoeien — zou 't niets anders wezen dan: 'sla toch in-godsnaam toe, man, 't mensch wacht er op!'[29]

[— But now I take a *painting* of the beheading of Mary Queen of Scots. [...] — you sit down in front of the picture, so as to enjoy it long and thoroughly — strange though it seems, we do *enjoy* the sight of horrible things — and what impression do you think it will make on you?
— Well ... terror, fear, pity, tenderness ... just as when I looked through the aperture in the wall. We have assumed that the painting is *perfect*, so it ought to make the same impression on me as the real thing.
— Oh no, it doesn't! Within two minutes you feel a pain in your right arm, out of sympathy with the executioner who has to hold that heavy piece of steel up for so long without moving ...
— *Sympathy with the executioner?*
— Yes! *Fellow-suffering, fellow-feeling*, you know! And also with the woman who has to kneel there in front of that block for such a long time, in an uncomfortable posture, and probably in an uncomfortable frame of mind, too. You are still sorry for her, but now not because she has to be beheaded, but because she is kept waiting so long before she is beheaded, and in the end — if you were to say or call anything to interfere — if you were to say or call anything it would be no more than: 'For goodness' sake strike, man, and get it over with, the woman's waiting!'][30]

Droogstoppel's and Havelaar's relations to art seem to be analogous on the ground of this quotation: the reality principle overwhelms the fictionality principle in both cases. Interestingly, the refusal of art in the name of the so-called reality principle functions here as a *mise en abyme*: *Max Havelaar* was given the form of a novel also only by necessity, in the hope that the message would more easily spread in the form of fiction. Even the writer's name, Multatuli, is a fiction opposed to the real Douwes Dekker. Multatuli wipes all his characters off the stage so as to place reality instead of fiction: this gesture prefers the reality principle against fictionality in just the same way that Droogstoppel and Havelaar do. The fictional form is a necessary means of reaching a broader public, but only in order to take it back to the world of reality.

Another similarity between Droogstoppel and Havelaar can be characterized by the statement by Benjamin Disraeli, the English prime minister and writer, in his novel *Tancred* (1847): 'The East is a career.' This thought is adaptable to the novel *Max Havelaar* by Multatuli in a twofold sense. On the one hand, the author has elaborated his own life in the novel in order to regain his honour and to receive acknowledgement and a higher position in the colonial administration. On the other hand, the novel is actually about career stories: the careers of Droogstoppel and Havelaar depend on the East, and vice versa these careers determine the 'career' of the East.

The analogue nature of the oppositions can also be observed in the structure of the novel: the frame and main stories are only seemingly oppositional. It is much more a matter of the penetration of the frame into the main story or of the mirroring of each other. Droogstoppel is the first-person narrator of the frame story. He is the one who asks Stern to edit the Scarf-man's manuscript to a coherent whole. Scarf-man is a character only in Droogstoppel's frame story. The Scarf-man's *manuscript*, however, embedded as it is in Stern's narration, is present from beginning to end of the whole novel. Havelaar is the Scarf-man's creation, or rather Stern's textual creation based on the Scarf-man's manuscript. This Stern sometimes takes on the Scarf-man's focalization and his narrative role. Speaking in the first person, he also claims to be a witness to the events he is narrating. Sometimes, however, he is an impersonal, extradiegetic narrator. Droogstoppel too comes forward in the Havelaar chapters as a narrator; he can nevertheless always be easily identified because he not only always speaks in the first person, but he also always reflects on himself. So the novel is not only thematically the 'greatest mess possible', as D. H. Lawrence wrote in his foreword to the second English edition in 1927, but it is also chaos from a narrative point of view.

Let us take an example from the Scarf-man's narration:

> Er was des morgens te tien ure een ongewone beweging op den groote weg die de afdeling Pandeglang verbindt met Lebak. [...] Het is myn doel niet, vooral niet in het begin van myn vertelling, den lezer lang bezig te houden met het beschryven van plaatsen, landschappen of gebouwen.[31]
>
> [One morning at about ten o'clock there was an unusual bustle and stir on the highroad in Java that connects the divisions of PANDEGLANG and LEBAK. [...] It is not my intention, especially at the beginning of my story, to take up much of the reader's time with descriptions of places, landscapes, or buildings.][32]

This can be Stern's voice on the whole, but it is surely a voice drawing on the Scarf-man's manuscript as Stern himself has never been to the Dutch East Indies. But it is undefinable to what extent Stern literally takes over the Scarf-man's text and to what extent this is his own wording (of course, even his own wording is based on Scarf-man's manuscript). Keeping narrative positions ambiguous in the Havelaar chapters makes the narrator's reliability or unreliability unclear and results in merging of perspectives.[33] Havelaar, who can be considered the Scarf-man's fictional creation or simply his fictional *alter ego*, is always and only an embedded focalizer. Havelaar and the colonial world appear to the reader through a dual focalization: that of the Scarf-man and Stern. And because both the Scarf-man and Stern focalize Havelaar in a very positive way, identification with Havelaar is automatically passed over to the reader. The indigenous people focalized by this already embedded Havelaar are situated a very great narrative distance from the reader. This great distance makes only partial identification possible. The ambiguous authorship of the story offered in the novel gives a good example of the invisibility and the incomprehensibility of many other authors who created discourses about the East, and it is also a good example of the manifold indirectness of these discourses.

Colony as 'Manuscript'

Ania Loomba argues that

> Colonialism [...] should be analysed as if it were a text, composed of representational as well as material practices and available to us via a range of discourses such as scientific, economic, literary and historical writings, official papers, art and music, cultural traditions, popular narratives, and even rumours.[34]

The Scarf-man's parcel and its later version edited by Stern *is* literally a text of colonization. Stern has hardly begun his work when he immediately meets difficulties: the manuscript is full of Javanese and Malay words which he does not understand. The manuscript is a corpus (it can be interpreted as the colony's body) which does not so easily succumb to subjugation. This is because the colonies have another language, foreign in both a grammatical and a cultural sense. Where there is a foreign word in the manuscript and it causes an obstruction of understanding for a Dutch person, this phenomenon can be interpreted as a metaphor of the colony's opposition to the colonizer.

The manuscript uses also other metaphors, i.e. some elements of the storytelling become metaphors also representing opposition to colonization. These metaphors emphasize contradictory elements inside the frame and the main story respectively on the one hand, and parallel elements between frame and main stories on the other. This is further evidence in support of my statement that the novel does not form a two-pole system which is realized in the opposition of the frame and the main story. The metaphors I am going to analyse are the following:

(a) mud/road
(b) digression
(c) relations between older and younger brother, parents and child

All these metaphors have something to do with power relations. The problem of speech/language will be discussed later because of its gender connotations.

(a) mud/road

In the first chapter on the Dutch East Indies — the fifth in the novel — there appears an antagonistic image between Europe and the colony. This image is represented by the road which connects Pandeglang with Lebak. This road is very muddy and it is extremely difficult to reach one's destination in a four-in-hand which every now and then becomes stuck in the all-pervading mud. Mud is a *leitmotif* of the novel and it functions as a *pars pro toto* of conditions in the Dutch East Indies. According to Max Havelaar, these conditions are laid down by the native leaders in the first place and by the Dutch bureaucracy in the second. If Max Havelaar wants to achieve anything in the Dutch East Indies he must wade through mud in both its literal and figurative senses. Besides being a hindrance, mud also has a metaphoric meaning which is its resistance to the colonizing power.

And there is, of course, the real highway built by so much human sacrifice under General Daendels. On the one hand there is mud and on the other hand there is civilization, which forges ahead even against the revulsion of the native populace. This opposition indicates that civilization and modernity have been introduced by the Dutch in the Dutch East Indies even against the will of the native people. This may be quite true, but it is important to know that Herman Willem Daendels (1762–1818) was a real, historical person who had this highway built so as to make the movements of the Dutch army on Java easier. This is not mentioned in the novel. But for any reader who knows all this, the highway becomes a metaphor not only of the civilizing mission but also of the violent nature of colonization.

(b) digression

One of the rhetorical figures of the main story is digression. Its narrator — Scarfman/Stern — is forced to take more and more detours in order to make the circumstances in the Dutch East Indies understandable: 'Een uitweiding over 't mechanismus van het bestuur in deze landstreken is hier, tot juist begrip van hetgeen volgen zal, noodzakelyk.'[35] [To enable you to understand what is to follow, I shall have to make a digression here regarding the machinery of government in these regions.][36] Not only do the texts explaining these circumstances function as a digression, but so do other texts belonging to several other genres: poems, fables, anecdotes, essays. The rhetorical figure of digression is also a metaphor: the European readers must take a circuitous path until they can gain any understanding at all of a world that is so far away and so strange to them. The Scarf-man's manuscript, too, can be interpreted as a digression — in this case for Stern, who had to make this digression in order to edit a profitable writing for Droogstoppel. What is more, even Multatuli's writing in novel form instead of a political pamphlet — as the author himself argued — functioned as a digression for his contemporary readers, who could only become acquainted with their own colonies and the 'truth' of the author through this literary text.

One kind of digression is self-correction. This plays an important role in Droogstoppel's text. Clarifying comments appear in his sentences repeatedly, such as:

> Zyn [Sterns — J.G.] uitzet is heel netjes, Ik heb hem aan 't kopyboek gezet, om zich te oefenen in den hollandschen styl. Ik ben benieuwd of er spoedig orders van Ludwig Stern zullen komen. Marie zal een paar pantoffels voor hem borduren ... voor den jongen Stern, meen ik.[37]

> [I have set him [Stern — J.G.] to work on the copybook, so that he can get some practice in Dutch style. I am curious to see how soon it will be before we get orders from Ludwig Stern. Marie is going to embroider a pair of slippers for him ... for young Stern, I mean.][38]

Droogstoppel's fussy specifications are miniature caricatures of the long, philosophical, and historical digressions in the Scarf-man's manuscript. They function, however, in a different way: while digressions in the main story lead to more knowledge, Droogstoppel's digressions in the frame story are circular; they do not open new ways of thinking but they always lead back to the point of departure.

(c) relations between elder and younger brother, parents and child

There are several references to such relationships in the text, but it is always Max Havelaar who takes the role of elder brother or parent while the native leader is the younger brother or the child:

> [...] de toon die in deze verhouding heerschen moet, vry wel wordt aangegeven in 't officieel voorschrift dienaangaande: de europesche ambtenaar hebbe den inlandschen beambte die hem ter-zyde staat, te behandelen als zyn jonger broeder.
> Maar hy vergete niet dat deze jonger broeder by de ouders zeer bemind — of gevreesd — is, en dat, by voorkomend geschil, zyn meerdere jaren zouden worden in rekening gebracht als beweegreden om hem euvel te nemen dat hy zyn jonger broeder niet met meer inschikkelykheid en takt behandelde.[39]

> [[...] the tone which should prevail in the relationship is fairly well indicated in the official instructions to it: 'the *European* official is to treat the *native* officer who assists him as his *younger brother*.
> But he must not forget that this *younger brother* is greatly beloved — or feared — by their parents and that, in the event of differences between them, his 'greater' age would be a reason for blaming him for not having treated his *younger brother* with more indulgence or tact.][40]

In the first sentence of the quotation there is a reference to 'official instructions' which regulate the tone between European and native officers. Here we have an unambiguous hierarchy. In the second part of the quotation 'parents' are supposed to mean the Dutch government, an authority having absolute power announcing the truth over two naughty children from a position of control: the issue is raised here of the ethical responsibility which the elder brother bears towards his junior. From this second part of the quotation we also learn about the ambivalent relation of the 'parents', that is, the Dutch government, to the 'younger brother', that is, to the native ruler: the younger brother is partly a 'greatly beloved' child, partly a 'feared' threat, the unpredictable 'other'. In the quotation there looms the story of Cain and Abel as a specific intertext whereby the intricate network of sub- and superordinate relations in the Dutch East Indies is placed in a Christian context. This association is again raised in the biblical style of Max Havelaar's famous inauguration speech to the native leaders:

> En wat zullen we antwoorden, als er na onzen dood een stem spreekt tot onze ziel, en vraagt: 'waarom is er geween in de velden, en waarom verbergen zich de jongelingen? Wie nam den oogst uit de schuren, en uit de stallen den buffel die het veld ploegen zou? Wat hebt ge gedaan met den broeder dien ik u gaf te bewaken? [...]'[41]

> [And what shall we answer when, after our death, a voice shall speak to our souls, and ask: 'Why is there weeping in the fields, and why are the young men in hiding? Who took from the barn the harvest, and from the stall the buffalo that was to plough the field? What have you done with the brother whom I gave you, to be to him as a guardian? [...]'][42]

The voice calling out to the soul is the voice of the superego, of the parent. The child–parent relationship is also apparent between the rich and the poor natives. It becomes a general metaphor of power and subjugation:

> Zulke geschenken zyn dan ook dikwyls van zoo weinig waarde, dat het afwyzen iets vernederends zou in zich sluiten, en vaak is alzoo deze gewoonte eerder te vergelyken met de hulde van een kind dat zyn liefde tot den vader tracht te uiten door 't aanbieden van een klein geschenk, dan optevatten als schatting aan dwingelandsche willekeur.[43]

> [These gifts are, admittedly, often of such small value that to refuse them would be tantamount to humiliating the giver; and often, therefore, this custom might rather be compared to the homage of a child, who seeks to express his love to his father by offering a small present, than to be conceived as a tribute to tyrannical despotism.][44]

The idiom of family ties functions as a metaphor of colonial power and the colonized subjugated, of the rich and the poor. Institutional colonization takes the shape of *parens patriae*, the parents of the nation who control, protect, and nurture their children. The family idiom also expresses ethnic and cultural differences: the younger brother is identical with the non-European.

Saskia Pieterse, in her book on the *Ideën* (*Ideas*) of Multatuli, does not agree with my statement that Havelaar plays the role of the elder brother (the European, the civilized) in the novel while the native regent (the non-European, the uncivilized) is cast in the role of the younger brother for whom the elder brother must take responsibility (while exercising control over him).[45] The oppositional rhetoric of Multatuli's text, however, supports my statement: the European has a way of life based on the puritan, civilian values of nineteenth-century Western civilization (living in a house, having one wife and two or three children, with a modest number of servants), while the regent lives like a prince according to a feudal code. The text implicitly praises European civilization against non-European feudalism. Havelaar sets an idealized notion of European democracy against the world of the regents and, referring to this dichotomy, he accepts the call of his contemporary Dutch establishment to conduct himself paternally towards native leaders.

Havelaar has the illusion that the Dutch establishment will be able to introduce an ideal democratic value system in the colonies. His story is an example of his disillusionment concerning his idealistic beliefs. But at this point of the novel it is indeed Havelaar's belief in the superiority of European civilization — in this case represented by the Dutch state — that gives him the assurance that he really has the right to act as an elder brother towards the native regent.

Saskia Pieterse even argues that it is not the European who is superior and the regent who is inferior, but the other way round.[46] There is some truth in this: the native regent has more local power and a greater local knowledge, so this assures him a superior position. The European officer is in this respect really dependent on him and is in an inferior position. What is important here, however, is that the narrator finds this constellation *strange*: 'Uit dit alles vloeit dus de vreemde omstandigheid voort, dat eigenlyk de mindere den meerdere beveelt'[47] [All this, then, results in the strange situation whereby the *inferior* really commands the *superior*].[48] That is to say that in the text of the novel the regent *is* the inferior. Further on the European officer is not only placed officially in the role of 'elder brother', but he undertakes this role consciously, identifying with it in contrast to the native regent, who is *cast* in the role of 'younger brother'. This is also supported by the repeated and unreflecting use of the 'older-younger-brother' metaphor throughout the novel.[49]

Female Subversion: Woman as 'Manuscript'

Not only colony but also woman is a manuscript in this novel. Max Havelaar considers 'elk meisje van van dertien jaren een manuscript waarin nog weinig of niets is doorgestreken'[50] ['every girl of thirteen a manuscript in which as yet little or nothing has been crossed out'.[51]. Colonies and women are both degraded to text – passive, manipulatable, dominated, controlled. As mentioned before, I argue that sexual and colonial relations have an analogous character. In the early phase of European colonial discourses, there were many overlaps between literary texts, visual representations, and other writings.[52] Women's position and gender problems in colonial discourse have been illustrated by Loomba in her analysis of Stradanus's sixteenth-century print *Vespucci discovers America*.[53] Vespucci, holding the flag with the Southern Cross in one hand and an astrolabe in the other, is looking at a naked woman, representing America, rising up from a hammock. Loomba argues that this representation shows us the drama of colonization: the naked woman being discovered by the man equipped with the attributes of civilization. The man is individualized in the person of Vespucci, a historical personality, while the woman is an allegory of America, a whole continent. Their encounter recalls the colonial paradigm according to which the European subject gains his individualization through his opposition to colonized peoples, while these represent in most cases a country, nature, an idea or a group. In 1570 the Flemish cartographer and geographer Ortelius (1527–98) published his *Theatrum Orbis Terrarum*, the first modern atlas. It depicts the colonial encounter in a similar way. Renaissance etchings and the new science of geography together promised 'new' land to men as if it were a woman. The allegorical depiction of continents as women has to do with a linguistic circumstance, namely that in Latin the gender of continents is feminine. So in earlier times the visual representation of continents in the form of women seemed natural. This is a nice example of the semiotic nature of ideology: the depiction of the meaning of grammatically feminine words as women was a fixed code when Latin was generally known. Later this knowledge faded away, but the 'naturalness' of the imagery was still held and became the indirect source of many cultural and social conceits in later times too. Language, fine arts, and literature do not only reflect but also form reality: female allegories of continents to be 'discovered' (they had already been there before Europeans 'discovered' them) affect social practices. These examples not only support the analogous nature of the relations to colony and woman, but they are also the results of an analogous language usage when speaking or writing about 'discovering' and subjugating continents and women. Freud, Loomba argues, called female sexuality a 'dark continent' purely because it has not been 'discovered' yet in psychology.[54]

Female characters are in a suppressed or subjugated position in the novel. It is true of the poets' wives in the introductory text to the novel; of Barbertje who is a protagonist in Multatuli's unpublished play and who was nurtured and looked after by Lothario; of Droogstoppel's wife who sews flannel vests for her husband, of Droogstoppel's daughter, Marie, who embroiders slippers for Stern and who makes a fair copy of the manuscript of Droogstoppel's and Stern's novel; of Tine, Max Havelaar's wife, who is not allowed even to sneeze; of Mrs. Slotering, the widow of Max Havelaar's predecessor, who is protected by Havelaar but who, in return, is not supposed to open her mouth; of Si Upi Keteh, the native *datu*'s daughter, to whom Havelaar tells the tale of the Japanese stone-cutter, and of Adinda who is married off in her childhood and who promises Saïdjah that she will weave batik until he comes back to her; but also of such minor characters as the native *babu* (nanny) or the Greek girl in the Amsterdam fair.

Suppression and subjugation are not synonyms. Gayatri Spivak argues that not all who are suppressed are at the same time subjugated. One is subjugated when one is excluded from the use of power discourses.[55] So according to this view the position of most white European women in Multatuli's novel can be considered suppressed while native women, such as Si Upi Keteh, the *babu*, and Adinda are in fact the ones who are actually subjugated.

In the first edition of the book the author dedicates his work to his wife in the following form: 'Aan E.H.v.W.' [To E.H.v.W.]. The initials are identical with those of Dekker's first wife. From the fourth edition on, Multatuli's dedication to this same first wife — the real and the fictional Tine — becomes lengthier (see Fig. 3.4). By that time the first wife is no longer alive. The longer dedication reads: 'Aan de diep vereerde nagedachtenis van Everdine Huberte Barones van Wijnbergen der trouwe gade der heldhaftige liefdevolle moeder der edele vrouw'[56] ['To the Revered Memory of Everdien Huberte, Baroness van Wijnbergen Faithful Wife, Heroic, Loving Mother, Noble Woman'].[57] This textual dedication appears only in the fourth edition of the novel, and Multatuli's wife 'pays' for it with her life. The dedication is not really intended for Multatuli's wife as a living person but to her 'revered memory'. To put it in another way, the female subject becomes text only after her death. In her life she is only signified by her initials.

FIG. 3.4. Portrait of Tine, Multatuli's wife. Multatuli Museum Amsterdam

The dedication is followed by the text of Henry de Pène, a French journalist of the time. His text describes woman as the ever-helpful companion and supporter of her husband. It is her glory if her husband's genius can fully develop. This development can only be made possible by the wife's background position. Not only is she a supporter to her husband in the labyrinth of everyday life, she is also his muse. Her figure is connected to the prose of everyday life, but her husband places his laurel wreath in her lap in return. This is, in fact, a reference to Antigone. She was the supporter of the blind genius, her father Oedipus entering the village of Colonus. She was also the first woman who ever received a wreath of laurel from a man. The background position of women is hereby situated in a mythological dimension and therefore takes the form of an old, unquestionable, natural tradition. The role of man — who is *per definitionem* the descendant of Homer, a creative artist of genius — is postulated also as an immemorially valid tradition. Being a creative genius is the role Dekker plays in real life, while Max Havelaar does the same in the fictional world of the novel.

The novel has still another 'introduction', a fragment from an unpublished play by Multatuli. It functions as a parable and refers to one of the basic questions of the novel: the injustice of official jurisdiction. Lothario is accused of cutting a young woman called Barbertje to pieces and of marinating her afterwards. Barbertje herself appears at the trial as the star witness, and contradicts everything: Lothario has not killed her; on the contrary, he was her benefactor. Lothario was condemned nevertheless. His crime was his arrogance. He had to be hanged.

What is Barbertje's role in this story? Her name makes us think of 'barbarian'. A barbarian is a foreigner, outside the borders of our civilization. This name is a deictic reference to another theme of the novel: the civilized Netherlands taking care of a foreign, barbarian world, the East Indies. In this hidden but obviously valid parallel the nurturing colonizer can be interpreted as a man (Lothario), the colony itself as a woman (Barbertje).

Barbertje is a name with a diminutive suffix, designating the weakness and dependence of its owner. Lothario confirms this in his answer to the charge: 'Ik heb haar gevoed en gekleed en verzorgd'[58] ['I have fed her, and clothed her and looked after her ...'].[59] This paternalism evokes the metaphor of the colonizer–colonized relationship. It is as if Barbertje were an orphan child while she is in fact a grown-up woman, as it also turns out when the judge asks: 'Wie zyt ge, vrouwtje?'[60] ['Who are *you*, my good woman?'].[61] She is not even called by her name but by a word referring to her sex, which is also given in the diminutive form in the original Dutch.

This unpublished play of Multatuli's from which this dialogue is taken refers to Lessing's *Nathan the Wise* (1779). Lessing's play shows the mechanism by means of which scapegoats are made. Whatever anyone says in defence of Nathan, the patriarch of Jerusalem always gives the same answer: it doesn't matter! To the stake with him! Multatuli's own dialogue, with Lessing's play as intertext, reflects his own life, as the Dutch colonial government made a scapegoat of him despite all his nurturing and paternal efforts to look after the colonized.

In these introductory texts the position of woman is that of the repressed who should be defended and maintained, who stays in the background from where she advances the career of men. Entering the world of the novel, this image is partly confirmed but it is also more complex than that.

In the frame story, that is, in the first four chapters, we see female characters through the eyes of Droogstoppel. Droogstoppel is an unreliable narrator.[62] His point of view is sympathetic to the repression of women. This may be Multatuli's criticism of Droogstoppel, because the text never offers identification with Droogstoppel. The question is whether the subordinated position of women radically changes in the main story, where identification with the protagonist Max Havelaar is emphatically offered. But first let us look at the frame story.

Droogstoppel's wife is the daughter of Last, the manager of the coffee company in which Droogstoppel has become a partner. The Dutch word *last* means burden or ballast. This is remarkable, especially when we take into consideration the fact that there are several other speaking names in the novel.[63] Droogstoppel has married her in order to build up his own career, so we never learn her first name. Droogstoppel never addresses her by her first name. All that we are told is that her main task is to sew flannel shirts and vests for her husband.

Another female character in Droogstoppel's story is the Greek girl, a figure from the common past of the Scarf-man and Droogstoppel. This episode has also the emblematic meaning that the two protagonists are connected by a 'foreigner'. She and her father used to sell perfumes in the Amsterdam fair.[64] Young Droogstoppel and his class-mate, the later Scarf-man, took a shine to the Greek girl and when Droogstoppel even tried to become acquainted with her, her father beat him up. The Scarf-man rescued him from the Greek. This may seem an innocent story, but, seen from the perspective of the whole novel, it is not. Like Droogstoppel's wife, the Greek girl has no name either, she is mentioned by her nationality, so she is not individualized but is representative of a group. She is also the object of desire in several boys' eyes. She is a foreigner because of her language too. Young Droogstoppel tries to talk to her in a kind of low Latin. The episode has all the attributes of 'the other': bodily features, clothing, characterization by sex and nationality, use of foreign language — all further complicated by the fact that the father tries to speak a kind of incomprehensible French.

I repeat: Droogstoppel is an unreliable narrator, so the author gives a caricatured, critical characterization of him; he is a ridiculous philistine. Thus his perspective too bears the same caricatured elements, which is why the reader never thinks of identification with him. The Scarf-man, however, is a positive character. His cooperation with Droogstoppel in their youth may be read as a prefiguration of future 'alliances' between Droogstoppel and Max Havelaar.

Back in the frame story, the Scarf-man's wife too is suppressed. The Scarf-man introduces her to Droogstoppel in a letter: 'Ik kan mijn lieve vrouw niet alles geven wat tot veraangenaming des levens noodig is [...]'[65] ['I cannot give my wife all that is necessary to make life pleasant [...]'].[66] A woman must be given things which make life pleasant. (Barbertje was in a similar position in relation to Lothario.)

Droogstoppel goes out to visit the Scarf-man because he wants to discuss the lexical problems of the manuscript. Droogstoppel's power is undermined by the many incomprehensible Malay and other foreign phrases. The manuscript represents partly 'another' world for him, but he himself becomes also 'another' in his relation to the manuscript. The Scarf-man — for Droogstoppel another 'other' because he is poor and connected to the East — can surely translate these foreign words and expressions for him. The Scarf-man is not at home, and Droogstoppel finds only his wife and children in the house. This is the first time that he personally meets the wife, and the impression that he receives is identical with the impression evoked by the foreign words in the manuscript. For Droogstoppel this impression evoked by the 'other' is a negative experience:

> Ze had, als een Chinese, de haren achter over gekamd, en die achter het hoofd in een soort van strik of knoop saamgebonden. Later heb ik vernomen dat haar kleding een soort van indische dracht is, die ze daar te-lande sarong en kabaai noemen, maar ik vond het heel lelyk.[67]

> [Her hair was combed straight back like a Chinese, and tied behind her head in a kind of knot. (I learnt afterwards that her dress was a sort of East Indian costume, which they call *sarong* and *kabaya* out there; but I thought it very ugly.)][68]

Droogstoppel compensates for his linguistic and situational uncertainty with a similarly linguistic and situational humiliation of Scarf-man's wife. He calls her 'juffrouw', Miss Scarf-man. Nor does he call his former class-mate by his proper name. Droogstoppel finds the address 'Miss' appropriate; his own wife, whom he ranks much higher than the Scarf-man's wife, is also addressed in that way. The Scarf-couple's son gives evidence of extreme class-consciousness when he talks to Droogstoppel:

> — M'nheer, waarom zeg je tegen mama: juffrouw?
> — Hoe dan, kereltje, zei ik, wat moet ik dan zeggen?
> — Wel ... zooals andere menschen! De juffrouw is beneden. Ze verkoopt schotels en priktollen.[69]

> [— Sir, why do you call Mama 'Juffrouw'?
> — What do you mean, laddie?, I said. — What else should I call her?
> — Why ... the same as other people do! The woman downstairs is 'Juffrouw', she sells cups and saucers.][70]

While little Max's class-consciousness is strong enough to defend his mother against Droogstoppel's humiliating address, he is at the same time a typical representative of an oppressive patriarchal consciousness. The 'juffrouw' is somebody who is 'downstairs' both literally and figuratively. She belongs to a social layer which is even lower than theirs. The Scarf-man's son can defend his mother against the social humiliation of someone who is 'above' them socially, but he does this by humiliating someone else who, in her turn, has a lower place in the same social hierarchy than little Max and his family.

It can be concluded that women in the first four chapters are all in the service of men. This could be interpreted as the author's implied criticism of oppression, because the reader sees all this from Droogstoppel's perspective and he is an unreliable narrator. However, the positive protagonist, the Scarf-man, also cooperates in oppressing women.

It is a challenge to examine silent places in a text such as that of *Max Havelaar*, in which speaking, telling stories, reciting poetry, narrating and the use of different languages play such a crucial role. According to Wolfgang Iser, so-called 'blanks' are inherent in all literary works.[71] These communicative gaps between the literary work and its reader can never be filled in unambiguously. Iser distinguishes two types of 'blanks': negation and negativity. Negation is when the *narrator* overtly refuses narration and denies the validity of that narration. An example of negation is when Max Havelaar and his family arrive in Rangkas Betung. The narrator gives a detailed description of Havelaar and his wife Tine as they alight from their coach. The narrator, however, refuses to give any detailed information on the family's native female servant:

> De baboe die hy uit den wagen had geholpen geleek op alle baboes in Indië, als ze oud zyn. Wanneer ge deze soort van bedienden kent, behoef ik u niet te zeggen hoe zy er uitzag. En als gy ze niet kent, kan ik het u niet zeggen.[72]
>
> [The *babu* whom he [Max Havelaar — J.G.] had helped out of the coach resembled all the other *babu*s in the East Indies when they are old. If you know this type of servant, I do not need to tell you what she looked like. And if you do not know, I cannot tell you.][73]

Both Sötemann and Oversteegen find that this scene illustrates the outstanding human quality of Max Havelaar.[74] The Dutch writer Hella S. Haasse (1918–2011), however, goes a step further by criticizing the same scene:

> Havelaar vermeldt hoe hij bij zijn aankomst in Lebak de inheemse gedienstige, de baboe, hoffelijk uit het rijtuig helpt, maar verder blijft die vrouw de lezer onzichtbaar. Havelaar kent de mensen voor wie hij in het krijt wil treden, en die hij op zijn zo nadrukkelijk vermelde inspectietochten in de streek ontmoet, niet werkelijk; ze zijn accessoires bij zijn optreden.[75]
>
> [Havelaar tells us how politely he helps the native servant, the *babu*, out of the coach on arrival in Lebak, but this woman remains invisible to the reader. Havelaar does not really know the people for whom he will fight and whom he meets on his inspection trips in the neighbourhood; they are his props for his performances.]

Haasse's statement echoes Said's observations that writers about the East consider it — the East — unable to represent itself. Therefore the West must represent it. Literary stories are therefore always told and focalized by white, European, male narrators. This is also the case in *Max Havelaar*. Not one of the natives speaks directly, their focalization is always embedded; we readers never see the world through their eyes. This function is reserved for Droogstoppel, the Scarf-man or Stern, and Havelaar. The subaltern cannot speak here either.

A post-colonial and gender approach to the above-mentioned scene can result in the following interpretation: the nanny (*babu*) has no face, she is only a member of her race and social group; she is not worth an individualized representation. She is the object of a fourfold discrimination: first on the ground of her race (East Indian), second, of her class (she is a nanny, a servant), third, of her sex (she is a woman), and fourth, that of her age (she is old). This is a good example of how class, gender, ethnicity, and age are parts of the colonial (ideological) context, and of how closely post-colonial and gender criticisms are intertwined.

Negativity, as opposed to negation, contains omitted, silenced, or implied elements of the *protagonists* themselves. These empty places are filled in by the readers according to their interpretation of the text. There are several tropes of negativity: one of them is when a character stops speaking, refuses to answer, or uses non-verbal language. My hypothesis is that because negativity in *Max Havelaar* is a systematically and structurally recurrent phenomenon, it tells an underlying story in addition to the manifest, spoken narrative.

This novel not only makes use of several languages, registers, and genres, it not only gives voice to different opinions and argumentations, but it is also *about* all these forms of communication. As to different languages, there is Dutch, the master language in which the novel is written and which is the linguistic context of the whole novel. There is German, thanks to Droogstoppel's assistant Stern, but even Havelaar sometimes mixes some German words in his texts. French is present among the Greek stallholders in Amsterdam, and there are the native languages of the East Indies. The presence of all these languages creates the sphere of being a stranger, an outsider in a culture other than one's own. That is one of the basic issues of the novel. It is also a book of several genres and modes of speech: everyday prose, poetry, essay, tale, parable, oration. Therefore one is inclined to agree with Beekman, who sees in Multatuli's novel a brilliant example of Bakhtinian heteroglossia.[76] It is indeed an overwhelming space of confronting voices and languages, a battlefield of arguments and counter-arguments. Zook, however, points out that in Multatuli heteroglossia

> is not a subversive attempt to undermine the colonial archive. [...] these other voices intrude not to problematize truth and literary perspective, but to help capture truth and control it. Through the obsessive desire to capture and control knowledge, to retain the power to label the categories of truth, *Max Havelaaar* is not merely a novel about imperialism, it is a literary text which mimics its aspirations for control and power.[77]

Following both Beekman and Zook, I suggest that there is another type of heteroglossia in *Max Havelaar* and that is — paradoxically — a heteroglossia of silences which, however, does work subversively. In other words: non-subversive heteroglossia of speech forms a symmetry with subversive heteroglossia of silence.

Mastery of language implies mastery of power, as Said and several other post-colonial researchers have pointed out.[78] What can and what cannot be said in a novel may reflect what can and what cannot be said in contemporary society and culture.[79] Following Elizabeth Wright, I argued in my 2001 book that women in *Max Havelaar* are deprived of this mastery.[80] If they have any voice at all it is embedded in the narrative of the male protagonists. On the basis of this argument I drew the conclusion that in the novel silenced women constitute a parallel to silenced natives. Colonizing non-Europeans and colonizing women actually constitute one and the same male project. I interpreted different kinds of female silences, but previously I saw only that of Si Upi Keteh as subversive. Now I see also other types of female 'blanks' in the text which form a chain, a substructure of subversive silences. Silence is one of the main, although hidden, rhetorical strategies in the text. It gains importance as a zero sign against the dominance of speech.

Duco van Oostrum's article 'Sneezes and Lies' has already touched upon the speech or speechlessness of women in *Max Havelaar*.[81] He points out that some women in *Max Havelaar* are not totally silent but use another kind of language which is conspicuously different from that of men. Tine, for example, sneezes at the moment when Havelaar, in talking about the beauty of the women in Arles, mentions that he saw one of them blow her nose. He says: 'Ik had ze liever dood zien vallen! Mag zulk een meisje zich profaneeren!'[82] ['I'd sooner have seen her drop dead! *May* such a woman desecrate herself?'].[83] Tine's sneeze, coming at that very moment, as Van Oostrum argues, is body-language of protest against the colonization of women by male eyes, and therefore is emphatically different from logocentric male language, and expresses a protest against Havelaar's idealization of woman. Agreeing with Van Oostrum's interpretation of that scene, I see here again a close relationship to patriarchal and colonial behaviour. According to Multatuli's note 66 (in the English translation) on this subject, female beauty is identical with that of white European woman, and therefore it is at its highest when it is not mixed with the blood of other races:

> *Arles* wordt gehouden voor 'n binnenlandsche kolonie van de Massiliers, en *Massilia (Marseille)* was door de Phoeniciers gesticht. Dat de waarlyk typische schoonheid der vrouwen te *Arles*, daar beter dan te *Marseille* bewaard bleef, kan liggen aan de mindere vermenging met vreemden. Op strandplaatsen als *Marseille* verbasteren de rassen zeer snel.[84]
>
> [Arles is considered to have been an inland colony of people from Massilia (Marseilles), which was founded by the Phoenicians. The fact that the truly characteristic beauty of the women of Arles has been preserved better there than at Marseilles may be due to the fact that there was less opportunity for intercourse with foreigners at Arles. In coastal towns such as Marseilles races lose their purity very quickly.][85]

I do not want to discuss the question of whether Multatuli's notes can be considered an integral part of the fiction *Max Havelaar*. However, the quotation above shows how deeply Multatuli was involved in colonial history and what his views were on the mixing of races.

Another example in Van Oostrum's article is Upi, the thirteen-year-old native girl who has no language of her own: 'Upi's language comes from men, and she has no access to a liberating body language.'[86] Havelaar tells about the episode when he had to make a tour of inspection of the pepper-gardens in Natal and — because of his insufficient knowledge of agriculture — he took a *datu*, a native leader, and his daughter Upi in a boat to help him with his work. Whenever he asked the girl anything, her answers echoed only the will of her father or that of Havelaar. It is also she to whom Havelaar tells the story of the Japanese Stone-cutter. After finishing the story, which is overtly a disciplinary text encouraging resignation to one's fate — how similar this is to the views of Nicolaas Beets on the static system of social classes in Chapter 2 — Havelaar asks Upi what she would ask for if an angel from heaven came and enquired. Her answer is that she would like to be taken to heaven by that angel.

In contrast to Tine's body-language, Van Oostrum sees sheer voicelessness in

Upi's monotone answers echoing the wishes of men. In my view, however, Upi is not voiceless: she — like Tine — is using another voice, the voice of parody of her own suppressed situation where there is no place for the individual voices of women. Upi deliberately suppresses her individual voice and this works subversively — not only because it echoes the male will and therefore is also provocative, but also because it echoes the deep silence of Upi's self. To Havelaar's questions as to whether she would like to come with him to Taloh Baleh next time, her answers — 'Zoo als toewan kommandeur beveelt', 'Als myn vader beveelt'.[87] [As the Tuan Commander decides, If my father wishes].[88]) — speak a double language: one which adapts itself to the colonial and distinctively male context, and a silent one which protests against this very context that is silencing the self. Also, her wish to go to heaven has, in my view, an aspect other than that which Van Oostrum suggests. According to Van Oostrum, Upi's wish expresses her desire for a non-male world rather than life in one with such gender asymmetries. Heaven is, however, not a desired theological *locus amoenus* where oppression by men does not exist. It is rather, I argue, a metaphor of death. Upi knows that for women there is no equality in life on earth. Suppression of the individual voice is connected to death, in which there is no language at all.

There is a conspicuous parallel to the thirteen-year-old Upi's story in the Amsterdam episode of Marie Droogstoppel, the daughter of Batavus.[89] Marie, also thirteen years old, refuses to read out a chapter from the Bible during breakfast. The chapter in question is about Lot and his daughters — Genesis 19. When the two daughters of Lot realize that there are no other men around by whom they could be made pregnant, they decide to make their father drunk and have intercourse with him so that they can preserve their family line through him. Marie Droogstoppel says that she would rather be beaten to death than read out this ominous passage. Droogstoppel punishes her by locking her in her room for three days with nothing but coffee and bread and she has to copy out the Lot episode ten times. The question may be asked: why is Marie unwilling to read the episode out? The question is neither asked nor answered in the novel, so readers must use their own imagination. According to the Dutch critic Elsbeth Etty, one possible answer is that father Droogstoppel sexually abuses his daughter.[90] Being confronted with approved incest in the most authoritative book of Western civilization destroys all Marie's illusions, and her protest is not only against her father's misconduct but also against the culture in which incest is sanctioned. These were issues which could not be discussed in Dutch society in the middle of the nineteenth century. Marie's refusal to read out and her cry that she would rather be beaten to death is another example of the textual relation between subversive silence and death.

There is a second parallel between Upi's and Marie's stories. This does concern sexual abuse. Among the several autobiographical links in the novel such as that between Multatuli (Eduard Douwes Dekker) and Havelaar, between Tine in the novel and Tine as the wife of Multatuli, this is also the case with the thirteen-year-old Upi: Dekker had a sexual relationship with a real Upi in 1843.[91] These links create in the novel a structural repetition of women's silence as connected to abusive sexuality and death — and the same applies even in the case of Tine, as I will try to demonstrate in what follows.

Van Oostrum sees a difference in the relationship between Havelaar and Tine on one hand and that between Droogstoppel and his wife on the other: whereas Havelaar at least acknowledges Tine's status as 'the angel of the house', for Mrs Droogstoppel there is no place whatsoever, not even in the separate sphere of woman. The latter is also the case for Upi, who, as a native female, is a chattel in a male world. Van Oostrum therefore sees a hierarchical sequence of women according to the status awarded them by their male partners: Upi, Marie and Mrs Droogstoppel have no status at all, whereas Tine is the 'proud possessor' of the self-denying spouse. The dedication of the novel by Multatuli to Tine, Van Oostrum argues, is also proof of Tine's relatively higher position. Van Oostrum forgets, however, the fact (already mentioned) that the dedication came only with the fourth edition of *Max Havelaar* — after the real Tine's real death. Therefore Van Oostrum also makes a slight mistake when he says that the novel is dedicated to Multatuli's *wife*. Let us emphasize it again: the novel is dedicated to the 'revered memory' of Tine. We could say: the text of the dedication has been born at the cost of Tine's death. In other words: sexuality and death, eros and thanatos, are in *Max Havelaar* structurally connected to different types of the silence of women: actual silence (Marie), textual silence (Mrs Droogstoppel), non-verbal communication (Tine), or pseudo-communication (Upi). Being silenced in any of these forms means effectively being dead in the fictive world of a novel in which articulate voices play a crucial role.

The use of alternative languages by Tine, Upi, and Marie reflects silenced aspects of culture in mid-nineteenth-century Holland. Multatuli shows three different modes of saying the unsayable. By sneezing, Tine makes non-verbal criticism of Havelaar's impossible idealization of women. By using a double language that does not actually express what the speaker really wants to say, Upi escapes from the logocentric masculine discourse in which she never can be an equal partner. Marie's refusal to read out the story of Lot and his daughters is an overt protest against the cultural narrative of the Bible and, by the same token, against the hypocritical morals of her father and contemporary Holland.

The question may be put whether *Max Havelaar* is a misogynous text or the opposite: it regularly touches upon the oppression of women. I myself read the text like Etty and Wright as misogynous, whereas Van Oostrum says: 'Through an emphasis on women's language of the body and women's alignment with Heaven rather than the world of business, Multatuli is able to expose female suppression.'[92] This argument can be supported by the episode of Tine's sneeze, in which Havelaar is represented in the same grotesque way as Droogstoppel:

> Als Duclari nog meende dat Havelaar 'gek' was, had men 't hem niet tenkwade kunnen duiden wanneer hy zich in deze meening versterkt voelde, by 't bemerken der korte verstoordheid die er, na en om dat neussnuiten, op Havelaars gelaat te lezen was.[93]
>
> [If Duclari still thought the new Assistant Resident was a 'fool', he could not have been blamed for feeling confirmed in that opinion on noticing the momentary irritation which could be read on Havelaar's face after and because Tina blew her nose.][94]

In the Upi episode Havelaar himself reflects on his own obnoxious behaviour:

> [...] ik zat dáár in die prauw met een zuur gezicht en slecht humeur, en was, wat de Duitschers noemen: ungeniessbar. Ik vond onder anderen dat het niet te-pas kwam my pepertuinen te laten inspekteeren, en dat ik lang had moeten aangesteld zyn tot gouverneur van een zonnestelsel. Hierby kwam het me voor als zedelyke moord, een geest als den myne in één prauw te zetten met dien dommen datoe en zyn kind.[95]
>
> [I was sitting in this proa with a sour face and a bad temper. I was what the Germans call *unenjoyable*. Among other things, I considered it was beneath my dignity to have to inspect pepper plantations, and that I should have been appointed governor of a solar system long ago. Then again, it seemed to me a sort of moral murder to put a mind like mine in one proa along with that stupid *datu* and his child.][96]

Does this kind of speech not remind us of Droogstoppel's mentality? Havelaar is not always the faultless, romantic hero, the 'good guy' in the story, with whom the reader can identify without reservation. Parallels between the two can be found not only in their patriarchal behaviour but also in their denial of art and their encouragement of social immobility. As I have already mentioned, we have here a case of a *Doppelgänger-motif*.

Droogstoppel ascribes Marie's revolt to the possible influence of Stern's manuscript, of which she has the task of making a fair copy. The story of Havelaar is, to Droogstoppel, a possible source of subversion, and not only because of his fight for a better life for the Javanese. Female protests — those of Tine and Upi — against male oppression can eventually influence his own daughter Marie Droogstoppel in her own small war of independence.

From a remark made by Droogstoppel, as Elsbeth Etty points out, the reader learns that the daughter of the rival firm of Busselinck and Waterman elopes with her German lover, leaving the petty bourgeois world of mid-nineteenth-century Holland behind. This almost unnoticed event is the most radical female protest in the novel against the suppression of female rights by males. It is, of course, utterly deplored by Droogstoppel, the unreliable narrator of the novel. *Max Havelaar* can be read as a misogynous book, but also as a book with hidden allusions to female revolt. The reader decides. In my revised reading, the suppression of women and their latent protest constitute complementary parts of the novel.

By showing parallels between colony and woman as they are both compared to manuscripts, I hope to have demonstrated the interrelations between colonial and misogynous ideologies. Showing parallels also between the characters of Droogstoppel and Max Havelaar demonstrates that they are extensions of each other rather than antagonistic. Max Havelaar, 'the good colonizer', can be interpreted as the superego of the colonizing subject, who has always also a Droogstoppel, the 'bad colonizer', within him, who can be compared to an unscrupulous, exploiting subconscious. They are both colonizing subjects under the control of the colonizing centre, and act as representatives of this centre, maintaining it from two different poles.

The role of the 'I' and the 'other' is not only shared between Droogstoppel and the Scarf-man/Havelaar, but also between the whites and the blacks, men and women, poor and rich. The main difference is only seemingly between white Europeans and black natives, but actually all the characters of the novel appear as the 'other' in relation to all other characters. Not even the Javanese are depicted as a homogenous group: they are both exploiters (the regent) and exploited. One of the proofs of the novel's outstanding quality is precisely the dynamic and manifold play of oppositions and parallels: the fact that Havelaar/the Scarf-man/Multatuli could formulate their emancipatory message despite their own contradictions.

Notes to Chapter 3

1. Rudolf Dekker, *Meer verleden dan toekomst* (Amsterdam: Bert Bakker, 2008).
2. See on this the debate 'Vorm of vent' (Form or Personality) and the great amount of secondary literature on this topic. This includes J. J. Oversteegen, *Vorm of vent?* (Amsterdam: Athenaeum, 1969); Wil-Jan van den Akker and Gillis Dorleijn, '15 december 1931. E. du Perron en Martinus Nijhoff gaan op de vuist. Vorm of vent' (15 December 1931. E. du Perron and Martinus Nijhoff Come to Blows. Form or Personality'), in *Nederlandse literatuur, een geschiedenis* (*Dutch Literature, a History*), ed. by M. A. Schenkeveld-Van der Dussen and others (Groningen: Martinus Nijhoff Uitgevers, 1993), pp. 642–47.
3. J. J. Oversteegen, 'De organisatie van Max Havelaar', *Merlyn*, 1 (1962–63), 20–45.
4. A. L. Sötemann, *De structuur van Max Havelaar* (Groningen: Wolters-Noordhoff, 1981).
5. The novel is based on Multatuli's own experiences in Lebak, where he was appointed assistant-resident in 1856 by the governor-general, Duymaer van Twist. Multatuli found evidence for the misuse of power by the native Muslim regent and his family members in the archives of his predecessor. When he himself was confronted with fraud and injustice and also received complaints from those who had been maltreated, he protested officially to his principal, the resident of Bantam, Brest van Kempen. He asked for the temporary removal of the regent from Lebak and the arrest of his accomplices. His request was ignored and the authorities decided to post him somewhere else. He did not accept this decision and gave notice to leave. However much he tried, his 'affair' was never properly examined in the Netherlands and the fact that he was right was never acknowledged. This was the so-called 'affair'.
6. See Cees Fasseur, *Onhoorbaar groeit de padi. Max Havelaar en de publieke zaak* (Amsterdam: Huis aan de Drie Grachten, 1987); Cees Fasseur, *Indischgasten* (Amsterdam: Bert Bakker, 1996); Dik van der Meulen, *Multatuli. Leven en werk van Eduard Douwes Dekker* (Amsterdam: Sun, 2002).
7. Saskia Pieterse, *De buik van de lezer. Over spreken en schrijven in Multatuli's Ideën* (Nijmegen: Vantilt, 2008), pp. 265–68; Elizabeth Wright, 'De kolonisatie van de tekst', in *Literatuur in psychoanalytisch perspectief: een inleiding met interpretaties van Multatuli's 'Saïdjah en Adinda'*, trans. by J. C. van Meurs, ed. by H. Hillenaar and W. Schönau (Amsterdam and Atlanta: Rodopi, 1990), pp. 148–64; D. C. van Oostrum, 'Sneezes and Lies: Female Voices in Multatuli's Max Havelaar', in D. C. van Oostrum, *Male Authors, Female Subjects: The Woman within/beyond the Borders of Henry Adams, Henry James, and Others* (Amsterdam: Rodopi, 1995), pp. 47–69; C. H. Niekerk, 'Race and Gender in Multatuli's Max Havelaar and Love Letters', in *One Hundred Years of Masochism: Literary Texts, Social and Cultural Contexts*, ed. by M. C. Finke and C. H. Niekerk (Amsterdam and Atlanta: Rodopi, 2000), pp. 171–90; Judit Gera, *Van een afstand: Multatuli's Max Havelaar tegendraads gelezen* (Amsterdam: Veen, 2001); Darren C. Zook, 'Searching for *Max Havelaar*: Multatuli, Colonial History, and the Confusion of Empire', *Modern Language Notes*, 121.5 (2007), 1169–89.
8. The Dutch essayist Elsbeth Etty also gives a rigorous criticism on the misogynous implications of the novel. Her article, however, came after the publication of Pieterse's book: Elsbeth Etty, 'Liever dood dan (seks)slaaf', *NRC*, 27 May 2010.
9. Anne-Marie Feenberg, '*Max Havelaar*: An Anti-Imperialist Novel', *MLN* 112.5 (1997), 817–35'; Reinier Salverda, 'Beeld en tegenbeeld van het koloniale verleden', in *Rekenschap 1650–2000*, ed. by D. Fokkema and F. Grijzenhout (Den Haag: Sdu Uitgevers, 2001), pp. 71–114.

10. Gera, pp. 12, 61.
11. This was the title of the pre-written Dutch lecture. Under the title we read: 'Samengesteld door het Multatuli Genootschap 2005' (Compiled by the Multatuli Society 2005).
12. Ian Buchanan, *A Dictionary of Critical Theory* (Oxford: Oxford University Press, 2010), p. 134.
13. Ibid., pp. 134–35.
14. Menno ter Braak, 'Multatuli, Droogstoppel, Havelaar', 'Douwes Dekker en Multatuli', 'Max Havelaar', and 'Huet en Multatuli', in Menno ter Braak, *Verzameld Werk. Deel 4.* (Amsterdam: G. A. Van Oorschot, 1951), pp. 49–61, 177–89, 333–36, 362–66.
15. See among others Erica van Boven, *Een hoofdstuk apart. 'Vrouwenromans' in de literaire kritiek 1898–1930* (Amsterdam: Sara/Van Gennep, 1992).
16. Arnold Labrie, 'Romantische politiek. Moderniteit en het ideaal van de zuivere gemeenschap', in *De zieke natie. Over de medicalisering van de maatschappij 1860–1914*, ed. by Liesbet Nys and others (Groningen: Centraal Boekhuis, 2002), pp. 58–73.
17. See Nop Maas, *Multatuli voor iedereen (maar niemand voor Multatuli)* (Nijmegen: Vantilt, 2000), pp. 7–49.
18. Kimberlé Crenshaw, 'Demarginalizing the Intersection of Race and Sex: A Black Feminist Critique of Antidiscrimination Doctrine, Feminist Theory and Antiracist Politics', *University of Chicago Legal Forum* (1989), 139–67.
19. Wright, 'De kolonisatie van de tekst', extended the colonial character of the novel to cover man–woman relationships.
20. Sötemann, p. 172.
21. Multatuli, *Max Havelaar of de koffieveilingen der Nederlandsche Handelmaatschappij* (Amsterdam: Wereldbibliotheek, 1932), p. 390.
22. Multatuli, *Max Havelaar or the Coffee Auctions of the Dutch Trading Company*, trans. by Roy Edwards (Leiden: Sijthoff; London Heinemann, London House & Maxwell New York, 1967), p. 320.
23. See Menno ter Braak, 'Multatuli, Droogstopple, Havelaar', in Menno ter Braak, *Verzameld Werk. Deel 4.* (Amsterdam: G. A. Van Oorschot, 1951), pp. 49–61; Oversteegen, 'De organisatie van Max Havelaar'; Sötemann.
24. Piet Emmer, 'De Max Havelaar: een pleidooi voor meer kolonialisme' (Max Havelaar as a Plead for More Colonialism) *Nieuw Letterkundig Magazijn* Jaargang XXVII, nummer 1, mei 2010, p. 12.
25. The following analysis is a revised version of my study *Van een afstand*.
26. See E. T. A. Hoffmann, *Die Doppelgänger* (1821); F. M. Dostoyevsky, *The Double* (1846); L. Stevenson, *The Strange Case of Dr. Jekyll and Mr. Hyde* (1886).
27. Multatuli, 1932, pp. 9–10.
28. Multatuli, 1967, p. 21.
29. Multatuli, 1932, pp. 180–81.
30. Multatuli, 1967, pp. 155–56.
31. Multatuli, 1932, pp. 59, 61.
32. Multatuli, 1967, pp. 62, 63.
33. The terms 'reliable' and 'unreliable' narrator were coined by Wayne C. Booth in his *The Rhetoric of Fiction* (Chicago: Chicago University Press, 1961). He is reliable to the extent that he is leaning on a real eyewitness's — that of the Scarf-man's — narration. But he is unreliable because he himself does not have direct experience of the things he is writing about. It is never quite clear when he is really and literally leaning on the Scarf-man's manuscript and when he is speaking according to his own preconceptions. Furthermore he is writing to Droogstoppel's commission, and this fact may also colour his voice.
34. Ania Loomba, *Colonialism/Postcolonialism* (London and New York: Routledge, 1998), p. 94.
35. Multatuli, 1932, p. 64.
36. Multatuli, 1967, p. 66.
37. Multatuli, 1932, p. 35.
38. Multatuli, 1967, p. 43.
39. Multatuli, 1932, p. 71.
40. Multatuli, 1967, p. 71.
41. Multatuli, 1932, p. 141.

42. Multatuli, 1967, pp. 123–24.
43. Multatuli, 1932, p. 77.
44. Multatuli, 1967, p. 75.
45. Pieterse, pp. 279–81.
46. Ibid., p. 279.
47. Multatuli, 1932, p. 70.
48. Multatuli, 1967, p. 70.
49. See Multatuli, 1932, pp. 71, 78–141, 226, and/or the English translation Multatuli 1967, pp. 71, 77, 123–24, 192.
50. Multatuli, 1932, pp. 186–87.
51. Multatuli, 1967, p. 160.
52. Loomba, pp. 76–78.
53. The Dutch name of the Flemish painter was Jan van der Straat (1523–1605).
54. Sigmund Freud, *The Question of Lay Analysis*, trans. N. Proctor-Gregg (London: Image Pub. Co., 1947), pp. 34–35.
55. Gayatri Spivak, 'Can the Subaltern Speak? Speculations on Widow-Sacrifice', *Wedge*, 7/8 (1985), 120–30.
56. Multatuli, 1932, p. 5.
57. Multatuli, 1967, p. 17.
58. Multatuli, 1932, p. 6.
59. Multatuli, 1967, p. 18.
60. Multatuli, 1932, p. 6.
61. Multatuli, 1967, p. 18.
62. According to Booth (1961) an unreliable narrator speaks mostly in the first-person singular and he or she is a narrator in the frame story. Droogstoppel is also such a narrator and his way of speech, his caricatured figure, his phobia of reading, his petty character, and his small-mindedness alienate him from the reader immediately.
63. Droogstoppel means 'scrawny staff', Slijmering is 'flatterer', Wawelaar is 'waverer', Stern is 'star', etc.
64. When Droogstoppel meets his old class-mate the first time he smells the fragrance of perfume. This fragrance is evoked in Droogstoppel's subconscious by an old, mutual adventure with the Greek girl. This associative and subconscious appearance of the past in the present is used later by Proust in the Madeleine episode from his *À la recherche du temps perdu* (1913–27).
65. Multatuli, 1932, p. 26.
66. Multatuli, 1967, p. 33.
67. Multatuli, 1932, p. 54.
68. Multatuli, 1967, p. 58.
69. Multatuli, 1932, p. 56.
70. Multatuli, 1967, p. 59.
71. Wolfgang Iser, *The Act of Reading: A Theory of Aesthetic Response* (Baltimore and London: The John Hopkins University Press, 1978).
72. Multatuli, 1932, p. 101.
73. Multatuli, 1967, p. 94.
74. Söteman, p. 119, Oversteegen, p. 43.
75. Hella S. Haasse, 'Overeenkomstig en vergelijkbaar', in Hella S. Haasse, *Lezen achter de letters* (Amsterdam: Querido, 2000), p. 10.
76. E. M. Beekman, *Troubled Pleasures: Dutch Colonial Literature from the East Indies 1600–1950* (Oxford: Clarendon Press, 1996), p. 229.
77. Darren C. Zook, 'Searching for Max Havelaar: Multatuli, Colonial History, and the Confusion of Empire'. *Modern Language Notes* 121.5, 2007, pp. 1169–1189.
78. Edward Said, *Orientalism* (New York: Vintage Books, 1979).
79. Michel Foucault, *The Archeology of Knowledge*, trans. by A. M. Sheridan Smith (London: Routledge, 1972).
80. Wright, 'De kolonisatie van de tekst'.
81. Duco C. van Oostrum, 'Sneezes and Lies: Female Voices in Multatuli's Max Havelaar', in D. C.

van Oostrum: *Male Authors, Female Subjects: The Woman within/beyond the Borders of Henry Adams, Henry James, and others* (Amsterdam and Atlanta: Rodopi, 1995), pp. 47–69.
82. Multatuli, 1932, p. 183.
83. Multatuli, 1967, p. 157.
84. Multatuli, 1932, n. 82, p. 428.
85. Multatuli, 1967, n. 66, p. 333.
86. Duco van Oostrum, p. 57.
87. Multatuli, 1932, pp. 190–91.
88. Multatuli, 1967, p. 163.
89. This episode has been drawn to my attention by Etty, 'Liever dood dan (seks)slaaf'.
90. Ibid.
91. Van Oostrum, p. 53; Beekman, pp. 348–49.
92. Van Oostrum, p. 62.
93. Multatuli, 1932, p. 184.
94. Multatuli, 1967, p. 158.
95. Multatuli, 1932, p. 186.
96. Multatuli, 1967, p. 159.

CHAPTER 4

A Novel of Hybridity: Louis Couperus's *De stille kracht*

The Outside Context

Innovation of Dutch Colonization in the Dutch East Indies: Ethical Politics

Dutch colonial practice begins to change at the turn of the twentieth century. Not only do colonial administration and economy change but so too do reflections and texts. The broader social, political, and cultural frames of Couperus's novel are also determined by this slowly changing colonial practice and the changing relationship of the Netherlands to its colonies. This new relationship has a textual character too: under the influence of Multatuli's *Max Havelaar* it was no longer possible to think about the Dutch East Indies in the old manner. This novel is one of the concrete examples of how literature can form and change reality. By calling attention to the dependence of the Javanese, the novel played a crucial role in revising not only colonial discourse but also colonial practice itself.

A cultural and ethical view of colonization came to replace an economy-centred colonial practice. This view was called officially 'ethical politics'. Not only was the pretext of this politics triggered by a text, *Max Havelaar*, but also its birth and maintenance are due to texts. Its official beginning was signalled by Queen Wilhelmina's speech in 1901, in which she underlined the moral mission of the Netherlands as a Christian state towards the population of the colonized territories and emphasized that this moral mission should also be present in politics. However, even this speech was preceded by other written texts, most notably the book by the social democrat member of Parliament Henri van Kol in 1896, *Land en volk van Java* (*The Land and Folk of Java*), and the article 'Een eereschuld' (A Debt of Honour) by C. Th. van Deventer, published in the journal *De Gids* (*The Guide*) in 1899. The latter proposed that the Netherlands should repay the natives the 7.5 million guilders of which, in Van Deventer's estimate, they had been robbed by the Dutch. This amount should be spent on improving education and economy for the natives in the Dutch East Indies, he argued. The colony should be guided rather than dominated or exploited. He wrote: 'Nog is het niet te laat: de groote meerderheid der inlanders is tevreden, onder Nederlands heerschappij; weet niet beter of het behoort zo. Maar — *les idées marchent*, zelfs in Indië en onder de inlandsche bevolking!'[1] [It is not too late yet: the great majority of the natives are satisfied under Dutch rule; they don't really know whether this is how it should be or not. However, *les idées marchent*, ideas are developing, even in the East Indies and among the native populace]. The quotation illustrates the relationship between knowledge and power, and that ideas spread not from above downwards but as in communicating vessels, as Michel Foucault argued.[2] These ideas very often lead to the revolt of the subjugated. Another piece of the textual fabric of changing colonial practice is the article 'De ethische koers in de koloniale politiek' (The Ethical Course in Colonial Politics) by Pieter Brooshooft (1845–1921), editor-in-chief of the Dutch-East Indian journal *De Locomotief* (*The Locomotive*), published in 1901. Brooshooft was one of the most important journalists of the time and spent quite a long time in the Dutch East Indies. The new trend in colonial politics took its name from the title of his article.

These texts form not only the context of the colonizing practice, but also that of the new articulations of colonial literature such as the novel *De stille kracht* (*The Hidden Force*, 1900). This broader political and cultural context is important not only because Couperus obviously followed the discussions related to the Dutch East Indies, but also because of the special characteristics of the ethical trend in Dutch colonial politics. This new trend, driven partly by guilty feelings, partly by practical considerations, wanted to raise the natives' standard of living by improving education, medical care, agriculture, and banking in the Dutch East Indies. The Dutch even talked of a future political and economic independence. Behind all this goodwill, however, a double intention was concealed. The motive behind developing the native population was not only the easing of a bad conscience but also the achievement of greater economic efficiency. That is how it was possible for the same Van Heutsz (1851–1924), who left behind him so many massacres in the Aceh wars (1873–1914) and who received the highest decorations and promotions from the Dutch government for all that, was also to found folk schools in villages in the Dutch East Indies at the turn of the twentieth century.

Meanwhile, however, it did not occur to anyone that ethical politics might actually give rise to the native population's dawning consciousness. Ethical politics was invented by Dutch colonizers who were undoubtedly driven by the best intentions; the actual loss of the colony, however, was not on their agenda. So ethical politics is a good example of ambivalence, in the sense in which the term is used in post-colonial discourse. I shall return to this later.

Louis Couperus (1863–1923)

Louis Marie Anne Couperus was born in The Hague as the youngest child of a large family (see Fig. 4.1). His father worked as a civil service officer in the Dutch East Indies. The youngest child could hardly meet his father's extremely high expectations. He spent his childhood in the company of his mother and his sisters, who determined his life in many aspects. He spent six years of his early childhood in the Dutch East Indies and returned to The Hague in 1878. Here he became a pupil of the Hogere Burgerschool (Civil High School), but he never finished his studies. In 1886 he took a high school examination in Dutch language and literature and that was that.

FIG. 4.1. Portrait of Louis Couperus by Jan Veth, 1900, litograph, Collectie Documentatie Nederlandse Letterkunde

His first literary endeavours were not successful: his poems, written in the style of the fashionable 'boudoir poems' of the time, were crushingly criticized by the most important literary journal, *De nieuwe gids* (*The New Guide*). As a prose writer, however, with his first novel, *Eline Vere*, which was published as a book in 1889, he had an immediate success. In 1891 he married his niece, Elisabeth Baud. From 1893 on he travelled continuously and spent much time abroad, sometimes in the South of France, sometimes in Italy. The First World War found him back in The Hague again. From 1903 he edited the journal *Groot Nederland* (*The Great Netherlands*) together with W. G. van Nouhuys and the Flemish writer Cyriel Buysse.

The works of Couperus, who lived the life of a decadent dandy, are divided into four groups in Dutch literary history: (1) psychological novels on contemporary problems, (2) symbolist tales and mythological novels, (3) historical novels, (4) short historical stories, travelogues, and journalistic writings. Several have been translated into a number of languages including, of course, English.[3]

Two main motifs are accentuated in Couperus's oeuvre: the presence of the almighty power of Fate and the sexualized opposition between North and South, in which the North represented the cool, rational, and emotionless male, whereas the South stood for the weak, emotional, decadent female principle. His characters are dependent on the irrational and incomprehensible power of Nemesis, and for that reason they must fall. Most scholars identify in this all-pervasive power of Fate the doctrines of the French critic and historian Hippolyte Taine on 'race, milieu, and moment'. The individual regards a break-out from his or her predestined course of life as impossible. In my opinion, however, Couperus adds a very sharp social criticism to this all-decisive role of Fate, and often depicts it ironically. This is because he is also interested in his protagonists' personal responsibility for their own lives. His 1890 novel *Noodlot* (*Footsteps of Fate*, 1891) is mostly interpreted as the depiction of the all-pervasive power of Fate. The three protagonists, Frank, Bertie, and Eve, actually become the victims of Fate, but only at first sight. At one point we read the following about Bertie, the decadent parasite and the source of the tragedy:

> Want, in zijn woede, nu opeens, zag hij het, ten dele met zekere trots: zag hij het, dat hij, wel degelijk hij, de omstandigheden had geleid om Frank en Eve te scheiden! Hoe had hij er nog een ogenblik aan kunnen twijfelen.[4]

> [For now, in his wrath, he suddenly saw and prided himself on the fact; he saw that he — very certainly he — had guided events to separate Frank and Eva. How could he even for a moment have doubted it?][5]

The novel really raises the question of individual responsibility together with criticism of a frivolous, dawdling, characterless creature who wants to become wealthy without working. It is much more than a mere tale of the power of elusive Fate.

The Contemporary Reception of Couperus

In 1896 Gerrit Hulsman, a Protestant minister, analysed Couperus's oeuvre up to that time in a three-part critique published in the journal *Stemmen voor Waarheid en Vrede* (*Voices for Truth and Peace*).[6] His main point is that in spite of his literary virtuosity Couperus's writings lack any kind of morality or ethical guidance. This is because the author is irreligious. According to Hulsman, Couperus adores aestheticism and sees beauty only in decadence, helplessness, and depression. He depicts only the surface of life, but never penetrates into its depths. Works like the 1892 *Extase* (*Ecstasy*)[7] and *Illusie* (*Illusion*) definitely offend the sensibility of believers because of the blasphemous abuse of the figure of Jesus. What is more, Couperus blurs Jesus with other prophets; he always depicts just those deities who come in handy for his themes, but always mocks the sensitivity of believers. Religious faith is always represented in his work by old women, hysterical young girls, or ignorant peasants. Despite all its virtuosity, his language must be also condemned because of the numerous Gallicisms, Germanisms, and Anglicisms. In Hulsman's opinion, Couperus's prose lacks humour. Society is not as bad as depicted by Couperus. Also, his characters are often repeated: all of them are brooding, weak, sensitive artistic souls. Hulsman indicates the pages in Couperus's eight works (published up till then) that express thoughts considered especially dangerous for young people: these pages spread the infectious diseases of pessimism, fatalism, unbelief, and immorality, he argued.

In contrast, Pol de Mont (1857–1931), the Flemish liberal poet and literary critic, who was the advocate of modern Dutch and French literature in Flanders, writes only in superlatives about the same period of Couperus. He praises the novel *Eline Vere* because of its profound psychology, and in his other works, such as the 1893 *Epiloog* (*Epilogue*) and *Kleine Raadsels* (*Small Secrets*), he thinks he can perceive the influence of occultism, Edgar Allan Poe, and E. T. A. Hoffmann.[8]

Willem Kloos, one of the most important poets of the time, and the novelist and critic Lodewijk van Deyssel found Couperus's novel *Majesteit* (*Majesty*, 1893) kitschy and unreadable.[9] This novel, however, was very popular at the time and it sold very well. The only one among the official critics who unconditionally acknowledged Couperus's achievements while the author was still alive was W. G. van Nouhuys in the daily paper *De Vaderland* (*The Fatherland*).[10] This ensured new publicity for him, as did his reading tours throughout the country. The author's person became more and more popular while his works no longer sold so very well. After his death, interest in his work decreased even more. Some revival came in the 1930s, when contributors to the journal *Forum* (1932–35), such as Hendrik Marsman, Menno ter Braak, and Jan Greshoff, wrote very positively about his work.

When the novel *De stille kracht* came out, it was received well on the whole. Some objected to the excessive presence of eroticism, and the different forms of the 'hidden force' were also felt to be unrealistic. Lodewijk van Deyssel prophesied that in about a hundred years the author would be spoken of as a second-rate feuilletonist who was unable to see any difference between spiritualism and the mysterious, enigmatic world of the Dutch East Indies.[11]

Ch. M. van Deventer, critic of the Semarang daily *De locomotief*, called the novel in his review an apology for colonialism. He saw in the protagonist of *De stille kracht*, Otto van Oudijck, an honest Dutch officer who only wanted the best for the Dutch East Indian natives. In this respect he found it a pity that Couperus seemed to be an occultist because, Van Deventer argued, the fabulous world of the Dutch

East Indies was not a worthy rival to the great stature of Van Oudijck. Later on Van Deventer went so far as to oppose Van Deyssel's negative criticism, reproaching him for overlooking the fact that the 'drama of the resident' symbolized the continuous fight of the Europeans against the hidden forces of Java.[12]

Interpreting Couperus Today

From the 1970s onwards, the evaluation of Couperus has been unanimously positive; the only difference has been in the differing emphases of critics and literary scholars. Nieuwenhuys reproaches Couperus for not really knowing Javanese culture well enough and therefore making several mistakes in depicting 'the hidden force'.[13] Nieuwenhuys does, however, have sympathy for mistakes regarding the total ethnic segregation of contemporary colonial society. While Marion Valent repeats that same criticism, she also calls attention to the fact that Couperus suggests a relationship between 'the hidden force' and Islam.[14]

An essential stage in the Couperus literature is F. L. Bastet's biography of him.[15] Bastet discusses Couperus's works, including *De stille kracht,* embedding them in his biography. We can gain a better understanding of the author's relationship to the East. In 1899 Couperus and his wife arrived in the Dutch East Indies for a family visit. At the beginning they stayed with his brother, John Ricus Couperus, who was a Vice-Resident of Meester Cornelis, later called Jatinegara, a small part of the town of Jakarta (Batavia).[16] Some months later they travelled up to Couperus's sister Trudy, who was the wife of the resident in Tegal, Gerard Valette, and who lived in a sort of palace. Here they had all kinds of entertainment, among others *tableaux vivants*, performing fragments from different plays and table-dancing. These motifs also play an essential role in the novel. While Couperus and his wife were staying in Tegal, their host, Gerard, heard that he was to be transferred to Pasuaran. During the removal the Couperuses stayed with Couperus's mother-in-law in Gabru. According to the author, it was here that all the strange, mystical things happened to him which he later also used in *De stille kracht*. Once, on entering the bathroom (which was in a separate building from his mother-in-law's house), he saw a white-clad figure with a turban on its head gliding past and vanishing from the place. This vanishing could only happen in a mystical way, because the other door of the bathroom — which offered the only chance for leaving other than the entrance — remained locked from the inside even after the strange shadow had vanished. This meant that the white figure could only have left through the wall. In a later newspaper article Couperus described the incident in detail, and stated firmly that it had all really happened.[17] In the novel *De stille kracht* the scene occurs again, and the white dressed *hadji* also appears at dramatic turning points. Couperus was still working on an earlier novel at the time. When his sister and brother-in-law had settled down in Pasuaran the Couperuses went to stay with them again. As he was then in a difficult financial situation, Couperus was already planning a new novel, to be set in the Dutch East Indies in prominent circles. His brother-in-law, being perfectly acquainted with the local circumstances and a high-ranking officer himself, would provide the necessary information for this new novel — the future

De stille kracht. According to Bastet, on the basis of the novel one can follow exactly the events of the year 1899, which Couperus spent on Java. The novel forebodes the end of colonialism, Bastet argues:

> *De stille kracht* is dan ook niet zozeer het verslag van een reeks paranormale verschijnselen waar de auteur ons mee wil begoochelen, als wel de beschrijving van verzwegen maar voortdurend — zij het niet altijd aanwijsbaar — zich manifesterende haatgevoelens van de inlandse bevolking ten opzichte van hun overheersers.[18]
>
> [*De stille kracht* is not so much a report on a series of paranormal phenomena with which the author wishes to enchant us; it is rather a description of a silenced but permanently manifested — although not always detectable — hatred of the native people for their rulers.]

Part of the plot is set in Tegal (called Labuwangi in the novel). The resident's house, which is described in full detail, was the real house of his brother-in-law: it was here that the above-mentioned *tableaux vivants* and theatrical performances were organized. The character of Eva Eldersma is based on Trudy, but in the novel she is the wife not of the resident but of his secretary. The main character, Otto van Oudijck, the diligent and conscientious Dutch officer, could be modelled on Couperus's own brother, John Ricus, and Otto's fictitious wife, Léonie, on Couperus's aunt on his father's side, Elisabeth, who had been disowned by the Couperus family because of her immoral way of living. Bastet emphasizes that Couperus changed the real persons who formed the basis of the characters in the novel so much that readers could not recognize any of them. So it was with the author's brother, John Ricus, whose stock was rising in contrast to Otto van Oudijck's drama. Other events and realia in the novel too went back to real events and persons, all of them precisely described by Bastet. The motif of the illegitimate child, Si-Oudijck, is also not a mere product of phantasy: several male members of the Couperus family had illegitimate children by native women, all of whom bore the name Couperus. The real sea-quakes in the vicinity of Ternate also play a role in the novel. Bastet also touches upon the real androgynous character of Couperus himself, which made it possible for him fully to identify both with Léonie's sensual, over-sexed character and with the beautiful young man, Addy de Luce.

The Dutch literary scholar Jacqueline Bel underlines the importance of the contemporary Dutch context in the interpretation of the novel.[19] The 'hidden force' also satisfied contemporary Dutch society's interest in the occult and in mystic and exotic phenomena. Bel also sets the novel in the context of those literary works which cautiously criticized colonial politics and Dutch colonizers living in the Dutch East Indies. She ascribes this sharpening criticism to 'ethical politics': it became clear that stopping the state monopoly in the colonies and replacing it with private holdings did not automatically solve the problems of the native people. In addition, decentralized Dutch power was easier for the colonized to undermine by individual actions and passive resistance. This is the reason, Bel argues, why white European characters were gradually replaced with non-Europeans in Dutch colonial novels of the time.

As mentioned above, Couperus is considered by many scholars as the writer of inevitable Fate. H. T. M. van Vliet, one of the Dutch Couperus experts and the editor of the *Complete Works* in fifty volumes, concedes that although in his first novels, such as *Eline Vere* (1889) and *Noodlot* (1890), Fate and weak characters are related, the responsibility of the characters and of society is also raised. According to Van Vliet, however, in later novels such as *Langs lijnen van gelijdelijkheid*[20] (*The Inevitable*)[21] or *De stille kracht* Fate expands to be an irresistible force. Life cannot be changed any more. So, for example, Cornélie de Rez, the main character in *Langs lijnen van gelijdelijkheid*, divorces her husband, writes a feminist manifesto on the situation of divorced women, and moves to Italy to live with her lover, an Italian painter; in the end, however, some irrational power draws her back to her husband and she resumes her life with him. In my opinion, however, Couperus also makes a very sharp criticism of society in this novel: the spoiled, aristocratic Cornélie has no taste for work, at least not for the kind of work which is incompatible with her social class. She prefers to leave her lover and become a lady's companion in an aristocratic family, and there she meets her ex-husband again, whom she cannot resist — at least not his fortune: the recurring attraction of riches overcomes her ambition to be independent.

Writing about *De stille kracht*, Van Vliet considers it to be a serious social criticism. In his interpretation this criticism concerns the decadence of the Dutch colonizers and the explanation of the principle 'flowering, growing and declining'. He sees the essence of the novel in the East–West opposition: Van Oudijck, the Dutch colonial officer, finds himself on foreign soil, and the mystic, incomprehensible power of the East leads to his decline. Van Vliet agrees with Hulsman that Couperus was an aesthete in the first place and not a philosophical writer, but that he was gifted with enormous visual power.

Rhetorical Context and Plot

De stille kracht, 1900 (see Fig. 4.2)

The Dutch officer Otto van Oudijck is a tireless and devoted resident of Labuwangi in East Java. He lives in a big, comfortable, beautiful residence, with numerous servants doing his bidding. He endeavours to do his job as best he can. In accordance with his value-system, he works hard from early morning to late at night. He believes himself to be a righteous, honest person who wants only the best for his subjects. From his first wife, a native woman now living in Batavia, Otto has four children: Theo, Doddy, René, and Ricus. Somewhere in the middle of the novel it turns out that Otto has another illegitimate child, called Si-Oudijck, from a relationship preceding his first marriage. His lover had once been his native housekeeper. Otto's second wife is the white but Dutch-East-Indies born Léonie, who has several lovers, among others Van Oudijck's own son, Theo. Van Oudijck's daughter, Doddy, is in love with Addy de Luce, the womanizing son of a rich family consisting of a set of mixed marriages. Addy also has a relationship with Van Oudijck's second wife, Léonie. In the beginning Otto is unaware of all these tangled love affairs, and has at most some suspicions. In addition to all this, Otto comes into conflict with the native lieutenant-governor's family, the Adiningrats,

FIG. 4.2. Cover of the first edition of the *Stille kracht*, Leiden University Libraries, 22537 D 11 001

who are high-ranking descendants of the sultans of Madura. While Adiningrat senior answered all Otto's expectations and they were on friendly terms, after his death his two sons who take over his office are not able to follow in their father's footsteps. One of them relapses into silence and passivity as a form of resistance to Van Oudijck, the other one drinks and gambles instead of working, so Otto warns him that he may be dismissed from his office. After this there come mysterious, uncanny powers to threaten Otto and his family: Léonie's naked body is spattered with red betel juice in the bathroom. Sometimes stones are thrown through the windows. The atmosphere in the resident's house gradually becomes unbearable. Otto loses all self-confidence and becomes mistrustful of his employees and his family. He receives letters from his illegitimate son Si-Oudijck, who continuously blackmails and threatens him. Léonie deserts Otto and goes to Europe. Otto resigns his office and moves to Garut with a native woman, Lena. Here he feels at home again.

In order to give more nuance to the interpretations of the novel up till now, here I shall attempt to give a new one. My approach draws on an article by Pamela Pattynama.[22]

Pattynama rightly analyses the novel in the historical context of Dutch colonization. One of her points of departure is the conflict between the Dutch resident Van Oudijck and the native lieutenant-governor Sunario. Behind this conflict we find Dutch colonial politics based on indirect power. Indirect power means that Dutch colonies were controlled by Dutch colonial officers not directly but through local leaders. These local leaders came from aristocratic families and were supporters of local sultanates, who in the beginning could choose their own means of exploiting the native population. Throughout the nineteenth century, however, Dutch control over these local leaders strengthened, because with the appearance of other European powers in the colonies, economic competition too began to grow. Local leaders became more and more puppets subjugated by the Dutch. They were allowed to retain the trappings of power, the ceremonies and other privileges, however, so that they would cooperate with the Dutch smoothly. But all this grandeur masked hollow functions.

Pattynama's theoretical point of departure leans on the post-colonial theorist Homi K. Bhabha's critique of Edward Said's *Orientalism*, and on combining post-colonial and gender approaches. According to Bhabha, colonial discourse is not only an instrumentalized construct of knowledge, nor can this knowledge be considered the intentional invention of the West.[23] Involving psychoanalysis in his inquiry, he argues that colonial discourse also operates by ambivalence generated by desire.

Feminist critics combine discourse analysis of colonialism with feminist theory so that they show points of intersection among race, gender, social class, and sexuality. Pattynama herself considers her own analysis a post-colonial approach refined by feminist theory and a mixture of colonial historiography and semiotic analysis. She complements Said's suggestion of 'contrapuntist reading' with the so-called 'resistant reading' developed by feminist critics. By 'resistant reading', the 'unsayable' — otherwise confined to the periphery of literary discourse — can be localized.

Pattynama's basic question is: what can be the meaning of the hidden force in the novel? In answering this question she focuses on the ambivalence in the book, which she finds in its literary devices, its psychological tensions, its hidden ideologies, and in coded imperialism.

Van Oudijck, the 'totok', that is to say, the white European colonizer, believes that control over natives is his natural right. His portrait is drawn in masculine terms. His figure reflects the 'ethical politics' which defines itself through teaching, nurturing, and guiding like a good father. The public character of his fatherhood is undermined by various factors. One factor is the passive resistance of Sunario, the native lieutenant-governor. Whereas Adiningrat senior could be fitted into the European stereotype of the 'noble savage', Sunario does not allow himself to be controlled. He resembles Si Upi Keteh from Multatuli's *Max Havelaar*. Their silence is their strongest weapon against colonial power. Van Oudijck can only describe Sunario as 'the negative other': 'not real', 'not a functionary', 'not a governor'. Local national consciousness, which develops as a result of 'ethical politics', also appears as a danger, a threat, in Sunario's personality. The real and greatest danger, however, comes from what Pattynama calls 'palimpsest narrative': just as Sunario escapes Van Oudijck's hierarchical control at work, Van Oudijck's wife Léonie and his children, Theo and Doddy, cannot be controlled either; all three undermine his authority as head of the family. The family line becomes mixed up with the public line and this leads inevitably to Van Oudijck's decline. Van Oudijck's sexual biography is clearly laid out in the palimpsest narrative. His first wife was born into a mixed marriage: she is an Asian-European (Eurasian) woman who illegally operates a gaming house somewhere in Batavia. Her mixed-race origin and her illegal activity create an aura of miscegenation and illegality around the figure of Van Oudijck too. Pattynama explains that miscegenation and illegal cohabitation with native women were tacitly permitted and considered a natural way of life in the first centuries of colonization. As a result there evolved a mixed, mestizo culture and society in the Dutch East Indies. Only in the nineteenth century, when fear became stronger that the white population in the Dutch East Indies would become 'degenerate' because of miscegenation, and in the long run could even vanish, did more serious segregation of ethnic groups become essential. So at the turn of the twentieth century racial mixing became less and less accepted. Suppression of mixed culture aimed to create a Eurocentric Dutch East Indies. The novel depicts this political and cultural situation. Van Oudijck's integrity, which seems to be intact at the beginning of the novel, is actually being undermined already from the outset by the invisible presence of his first mixed-race wife. There is a similar case with his second wife, who is of white European parents but was born in the Dutch East Indies. She is endowed with stereotypes such as her egotism and being a cruel *femme fatale*. At the same time she crosses borders between East and West, both her lovers — Theo and Addy — being men of mixed race. Her interracial sexuality and her place of birth make her the embodiment of stereotypes of the East as well: she is irrational, lazy, mystical, narcissistic, and over-sexed. As a counterpart there is Van Oudijck, symbol of the Western male stereotypes: masculine, rational, autonomous, a workaholic. So the opposition of East and West is sexualized.

Van Oudijck's daughter Doddy resembles her mixed-race mother in appearance. Her father can only accept a full-blooded white husband for her, while Doddy is in love with Addy, who is also of mixed-race origin. Van Oudijck would like to control this relationship, as miscegenation has by then become unacceptable. Control is, however, impossible, and he fails to intervene.

The last calamity for Van Oudijck comes from 'the heart of darkness'. As mentioned above, he had cohabited with his native housekeeper before his first marriage. From this relationship Si-Oudijck was born; he was rejected by Van Oudijck, who never wanted to know about him. Si-Oudijck, Pattynama argues, displays Van Oudijck's past and future: the past and the future native woman. That is how Van Oudijck's defeat becomes absolute: his second wife, Léonie, deceives him with mixed-race men (with his own son, among others), Doddy is also in love with a half-blood young man, Addy, and his illegitimate son, Si-Oudijck, is blackmailing him. By the end of the novel, in the Van Oudijck family — initially at the top of the social hierarchy — nothing remains clearly defined, nothing remains 'pure' or unambiguous, nothing is devoid of deceit. It turns out that borders are created by imaginary fictions, while reality is miscegenation. Everyone is fleeing distractedly from the father's white law.

I agree with Pattynama that the main theme of the novel is the process of mixing of the Dutch with the colonized 'other'. In this process seemingly unambiguous identities are destabilized. The novel can be best described by Bhabha's three interrelated notions: ambivalence, mimicry, and hybridity. Furthermore, I contend that the hidden force in the title is itself a mimicry: it is not a one-way process, it emanates not only from the indigenous population towards the Dutch but also the other way round, from Dutch colonizers towards Dutch East Indian subjects. *De stille kracht* is a novel of repetitive mimicry sequences of colonial power and family relationships.

The notion of ambivalence was introduced into colonial discourse by Homi Bhabha.[24] The concept originates in psychoanalysis. In post-colonial theory it means the complex amalgamation of fascination and hatred characteristic of the relationship between colonizer and colonized. Colonized subjects do not merely cooperate with or rebel against the colonizer, just as colonizers are not only oppressive either, they are often also nurturing. These contradictory attitudes are present at the same time in both oppressors and subjugated subjects in continuous fluctuation. Ambivalence undermines unambiguous authority, because again and again it destabilizes this very unambiguity of the relationship between colonizer and colonized. Colonial discourse itself is also ambivalent, because it is exploitative and nurturing at the same time. One of the problems of colonial practice is that it aims to create cooperative, subservient subjects who can reproduce colonial preconceptions, habits, and values — in other words, colonized subjects who 'mime' the colonizer. Instead of this, colonizing practice produces ambivalent subjects among colonizers and colonized alike.

A typical example of colonizing ambivalence is Otto van Oudijck, a full-blooded Dutch official, Resident of Labuwangi, who wants the best for his subjects — from a Dutch perspective, of course. He makes use of the wealth which goes with his position with the utmost nonchalance. The following scene shows not only his place in the hierarchy but also his real character:

> De rezident ging terug naar zijn kantoor, waar de hoofd-djaksa wachtte; het verhoor begon. Door een politie-oppasser opgeduwd, kwamen de beklaagden, een voor een, hurken op de trap, voor de drempel van het kantoor, terwijl de djaksa hurkte op een matje, de rezident zat voor zijn schrijftafel. Terwijl de eerste strafzaak behandeld werd, luisterde Van Oudijck nog naar de stem zijner vrouw in de middengalerij, toen de beklaagde zich verdedigde met de luide kreet van: 'Bot'n! Bot'n!'[25]
>
> [The resident went back to his office where the chief *djaksa* was waiting; the hearing began. Pushed along by a police-*oppasser*, the accused came one by one and squatted on the steps, outside the office door, while the *djaksa* squatted on a mat and the resident sat at his desk. During the first case, Van Oudijck was still listening to his wife's voice in the middle gallery, when the prisoner defended himself with a cry of: '*Bot'n! Bot'n!*'][26]

The resident is not listening to the prisoner's shouts but to his wife's voice. The Dutch officer, who is repeatedly characterized as a very conscientious man, is deeply indifferent towards his subjects. In addition, violence is also present — which can be considered as 'the hidden force' of Dutch power — but almost unawares: the accused are 'pushed along' by the police-*oppasser*. Hierarchical positions are visualized by the different postures of the protagonists: the accused squat on the steps outside the office door. They are not allowed to cross the border between their own world and that of the resident. The *djaksa* (a native officer of justice) squats on a mat, the resident sits at his desk. This is a visual reconstruction of the hidden force of Dutch colonial power. It is in this scene, however, that protest occurs for the first time in the form of the Malay shout '*Bot'n!*', meaning 'No!'. Otto's attitude is ambivalent: he is erudite, diligent, hard-working, self-confident, and the embodiment of jurisdiction on the one hand, and he is uncertain, anxious, exploiting, and indifferent on the other.

One form of ambivalence is mimicry: colonial power expects its colonized subjects to take on its values and norms, to mime them. The aim is, however, not to create exact replicas of the colonizing culture. In that case the borderline between oppressor and subjugated would vanish. Mimicry is itself ambivalent because it is operated by the colonizing power in accordance with its own interests, but at the same time it also strives to maintain the difference between oppressor and subjugated. Further on, the colonized are aware of the limits of this forced mimicry so they often change it into parody, tacitly mocking the oppressor. The native lieutenant-governor's function can be seen as the Dutch resident's function ('almost the same but not quite').[27] The function of the former has been created by the latter, that is, modelled by the colonizing power on its own power relationships in order to preserve its own existence. In such a way, exploitation of natives by natives became a crucial part of Dutch colonial policies as a whole. Mimicry is of a metonymic, therefore asymmetric, nature. There is a relationship between part and whole (*pars pro toto*). As a result, the Dutch resident could always call the native lieutenant-governor to account, but it could never happen the other way round.

But if the lieutenant governor protested or if he did not do his work well enough, this could become threatening for the colonizing power. So mimicry could serve both to strengthen and to undermine the authority of the colonial power. Ethical politics is itself a mimicry: it wants to build up Western civilization in the colonies, but not exactly the same civilization ('almost but not quite'): difference is needed to maintain colonial power, but difference also bears the possibility of revolt.

The relationship between the resident Otto van Oudijck and the lieutenant-governor's family, the Pangérans, is a concrete example of mimicry. The old lieutenant-governor, who had already passed away, was a scion of the Adiningrats: this family had been the sultans of Madura already in the time of the East India Company. According to Otto, the old lieutenant-governor was the embodiment of the ideal local leader who met Dutch expectations perfectly. His presence in the novel is virtual, like that of Otto's first wife, also a native living in Batavia, but it is just this virtual presence which bears a special meaning: as subjugated persons they have a serious influence on Otto even in their absence — the ex-wife is far away in space, the late lieutenant-governor in time. Otto tries to expect the same from the successors of the former lieutenant-governor. The two sons, however, embody only the imperfect mimicry of their father: they have received local power from the Dutch as a heritage, but they abuse it. The native widow's solidarity with her two sons, Sunario's continuous silence, and the younger son's drinking and gambling addiction seem also to be the reason for and manifestation of 'the hidden force'. Otto holds them responsible for the incomprehensible situations. That is even true, in that the two descendants' behaviour symbolically indicates the disintegration of the whole colonial system. But while Otto thinks that this disintegration is taking place only in the outside world, the fact is that he himself too is a cause and a bearer of disintegration. This, however, he does not recognize until the end of the novel. This is the deepest meaning of mimicry in this novel: the 'sameness but not quite' of the inside and the outside world. Both begin to decay, but while the colonizer's inside world disintegrates totally, the decomposition of the colonized outside world is a necessary prelude to a future integrity. The figure of Sunario, reminiscent of a *wayang*-puppet, and the decadent way of life of the lieutenant-governor(s) of Ngadjiwa form a parodistic mimicry of the larval, decadent members of the whole Dutch colonial community: of Léonie's egotism, indifference, and laziness, of Theo's love of his own stepmother, and of the table-tapping company around Eva Eldersma. This latter is a counterpart of Eastern mysticism: the strange activities of mystical stones thrown through windows and red betel juice.

Hybridity is another form of ambivalence beside mimicry. The word comes from the Latin *hybrida* meaning a cross between a domestic sow and a wild boar. The word was used in different meanings: in the biological sense it concerns plants and animals but it also has linguistic, ethnic, and cultural semantic fields. In the nineteenth century, when the ethnic and cultural meanings appeared in European discourses, it had mostly a negative connotation. This century was characterized by a dogged pursuit of purity.[28] The process began with Romanticism and went on until the middle of the twentieth century. The cult of purity was naturally connected with the ambition unambiguously to define national identity. One's own identity could only be defined in opposition to the identity of somebody else. In the case of hybrid forms this became impossible. Outlining the 'other' was not a problem if they were of unambiguous limits. Anxiety arose only when the 'other' could not be clearly differentiated. Colonization is a characteristic space of hybrid formations in both the ethnic and the cultural sense. There is no greater fear for colonizers than that of losing the limits of their identity, which was thought to be unambiguous, because this would mean losing their power at the same time. *De stille kracht* is exactly about these processes. The novel thematizes hybridity by focusing on the most diverse variations of it.

In the foreground of the novel we have the Dutch community. Otto and Léonie have no children in common. The four legitimate children come from Otto's first marriage to a half-blood woman. These four children are all racially mixed. Otto's several relationships with native or half-blood women 'result' not only in hybrid children but also in his vanishing from the stage of colonial enterprise. He fades away into the whirling world of the Dutch East Indies. His vanishing points towards the vanishing of Dutch colonial power itself.

Theo, Otto's hybrid son, has an affair with his stepmother. This affair is not only forbidden by nineteenth-century white European, Victorian morality but it also threatens to hybridize Léonie. So her character is not only ambivalent, but by her attractive power over hybrid men she herself becomes a representative of actual miscegenation and hybridity. Léonie's experience with 'the hidden force' in the bathroom scene is the central event of the novel: the bespattering of her body with betel nut juice is a symbol of her oncoming hybridization. Her snow-white European skin gets 'dirty' and Léonie no longer meets European expectations of purity. In this same scene Léonie, who is literally the embodiment of Dutch colonial power because of her white skin, becomes the object of the gaze of the subjugated: the red colour of betel spirits away white skin. Franz Fanon, a Martinique-born Afro-French psychiatrist, philosopher, revolutionary, and writer wrote about the fetish of colonial discourse, the 'epidermal schema' which, unlike the sexual fetish, is not private, not secret. In his book *Black Skin, White Masks* he reports the words of a white girl to her mother which she shouted in Fanon's sight: 'Look, a Negro ... Mama, see the Negro! I'm frightened!'[29] After this Fanon adds: 'What else could it be for me but an amputation, an excision, a hemorrhage that spattered my whole body with black blood?'[30] While in the scene described by Fanon we see the everyday drama of colonial societies where discrimination against black skin (considered negative, anomalous as opposed to narcissistic white) is manifest, in the novel we see the colonizer becoming the object of hate expressed by the violation of the fetish of white skin. In its simplicity this is the climax of the novel. With Fanon, we can say that the episode in the novel is a 'scene' in the psychological sense of the word, which underlines the visual (seen). Fanon's scene and the scene in the Dutch novel are parallel only in externals and not in their meaning. With Couperus it is the branding of the colonizer which is forever incomprehensible for the colonizer him/herself, while with Fanon it is the discriminative expression of colonial discourse far too well known to the subjugated.

Another group of white Europeans is the company around Eva Eldersma: her husband Onno, the resident's secretary, and their little son; a German couple, the Rantzows; Doorn de Bruijn, the chief engineer, and his wife; Ida van Helderen and her husband Frans, who in the meantime falls in love with Eva. Ida, Frans van Helderen, and Léonie were born in a non-European continent from European parents: they are Creoles. They have grown up and been educated in the Dutch East Indies, yet they do everything to be more European than the Europeans themselves: they would like to speak a more standard Dutch than the native Dutch do, they long for European culture, and the narrator is continuously emphasizing their white skin. Their Dutch Indies background refers to their doubly foreign identity; in the Dutch East Indies they belong to white colonizers, in the Netherlands they count as elements of the colonial world:

> Ida van Helderen was een typetje van blanke nonna. Ze probeerde altijd heel Europees te doen, netjes Hollands te spreken; zelfs gaf zij voor, dat zij slecht Maleis sprak, en dat zij noch van rijsttafel, noch van roedjak hield.
> [...]
> Er was een verwonderlijke distinctie en ingeboren stijl in deze jonge man, als was hij niet een kind van Europese ouders, die steeds in Indië waren geweest, als was hij een vreemdeling van een land onbekend, van een nationaliteit, die men zich niet dadelijk wist te herinneren ... Nauwelijks was er een zekere molligheid aan zijn accent — invloed van het klimaat — ; [...] Misschien had hij van een Franse moeder dat exotisch beleefde en hoffelijke; ingeboren, prettig, natuurlijk. In zijn vrouw, ook van Franse origine, gesproten uit een kreolenfamilie van Bourbon, was dat exotische een geheimzinnige mengeling geworden, die niets dan kinderlijkheid was gebleven ...[31]
>
> [Ida van Helderen was a typical little white *nonna*. She always tried to behave in a very European fashion, to speak Dutch well, and even pretended to speak bad Malay and to care for neither *rijsttafel* nor *rudjak*.
> [...]
> There was a wonderful distinction and innate style about young Van Helderen, as though he were not the offspring of European parents who had always lived in the Indies, as though he were a foreigner from an unknown country, of a nationality that you could not place immediately. His accent barely betrayed a certain softness, resulting from the climate [...]. Perhaps he owed to a French mother that exotic politeness and courtesy, innate, pleasant, and natural. In his wife, who was also of French extraction, springing from a Creole family in Réunion, this exoticism had become a mysterious mixture that had never developed beyond a kind of childishness [...]][32]

These people are neither Europeans nor native Dutch East Indians; their identities are elusive, situated in the post-colonial third space, to use the term coined by Homi Bhabha. This space is a space of miscegenation — this time of a cultural nature — containing dangers, threats, and secrets.

A prominent example of hybridization is the De Luce family. This family consists of what the Dutch call Indos, that is, mixtures of natives and Europeans — half of them half-bloods, the remainder people from Solo, a city in Central Java. The grandmother, the wife of Ferdinand de Luce (himself a scion of a French aristocratic family from Mauritius), is a princess of Solo and cannot speak Dutch. Ferdinand began as a cook and gained a reputation in Solo with his Dutch East Indian recipes.

After leaving his lowly occupation as a cook he begins a typical colonial enterprise: production of sugar. From the marriage of the native princess and the French sugar planter several children are born. Their eldest daughter marries a full-blooded Dutch man; the eldest son marries an Armenian girl, while two other daughters become wives of Indos and the youngest son pays court to the hybrid Doddy, daughter of Otto van Oudijck. As for different types of people, the reader gets to see a real ethnic richness:

> Vreemd was het te zien die verschillende types; de mooie melkblanke Léonie naast de geel gerimpelde Raden-Ajoe-douairière; Theo, Hollands blank en blond met zijn volle lippen van sensualiteit, die hij van zijn nonna-moeder had; Doddy, als een rijpe roos al met hare vonkel-irissen in de zwarte pupillen; de zoon-administrateur, Achille de Luce, — groot, fors, bruin, — wiens gedachte alleen ging over zijn machinerieën en zijn bibit; de tweede zoon, Roger, — klein, mager, bruin, — boekhouder, wiens gedachte alleen ging over de winst van dat jaar, met zijn Armeniaanse vrouwtje; de oudste dochter, al oud, — dom, lelijk, bruin, — met haar volbloed Hollandse man, die er uitzag als een boer; de andere zonen en dochteren, in alle nuances van bruin, en niet dadelijk uit elkaâr te kennen.[33]

> [It was strange to see the different types: the pretty, milk-white Léonie beside the yellow, wrinkled *radèn-aju* dowager; Theo, pale and blond as a Dutchman, with his full, sensual lips, which he had inherited from his *nonna* mother; Doddy, already looking like a ripe rose, with the sparkling irises and black pupils in her dark eyes; the manager's son, Achille de Luce, brown, tall, and stout, whose thoughts were only concerned with his machinery and his *bibit*; the second son, Roger, brown, short, and thin, the bookkeeper, whose thoughts were only about the year's profits, with his little Armenian wife; the eldest daughter, old already — brown, stupid, ugly — with her full-blooded Dutch husband, who looked like a peasant; the other sons and daughters, in every shade of brown and not easily distinguished one from the other.][34]

In the characterization of the youngest son, Addy, the narrator emphasizes the intellectual consequences of miscegenation: Addy's intellectual powers are zero, but he is endowed with the beauty of a young *sinjo*, a Dutch East Indies-born European. From a European perspective, miscegenation goes together with the decline of intellect (culture) and with the growth of physical beauty (nature). It is no surprise that Addy is at the centre of the oncoming drama between Theo, Léonie, and Doddy.

Hybridity has also a linguistic aspect in the novel. The text of *De stille kracht* is full of Malay words. These words are not integrated into the Dutch text: they float like isolated islands in the sea of Dutch, and the author does not attach notes to the novel, as Multatuli did. In consequence, the language of the local people is more visible, and this undermines the coherence of the colonizers' language. The numerous Malay words work in a subversive manner in the text: they remind readers that the language of the colonized is forced to the periphery and that we readers, just like colonizers, are treading foreign soil. It is not a balanced, co-equal relationship. The Dutch text colonizes the Malay words, as it were. If this were not the case, the text would not be readable for Europeans. On the other hand, only those who have a knowledge of Malay can fully understand the text of the novel. Those who lack this knowledge are confronted with an awkward feeling of not understanding. Thus Malay words also represent power relationships in an iconic way: on the one hand, textually they are in a minority position, their strangeness is constructed from a Dutch perspective, and they recall the language of the 'other'. On the other hand, they undermine the balanced harmony of Dutch readers' reading. The Malay words function also as a 'hidden force' which repeatedly disrupts the homogeneity and 'purity' of the Dutch language.

The background of the novel is populated by people considered locals. I would like to consider in more detail only on Si-Oudijck. As mentioned above, he was born from Otto's relationship preceding his first marriage. His mother was Otto's housekeeper. Si-Oudijck and Theo are introduced to each other by Addy. Si-Oudijck mixes up Dutch and Malay — speaks a hybrid language. In his brown, canny, furtive eyes he hides his hate, jealousy, and bitterness. His background and Theo's are identical: they are both children of a native mother and a Dutch father. Si-Oudijck still belongs to the colonized, Theo to the colonizers. The reason is clear: Otto van Oudijck had accused his housekeeper of being unfaithful and thrown her out undeservedly, while Theo's mother was, after all, his wife. The erudite, hard-working, melancholic Otto is in this respect the harsh, patriarchal colonizer again: the child of civilized, Protestant, ethical Holland, and as such a cold-blooded, cruel potentate. Beside the bathroom scene, I find the description of Theo's feelings towards his half-brother another climax of the book:

> Het deed de echte zoon goed hiervan te horen, omdat hij in het diepst van zich, hoe blond en hoe blank ook, meer was de zoon van zijn moeder, de nonna, dan de zoon van zijn vader; omdat hij in het diepst van zich die vader haatte, niet om die aanleiding of deze reden, maar om een geheimzinnige bloed-anthipathie, omdat hij zich, trots zijn voorkomen en voordoen van blonde en blanke Europeaan, geheimzinnig verwant voelde aan deze onechte broêr, een vage sympathie voor hem voelde, beiden zonen van een zelfde moederland, waarvoor hun vader niet voelde dan alleen met zijn aangeleerde ontwikkeling: de kunstmatig, humaan aangekweekte liefde der overheersers voor de overheerste grond.[35]

> [It did the legitimate son good to hear all this, because in his innermost self, blond and fair-skinned though he might be, he was more the son of his mother, the *nonna*, than of his father. In his innermost self he hated his father, not for this or that reason, but from a secret antipathy in his blood, because, despite the appearance and behavior of a blond and fair-skinned European, he felt a secret kinship with his illegitimate brother, felt a vague sympathy for him. Were they not both sons of the selfsame motherland, for which their father felt nothing except as a result of his acquired development, the artificially, humanely cultivated love of the ruler for the territory that he rules.][36]

Very rarely do we read a more serious criticism of the white Dutch colonizer in Dutch colonial literature. This time the 'hidden force' emanates from Theo, who is seemingly white, but in his deepest self a Dutch East Indian who secretly hates his father, the embodiment of patriarchal, colonizing power. In Theo's character we see the amalgamation of ambivalence, mimicry, and hybridity, the aspects of how colonial desire functions.

* * * * *

As already mentioned, most scholars see this novel as the expression of the exotic East, which is impenetrable for the European eye. On the basis of Couperus's own utterances, Bastet sees in the 'hidden force' not so much the symbol of exoticism but rather the expression of hate among the local population for white power.[37] Pattynama and I see the essence of the novel in the fabric of interracial relationships — relationships taking the forms of ambivalence, hybridity, and mimicry. The novel does not only describe, but is also a linguistic embodiment of, the processes of miscegenation: the loss of full-blooded Dutch identity and colonizing authority.

The interpretation of this literary work would not be complete without taking the author's personal life into consideration. Couperus's father was connected to colonial life in the same way as Multatuli's, as a consequence of which their sons' lives too could not remain untouched by the theoretical and practical questions of colonization. Couperus spent five years of his childhood in the Dutch East Indies with his parents and siblings, from 1872 on. Later he called this period the happiest of his life. He could never become accustomed to the cold, rainy Netherlands. He spent some time in Nice, some time in Italy, and later he travelled again to the Far East as a journalist. His own real life too was about crossing borders: borders between cultural, ethnic, and sexual identities. As in almost all his work, so in *De stille kracht* he blends real life and fiction. The *hadji* stepping through the wall, hybrid characters, relationships and positions straddling ethnic and psychological borders are manifestations of repeatedly occurring sequences of ambivalence, mimicry, and hybridity. Couperus could foresee the loss of Dutch colonial power because he recognized and depicted transitions, blending, ambivalence, and the inherent chaos of the colonial world as an inevitability and a necessary devastation of this world.

Notes to Chapter 4

1. C. Th. van Deventer, 'Een eereschuld', *De Gids*, 63.3 (1899), 205–57.
2. Michel Foucault, *The Archeology of Knowledge and the Discourse on Language*, trans. by A. M. Sheridan Smith (London and New York: Routledge, 2002).
3. See Paul Vincent, 'Louis Couperus (1863–1923), Dutch Novelist, Short Story Writer and Poet', in *Encyclopedia of Literary Translation into English: A–L*, I, ed. by Olive Classe (London: Fitzroy Dearborn Publishers, 2000), pp. 314–15.
4. Louis Couperus, *Noodlot* (Wageningen: L. J. Veen, 1978), p. 92.
5. Louis Couperus, *The Footsteps of Fate*, trans. by Clara Bell (London: William Heinemann, 1891), p. 46.
6. Hulsman, G., 'Louis Couperus I-II-III', *Stemmen voor Waarheid en Vrede*, 33, March (1896), pp. 36–76; 113–52; 209–55.
7. Louis Couperus, *Extasy*, trans. by Teixeira de Mattos and John Gray (London: H. Henry, 1897).
8. Pol de Mont, 'Louis Couperus', in Louis Couperus, *Een zieltje* (Gent: Hoste, 1893), pp. 1–2.
9. Lodewijk van Deyssel, 'Over Louis Couperus', *Tweemaandelijksch Tijdschrift*, I. 4 (1895), 1–20.
10. W. G. van Nouhuys, 'De stille kracht', *Het Vaderland*, November 1900.
11. Lodewijk van Deyssel, 'G. van Hulsen en Louis Couperus', in *Verzamelde opstellen*, VII (Amsterdam: Scheltema en Holtema's Boekhandel, 1904), pp. 1–10.
12. Quoted by Rob Nieuwenhuys, *Oost-Indische spiegel. Wat Nederlandse schrijvers en dichters over Indonesië hebben geschreven vanaf de eerste jaren der Compagnie tot op heden* (Amsterdam: Querido, 1978), pp. 252–62 (p. 258).

13. Rob Nieuwenhuys, 'De onbegrepen stille kracht', *Haagse Post*, 14 September 1974, pp. 46–49.
14. Marion Valent, 'Over "*De stille kracht*" van Louis Couperus', *Literatuur*, 1 (1984), 203–09.
15. F. L. Bastet, *Louis Couperus. Een biografie* (Amsterdam: Querido, 1987).
16. This small part of the town of Jakarta was called by the Dutch after a seventeenth-century Calvinistic teacher, minister, and landowner Meester (Master) Cornelis van Senen, born on one of the Banda Islands. After his death in 1661 the place kept his name for three centuries.
17. Louis Couperus, 'Wonderlijke historiën. De badkamer', *Haagsche Post*, 20 January 1917.
18. Bastet, p. 232.
19. Jacqueline Bel, *Nederlandse literatuur in het fin-de-siècle. Een receptie-historisch overzicht van het proza tussen 1885 en 1900* (Amsterdam: Amsterdam University Press, 1993).
20. Louis Couperus, *Langs lijnen van geleidelijkheid* (Amsterdam: L. J. Veen, 1900).
21. Louis Couperus, *The Inevitable*, trans. by Alexander Teixeira de Mattos (New York: Dood, Mead & Company, 1920).
22. Pamela Pattynama, 'Secrets and Danger: Interracial Sexuality in Louis Couperus's *The Hidden Force* and the Dutch Colonial Culture around 1900', in *Domesticating the Empire: Race, Gender and Family Life in French and Dutch Colonialism*, ed. by Julia Clancy-Smith and Frances Gouda (Charlottesville and London: The University Press of Virginia, 1998), pp. 84–107.
23. Homi Bhabha, *The Location of Culture* (London: Routledge, 1994).
24. Ibid.
25. Louis Couperus, *De stille kracht* (Amsterdam: Querido, 1991), p. 21.
26. Louis Couperus, *The Hidden Force*, trans. by Alexander Teixeira De Mattos, with an Introduction by E. M. Beekman (London: Quartet Books Ltd., 1992), p. 57.
27. Bhabha, p. 85.
28. Arnold Labrie, 'Romantische politiek. Moderniteit en het ideaal van de zuivere gemeenschap', in *De zieke natie. Over de medicalisering van de maatschappij 1860–1914*, ed. by Liesbet Nys and others (Groningen: Centraal Boekhuis, 2002), pp. 58–73.
29. Frantz Fanon, *Black Skin, White Masks*, trans. by Charles Lam Markmann (London: Pluto Press, 2008), p. 84.
30. Fanon, p. 85.
31. Couperus, 1991, pp. 56–58.
32. Couperus, 1992, pp. 85–86.
33. Couperus, 1991, p. 79.
34. Couperus, 1992, p. 103.
35. Couperus, 1991, p. 100.
36. Couperus, 1992, p. 121.
37. Bastet, pp. 239–49.

CHAPTER 5

Victory of the 'Other' over Colonial Power: Madelon Székely-Lulofs, *Tjoet Nja Din*

The Outside Context

Colonial novels sometimes retain current interest even today. Different aspects of the colonial past can generate discussions in the present about the political, economic, and cultural importance of the former colonies. Our relationship to the colonies is continuously changing and is also connected to our political value system. The name of J. B. van Heutsz (1851–1924) is linked to the Aceh war and it is this war that Madelon Székely-Lulofs's (1899–1958) novel is about. Van Heutsz was one of the leading figures of the war, a general who opted for military attack against Aceh. He led several bloody campaigns which resulted in many victims. The Dutch state awarded him several decorations for his part in the war. In 1904 he was appointed governor general of the Dutch East Indies, and it was then that he founded several *dessa* (village)-schools in accordance with 'ethical politics' (see chapter 4). The aim of these schools was to raise the native population through education. In 1908 Van Heutsz moved back to the Netherlands, where he continued to deal with colonial affairs, among other things founding the Colonial Museum (today: Koninklijk Instituut voor de Tropen, Royal Institute of the Tropics).

The Aceh war, which was started by the Dutch colonial power, lasted from 1873 till 1914, at least according to the Dutch. Its aim was to protect the Strait of Malacca, which was continually exposed to piratical raids from Aceh. In the 1824 Sumatra contract the Netherlands undertook the protection of passengers traveling through the Strait of Malacca, while respecting the independence of Aceh. This contract was overwritten in 1871 by another agreement, so that from this time on Britain allowed the Netherlands a free hand in Aceh. The increased importance of the Strait of Malacca — which came under the jurisdiction of Aceh — as a result of the opening of the Suez Canal played an essential role in both the beginning and continuation of the war in Aceh, which was also a prosperous agricultural territory, especially because of pepper. Thus there was also an economic reason for the Netherlands to conquer Aceh, which had been independent up till then. Fighting continued also after 1914. According to the Aceh people, this war ended only in 1942, when the Japanese appeared and the Aceh people were able finally to drive out the Dutch.

The history of the monument on the Apollolaan in Amsterdam is a good example of the evergreen nature of the Dutch colonial past (see Fig. 5.1). The monument named after Van Heutsz was inaugurated by Queen Wilhelmina in 1935. Lack of critical confrontation with the colonial past led to revolt in left-wing circles against the monument, which bore evidence of the past by bearing the name of a bloody killer. After long discussions and after being damaged several times, it was renamed in 2004 'Indië — Nederland' (East Indies — the Netherlands). It is a reminder of the whole colonial period from 1596 to 1949. All references to Van Heutsz were removed from the monument. A similar fate was shared by the bust erected in the general's birthplace in Coevorden, inaugurated in 1933. In 1965 Alard van Lenthe and Relus ter Beek, later Minister of Defence — both editors of the *Rooie Drentse Courant* (*The Red Drenthe Herald*) — placed the following caption on the bust: 'Ontslapen onder het hakenkruis; gesneuveld bij het uitmoorden van het 39ste Atjehse dorp; bij het verkrachten van de 79ste Acehse vrouw; om het geschokte vertrouwen van het Ned.-Indische bestuur opnieuw te funderen' [Died under the swastika; killed in action while extinguishing the 39th Aceh village; while raping the 79th woman of Aceh; in order to restore the shaken confidence of the Dutch East Indian government]. The bust has been replaced several times since this incident, it has been given a new caption, and in 2009 persons unknown made the caption 'Van Heutsz' illegible and carved the word 'Aceh' on it instead. That is why it is remarkable that we read in the last volume of the ambitious series *Nederlandse cultuur in Europese context* (*Dutch Culture in European Context*) the following:

> Ook in het geval van Indië staan we nu voor een verleden dat omstreden is geraakt, en naar goed Hollands gebruik gaat dat gepaard met een beeldenstrijd. Soms gaat die strijd ook letterlijk om beelden, zoals bij de aanslag op het Indische veteranenmonument te Leiden in oktober 1999. Veel vaker is het een strijd om namen en betekenissen, zoals in het recente besluit om het Van Heutsz-monument in Amsterdam om te dopen tot 'Monument Indië — Nederland 1596–1949'. Daarmee dreigt de herinnering aan de man die eens als bedwinger van Indië werd vereerd en tegelijk gehaat als slachter van Atjeh, te worden uitgewist.[1]

> [In the case of the East Indies, too, we confront a past which has become controversial and, in accordance with good Dutch custom, goes together with the destruction of images. Sometimes the fight is literally for sculptures, as in the case of the assault on the East Indian Veterans' Monument in Leiden in October 1999. More often it is a fight for names and meanings, as in the recent decision to rename the Van Heutsz monument in Amsterdam 'Monument East Indies — the Netherlands 1596–1949'. Herewith the memory of a man, once respected as the conqueror of the East Indies, but at the same time hated as the butcher of Aceh, is threatened with oblivion.]

Almost each sentence in this quotation is ambivalent or not quite accurate. The past connected with the Dutch East Indies not only 'became' but it *was* already controversial at the time when the Van Heutsz monument was erected in 1933, so much so that it caused the Socialists to protest. The following sentences seem to suggest that the assault on the veterans' monument in Leiden and the protest against the naming of the Van Heutsz monument were not of the same nature. Both repudiated the same thing: the integration in the institutionalized national memory

FIG. 5.1. The Monument East Indies — The Netherlands by Frits van Hall, 1935. Photograph by Wikimedia Commons user PjotrP.

of Dutch colonizers as heroes. The last sentence of the quotation is the most ambivalent: on the one hand it suggests that we have to do with a historical figure — Van Heutsz — whose memory should be preserved in the form of a monument. On the other hand, 'the conqueror of the East Indies' and 'the butcher of Aceh' function in the sentence as if they were entities independent of each other, while they are closely connected. According to some sources Van Heutsz was responsible for the death of 70,000 people.

In this chapter I examine to what degree the novel *Tjoet Nja Din* was written from a colonial perspective and to what degree it is an anti-colonial novel. This question can be partly answered if we look at the narrative strategies which the writer uses and if we answer the question: in what way is Van Heutsz referred to in the novel? The analysis of these issues will, I hope, show that this work — in spite of its ambivalence — is one of Madelon Székely-Lulofs's strongest anti-colonial novels.

Prelude and Background

In the 1930s Madelon Székely-Lulofs (see Fig. 5.2) was a writer well known not only in the Netherlands but also in Europe. Her fame was based on her first novel *Rubber* (*Rubber*), published and translated into English in 1931.[2] Her second novel *Koelie* (*Coolie*), published in 1932, increased her reputation.[3] Both works give a psychologically realistic picture of the situation in the Dutch East Indies. Dutch progressive circles saw in them a protest against colonialism.[4] Their importance was often compared to that of Multatuli's *Max Havelaar*. The most respectful critics of the Netherlands at that time, Menno ter Braak and Edgar du Perron, the legendary editors of the journal *Forum*, however, did everything possible to undermine the writer's good reputation, and they did not waste too many words in praising her work.[5] They considered success as a bad sign, a factor inversely proportionate to quality. They put her novels in the category of the so-called 'damesroman' [ladies' novel], and this label counted as one of the most degrading criticisms of the day: it was used as a synonym for irrelevance and cheap kitsch. As Praamstra argues, although both were dead by the beginning of the Second World War the two literary giants maintained their authority also after the war to such a degree that not only could Székely-Lulofs hardly find a publisher for her work, but she herself became uncertain about her own talent. When she died she became a forgotten writer. After the war she was hardly published any more, and Rob Nieuwenhuys, the expert on the literature of the Dutch East Indies, devotes only a short chapter to her work in his monograph *Oost-Indische Spiegel* (*Mirror of the East Indies*).[6]

The writer's work was rediscovered only in the 1980s. Her work is being republished; literary scholars are re-reading her oeuvre and finding new aspects and great literary values in it. Rudy Kousbroek, Gerard Termorshuizen, Olf Praamstra, and Gábor Pusztai have played an essential role in its rediscovery.[7] They have published articles, longer studies, and monographs on her and her Hungarian husband László Székely, who was also a writer. All this work was crowned by two biographies published in 2005 and in 2008 respectively. The first was by Kester

Fig. 5.2. Portrait of Madelon Székely Lulofs,
Collectie Documentatie Nederlandse Letterkunde

Freriks, who wrote it in the form of a biographical novel.[8] The second, with scholarly ambitions, was written by Frank Okker.[9]

There has also been an important theoretical discussion going on around the novel *Rubber*, generated by the emergence and practice of post-colonial criticism. The Dutch literary scholar Maaike Meijer has analysed the novel using a post-colonial approach.[10] Her point of departure was that no text can ever exactly reflect reality. It can only create the illusion of reality. She follows Said's perception, according to which images of the East are always representations and not direct depictions of reality.[11] Representations of the East are never devoid of some kind of interest. Interests and power relations play an essential role in the way of depiction. In analysing the text Maaike Meijer put the question: to what extent does it reproduce the clichés and stereotypes of the East? She draws the conclusion that the novel makes use of several colonial and racial conventions of representation. René Marres challenges this opinion, saying that the realism of the novel does depict reality and it cannot be labelled as racist.[12] As Olf Praamstra points out in reviewing this discussion, the basic difference between Meijer and Marres lies in how they define realism.[13] While for Marres realism means the true depiction of reality, Meijer argues that every text offers a kind of construct of reality, and realism is only the application of a certain set of conventions of representation. In order to resolve the argument, Praamstra suggests examining the ideology of the novel. This he does, comparing the text and the film made of the novel and further analysing two other novels by Székely-Lulofs. According to Praamstra, in Meijer's analysis the colonizing character of *Rubber* is given greater emphasis than the critical depiction of colonialism and colonizers. Yet at the time of the novel's publication, Praamstra argues, it was just its anti-colonial tone which was dominant and that is how it functioned in the discourse of the time. In contradiction to the novel, the film distorted the conception of the original work, so it really gave an uncritical image of the colonizers.

One of Praamstra's most exciting ideas is when he explains what could be the reason of Székely-Lulofs's critical attitude. On the one hand he refers to an interview made with her in which she ascribes her critical attitude to her Hungarian husband. It was he, she said, who taught her to look at colonial society with another eye:

> Mijn man als iemand, in Europa opgevoed zag Indië altijd met andere oogen aan dan ik als in Indië geborene. Voor mij was vroeger alles gewoon en daarom zag ik in het begin veel niet, wat hij wèl zag. Ik vond alles doodgewoon. Hij wees me op tal van bijzonderheden, die ik zoo geleidelijk ging leeren zien [...][14]

> [My husband, brought up in Europe, always took a different view of the East Indies than I did myself, who had been born there. For me everything was familiar from earlier times and that's why I did not see a lot of things in the beginning which he saw very well. I found everything quite usual. He showed me lots of specific things which I also began to see gradually [...]]

It is perhaps even more relevant that the writer, who had lived in Deli, a state in East Sumatra, for several years with her first husband on the rubber plantations, felt herself a foreigner, an outsider. The first four years of her life she spent in Aceh,

North Sumatra, and after that lived in Manindjau, Middle Sumatra, until the age of nine. These were the formative years of her life. In Deli, as a new arrival, she could see the colonial situation more sharply, objectively, and critically.

Székely-Lulofs had already dealt with the theme of the Aceh war. In her novel *Hongertocht* (*Hunger Patrol*) published in 1936 she described the events from a Dutch perspective.[15] The Aceh war is otherwise a theme that hardly occurs in Dutch literature.

Tjoet Nja Din, Madelon Székely-Lulofs's last novel to be published during her lifetime, can be described as a historical novel with strong political connotations. We have to consider the historical background of the time when the novel was being written. Székely-Lulofs began writing it in 1944 in Santpoort. Later she had to leave her house in Santpoort because the Germans began building their defences there. It is also known that Madelon Székely-Lulofs's husband was a Jew and they had a daughter together, Kotjil.[16] In 1940 Székely returned to Budapest, partly for health reasons, partly because he did not want to put his wife and daughter in danger.[17] So politics too played an obviously essential role in the formation of the novel because of the specific historical circumstances, so crucial in their consequences for the writer's personal life. In the Netherlands, for example, she was forced to become a member of the Cultuurkamer [Chamber of Culture] founded by the Germans in 1941 in order to move Dutch authors in a national socialist direction. Every author was called upon to join this organization or be threatened with a ban on publication. Székely-Lulofs did not comply with this notice at first, but because she was hiding people — among others, the communist Theun de Vries — she did not want to risk their being discovered and so became a member. After that she stopped writing. Moral dilemmas triggered by the Second World War, treason, forced moves from one house to another, threats of persecution were all personal experiences and as such may have served as motifs for her novel.

When the novel appeared it was the time of the so called 'politionele acties' (police actions) of the Netherlands against Indonesia. In 1942, when Japan occupied the Dutch East Indies, the Dutch living there had to flee and those who could not were interned in local work camps set up by the Japanese. When the latter capitulated there followed a power vacuum in the country. This was exploited by the two leaders of the local nationalist movements, Sukarno and Hatta. The Republic was proclaimed in 1945. The Netherlands did not recognize Indonesia at that time and tried to regain power. There were many people who simply could not imagine the future of the Netherlands after the loss of such an old and established source of economic development. It was also at this time that the idiom was coined: 'Indië verloren, rampspoed geboren' [East Indies lost, disaster born]. So the Netherlands opted for military intervention in order to regain control over Indonesia. Regaining power was intertwined with economic interests, which is why they attacked mainly those territories where there were Dutch enterprises, that is, on Java and Sumatra. The first police action took place on 7 July 1947. Fighting went on until 5 August. More than 1,100 rubber, tea, coffee, cocoa, and palm oil plantations were regained by the Dutch. The second action took place from 19 December 1948 until 5 January 1949. These military interventions were called police actions by the Dutch so as to pretend for the benefit of international public opinion that they were only intended to repress the usual national revolts. The Netherlands recognized the independence of Indonesia and finally relinquished up its colonial power only in 1949. This happened under the influence of international public opinion. The birth of the Indonesian Republic was regarded by the Dutch for a long time as collaboration with the fascist Japanese forces.

The publication of the novel in 1948 coincides with these police actions. The text of the jacket flap warned readers in vain not to draw parallels between the Aceh war and the police actions: the book was removed from the bookshops and the press ignored it totally. And, knowing the writer's political commitment against the Indonesia politics of the Netherlands at the end of the 1940s, it is almost inevitable that we see some kind of palimpsest: behind the story of the Aceh war we see and feel the influence of not only the Second World War but also the narrative of the police actions.

There is a further interesting circumstance, namely that in her will, written in Hungarian, Madelon Székely-Lulofs left everything to her third daughter, Kotjil, born from her second marriage, including the copyright of the novel *Tjoet Nja Din*. As John Jansen van Galen argues, the Hungarian will was without force, because after the death of her Hungarian husband the writer lost her Hungarian citizenship.[18] Nevertheless, the two elderly daughters of the first marriage of the writer decided to publish the novel again. This made possible the second edition in 1985, although without the formal consent of Kotjil who, identifying with her father's Jewish identity, had moved to Israel and could not be found by the publisher. This is an example of what an essential role is played by language and politics, language and culture, identity and images of the past in publishing and republishing books.

The subtitle of the novel is *De geschiedenis van een Atjehse vorstin* (The History of an Aceh Sovereign). Title and subtitle seem to suggest that the protagonist, Tjoet Nja Din, stood in the middle of the story about the Aceh war. This, however, is only partly true. I shall come back to this later.

In her introduction to the novel, Székely-Lulofs writes about the personal relationship between her own life and the Aceh war. Around 1900 her father was working as a senior officer at Meulaboh, on the west coast of the Aceh Province. It was here that Teku Umar, one of the Aceh heroes, was killed in action in one of Van Heutsz's attacks. In 1900 Madelon Lulofs was one year old. Meulaboh is the very place which connects her life with the Aceh war and its participants. The following quotation illustrates that the writer was well aware of the fact that all images created about reality are constructions and transmissions and she also gives a psychological explanation of why she was deeply touched by the Aceh war:

> Zó en aldus leefde destijds Oemar in een donkere uithoek van mijn wezen, als een schim, die werd tot een dogmatisch, overgedragen begrip van valsheid en trouweloosheid. Als een overgedragen begrip! Niet als een zelf doorleefde ervaring of zelfs maar als een zelf doordachte wezenlijkheid. Váák dragen wij zo door ons leven de mensen, dingen en gebeurtenissen mee uit het onbewuste begin van ons bestaan en uit het leven van onze ouders en voorouders en veel daarvan bezinkt in de lagen van ons groeiend Ik en wordt daarin tot fossiel, maar soms, plotseling, blijkt iets daarvan in ons opnieuw gekiemd, in alle stilte,

in de donkerte, en op het moment, dat wij licht en warmte toelaten, ontplooit het zich tot nieuwe bloei.[19]

[In this way and in this manner Umar was living in a dark corner of my mind, as a ghost who became a dogmatic and transmissive abstraction of falsity and unreliability. As a transmissive abstraction! Not as a personal experience or even as a privately conceived reality. We often carry with us people, things, and events throughout our lives in this manner, from the unconscious beginnings of our existence and from the lives of our parents and grandparents. Much of all this sinks into the layers of our growing Self and becomes a fossil there. But sometimes, suddenly, it seems that something of all this begins to bloom in silence, in the darkness, and the moment we let light and warmth through, it develops into a new flowering.]

The quotation can be interpreted in a colonial frame: members of the colonizing community are carrying the 'burden' of the colonial enterprise of their country and they cannot get rid of this 'burden' until the end of their lives. The phenomenon of this colonial enterprise becoming a fossil in the citizens of the colonizing community is called repression in psychological terms. The novel becomes possible as a result of the writer's tidying up her bookshelves, as we read in the introduction. This is a metaphor for straightening up her subconscious where colonial events had become fossilized.

The Strategic Position

As already mentioned, the writer's relationship to the East has been 'translated' in her works: it is written into the narrative mode and into those images, themes, and motifs with which the text is intertwined. First I shall examine what kind of a strategic position — a term coined by Edward Said — Madelon Székely-Lulofs had, to the Dutch East Indies in general and in her novel *Tjoet Nja Din* in particular.

Madelon Székely-Lulofs is said to be a real 'child of the Dutch East Indies' because — unlike Daum, Multatuli, or Couperus — she was actually born there, to be more exact, in Surabaja.[20] Her father, Claas Lulofs, worked first as an officer in the Java administration. In a 1949 interview Madelon Lulofs said that her father considered his job a real mission and behaved towards the native population as a benevolent guardian.[21] This approach to the colonial office is a typical case of the so-called *mission civilisatrice*. The guardian role of the white father also evokes the characteristically patriarchal relationship between colonizer and colonized: the native population, considered as a forlorn child, must be controlled by a benign guardian.[22] We saw the same attitude in the case of Max Havelaar and Otto van Oudijck in the previous chapters. This subjective vocation is complemented with an institutional vocation. Apropos of the Linggadjati Agreement which proposed a federal union between Indonesia and the Netherlands, J. A. Jonkman, Dutch minister of the Overseas Territories, said in one of his speeches in the second chamber: Indonesian nationalism could enjoy full freedom to develop, in all its nuances, while the Netherlands went on fulfilling its mission. As Van den Doel remarks, Indonesian people just wanted to get rid of the Netherlands, which wanted to fulfil its 'mission' in South East Asia at any cost.[23]

Wijngaard describes the writer's father's life as that of the systematically developing, righteous leader. As already mentioned, Madelon Lulofs was one year old when her father was sent to Aceh. This happened in the middle of the Aceh war, which became the theme of *Tjoet Nja Din*. Little Madelon played among prisoners of war and criminals who were doing penal servitude. To illustrate this phase in the life of the writer, Wijngaard quotes from the 1957 autobiographical work by Madelon Székely-Lulofs, *Weet je nog wel? (Do You Still Remember?)*:

> In mijn hansop sloop ik met blote voeten over het warme gras naar de bloemen en wachtte met ingehouden adem tot een libel zich daarop neerzette. Dan trachtte ik met de toppen van duim en wijsfinger het lange, naaldunne lijfje te pakken. Het lukte mij nooit en, teleurgesteld, heb ik toen eens één van 'onze' gestraften het bevel gegeven zo'n 'tjapoeng' voor mij te vangen ...[...] Mijn vader, die het van zijn kantoortje uit zag, kwam met grote stappen en daverende stem de gouvernementele orde herstellen; de gendarme kreeg een behoorlijke schrobbering, maar hij verweerde zich met de voor hem kennelijk onaanvechtbare verontschuldiging: 'Nonnie had het bevolen.'[24]

> [In my all-in-one suit I was sneaking barefoot in the warm grass to the flowers and holding my breath I was waiting until a dragonfly descended on one of them. Then I tried to catch its long, thin, little body with the tip of my thumb and first finger. I never succeeded and disappointed as I was, I ordered one of 'our' prisoners to catch me such a 'tjapung'... [...] My father, who saw all this from the window of his office, came along with big strides and a roaring voice to re-establish the official order; the guard was rebuked harshly but he defended himself with an excuse which seemed an irresistible argument to him: 'Nonnie ordered it.']

All that is described in this scene is the experience of the colonizer with 'prisoners'. Madelon Lulofs was socialized as the child of well-to-do colonizers. The reflexes of giving orders, the approach to the natives as 'our prisoners' are inherent traits. This socialization is also reflected in Madelon Székely-Lulofs's later writings.

A remarkable feature of the novel is the circumstance that children born and educated in the Dutch East Indies — including Madelon Lulofs — were raised by a native nanny, the so-called *babu*. As Praamstra explains in the article referred to above, the relationship of Dutch children to their *babu* is a typically ambivalent one: the *babu* is above them as a second mother, but in reality she is their servant. These children have the same strong bonding to the *babu* as to a family member while they, the children, stand in the hierarchy high above her, the person who is responsible for their early upbringing. So master–servant relationships are inevitably entangled in these strong emotional bindings. The ambivalence in the depiction of the native freedom fighter Tjoet Nja Din can be explained partly with this special relationship between the Dutch child as master and the native nanny as servant.

In Székely-Lulofs's descriptions there are not only divides between whites and natives, but also between rich and poor. This last social difference appears as a natural one in *Tjoet Nja Din*. The common people of Sumatra on the lowest steps of the social ladder are shown as the servants of the native potentates. The reason for this is, however, not only to be found in the writer's social background. It is conspicuous that novels by other Dutch authors also confine themselves to the representation of the native upper class: these higher circles actually formed that very social group with which Dutch officers directly associated in practice. This is true of Multatuli's *Max Havelaar* just as it is of Couperus's *De stille kracht*. Lower social groups are represented only sporadically, on the periphery, although they bear threatening, disturbing messages in all three cases. According to Salverda this literary imagery is partly due to the influence of Johan Huizinga's *Herfsttij der Middeleeuwen* (*The Waning of the Middle Ages*) from 1919:

> Via Van Vollenhoven en anderen, zoals G.J. Nieuwenhuis, kreeg Huizinga's aristocratische cultuurbegrip vervolgens een centrale plaats in de opvattingen waarmee Nederlandse geleerden en beleidmakers de inheemse cultuur tegemoet traden. Daarbij ging dan vooral op Java en Bali, de aandacht primair naar de Oosterse hofcultuur van een inheemse elite van regenten in al haar veelzijdige exotische en esthetische pracht. In deze oriëntalistische cultuuropvatting was echter geen plaats voor de eigentijdse, moderne, gemengde, multiraciale, islamitische cultuur van het gewone volk in de stadscampongs.[25]

> [Later, Huizinga's aristocratic notion of culture received a central place via Van Vollenhoven and others like G. J. Nieuwenhuis in the approaches of Dutch scholars and politicians in which they were dealing with the native culture. So, attention was paid especially on Java and Deli, primarily to the Eastern court culture of the native elite of regents in all its versatile, exotic, and aesthetic magnificence. In this orientalist approach to culture there was no place for the contemporary, modern, mixed, multiracial, Islamic culture of the simple folk in the town-*campong*s.]

In Székely-Lulofs's novel, too, the reader only sees the exotic grandeur surrounding Tjoet Nja Din:

> Maar natuurlijk, bij de rijken en voornamen en vooral bij zulke machtige lieden als de Nanta's, dáár was de kamerhemel van laken, rijk geborduurd met blad- en bloemmotieven en met bonte kwasten versierd. En daar was de koele pandanmat op de slaapbank bedekt met een kleed en aan het hoofdeinde waren de pronkkussens opgestapeld, daar lag de ganse rijkdom der Nanta's weggeborgen: feest- en bruiloftskleren broeken jakken, sjaals en lendedoeken, donkerpaars, wijnrood, diepgrijs en zwart, zwaar van goud- en zilverdraad; en de sieraden: diademen, halskettingen en borstversierselen, enkelringen en armbanden van rood goud in de edelste bewerking, gordels met juwelen gespen, polsbanden met diamanten slot, flonkerende vingerringen, puntige gouden jasknopen en oorhangers en de gouden bloemsluier voor bij het bruidsgewaad.[26]

> [But of course, in the houses of the rich and the aristocracy, especially such powerful people as the Nantas, the ceiling of the room was of richly embroidered linen and it was decorated with colourful fringes. The cool palm seat of the coach was covered with a carpet, at the headend colourful, shiny, valuable cushions shot with gold, were piled high. In the chests there hid all the Nanta treasures: robes and bridal clothes, trousers, jackets, shawls and loincloths, dark purple, wine red, dark grey and black, heavy with golden and silver trimmings; and jewels: tiaras, necklaces and brooches, anklets of red gold, finely decorated, bracelets and girdles decorated with gems and clasps, wrist bands studded with diamonds, glittering rings, bright golden buttons and earrings and a wedding veil embroidered with golden flowers.]

Similar passages reminiscent of the exuberant *fin-de-siècle* style can be found in large numbers in the novel. The subservient role of the simple folk appears as a background motif with a self-evident naturalness:

> Op het erf staan de dragers met de draagstoel gereed en zij neemt daarin plaats met de beide kinderen. Dan zetten de mannen hun schouders onder de lange bamboezen staken, ze heffen het gestoelte op, de vrouwen voegen zich met hùn kinderen tot een stoet, de lijfwacht omringt hen. Zo verlaat Tjoet Nja Din huis en erf om niet te hoeven buigen voor het gezag van de Ongelovige. [...] Zij verlaat het met alles en iedereen, met goud, goederen en juwelen, met al haar volgvrouwen en slavinnen. [...] Din heeft alleen de kaken hard opeen gebeten en heel recht op zit zij in het draaggestoelte, dat deint op de rythmische gang van dragers, en haar kleine, van ringen flonkerende handen omklemmen elkaar onder de afhangende einden van de doorzichtige, witzijden sjaal [...].[27]

> [The palanquin-bearers are waiting on the estate and she takes her seat with her two children. Then the men put their shoulders under the long bamboos, they lift the palanquin, the women with their children line up, the guards stand around in a circle. That is how Tjoet Nja Din leaves her house and estate so that she does not have to bow to the Infidels. [...] She leaves everything and everybody behind, with gold, belongings and jewels together with her chaperones and slaves. [...] Din merely bites her lips hard and sits upright in the palanquin, which rocks gently to the rhythm of the carriers' footsteps, her small hands covered with glittering rings clasped under the diaphanous, white silk shawl falling from her shoulders [...].]

I do not know whether these colourful and aesthetic descriptions were really born under the influence of Huizinga's *Herfsttij der middeleeuwen*. In any case, the style reminds one of that of the famous historian. Tjoet Nja Din's perspective is confined only to her enemies; those who are socially inferior to her are of no interest to her. She is fighting against the unbelieving Dutch, not against her own class. Her interest is of a political, not of a social nature. She is insensitive to social conflicts.

We should not forget either that Madelon Székely-Lulofs did not have direct experience of the Aceh war. As can be seen from the bibliography at the end of the novel, she learned about this war from books. The description of the Aceh war is therefore a multiply transmitted — that is, indirect — representation and not a 'natural' mirror of the East. One of the writer's most important sources was the 1893 book *De Atjehers* (*The Aceh People*) by the Dutch Arabist and scholar of Islamic Studies, C. Snouk Hurgronje (1857–1936). When there was a ceasefire in the Aceh war in 1884, the Dutch asked Hurgronje for help for a better understanding of the Aceh people. Hurgronje had studied theology and Semitic languages at Leiden University. After taking his doctorate he became a lecturer at the institute training officers for the Dutch East Indies. He devoted himself to studying Islamic jurisprudence and later was appointed lecturer in Islamic social institutions at Leiden University. He travelled to the Arabian peninsula, had himself circumcised, and converted to Islam in order to take part in the Hajj.[28] Here he met pilgrims from Aceh from whom he obtained a lot of information about the situation in the Dutch East Indies. Returning to the Netherlands he persuaded the minister of Colonial Affairs to send him on a field trip to Aceh. So it happened: he stayed from 1891 to 1892 inside the so-called Concentrated Fortress Ring.²⁹ At this time he succeeded again in gaining the confidence of the Aceh people and was also able to see the circumstances of the native society in practice. He recorded his experiences in a report which he presented to the governor general, C. P. Hordijk. Later he worked as a colleague and adviser to General Van Heutsz who was a fierce believer in defeating the Aceh people. Van Heutsz's brochure *De onderwerping van Aceh* (*Defeating Aceh*) also has a distinguished place in Székely-Lulofs's bibliography. A quotation from the brochure goes like this:

> Alleen hij, die toont de macht te bezitten om zijn wil te doen eerbiedigen, overal en onder alle omstandigheden, ook waar nodig, door doeltreffende gebruikmaking van den sterken arm, zal de man zijn die Atjeh tot volkomen onderwerping brengt, die het dappere en vrijheidslievende Atjese volk den voet op den nek zet, [...].³⁰

> [Only he who shows that he has the power to carry his purpose everywhere and under all circumstances, and where needed even using strong-arm methods, only he will be the man who will finally defeat Aceh, who will put his foot on the neck of Aceh's brave and freedom loving folk, [...].]

Another real historical figure was Teku Umar, also recorded in the novel. He came from an aristocratic family and he led the local people during the fighting in Aceh. Since the Dutch thought for a while that it would be more efficient if they won loyal natives for their case, they offered Teku Umar a remarkable amount of money and weapons for his desertion. They also gave him a new name, which is a cultural aspect of colonization overwriting the personality and original culture of the colonized. The same happened to Jacatra, which was renamed Batavia by Coen. Besides a new name, Teku Umar also received a new home with new furniture. However, he turned the weapons against the Dutch and returned to his own people. After this the Dutch broke into his house in order to rob him. The interior described in the novel is a good example of the contact zone of two cultures, European Dutch and East Indian:

> Daar is Oemar's Europees meubilair, de wipstoelen met hun fijne matting, de gebeeldhouwde fauteuils, de tafels met marmer blad en gedraaide poten, de pronkende spiegels, de prachtige oude kasten, de zware ijzerhouten kisten met koperbeslag, het Europeese ledikant met het tulen bedgordijn, een tafeltje met een stapel oude kranten. Het is daar alles, weerloos uitgeleverd aan de sarcastische verbazing, aan de hoon, aan de indiscretie, aan de gewelddadigheid. Wat geroofd kan worden, dat wordt geroofd: sirihstellen, een zitmatje, een waardevol kussen, een kris, een prachtige antieke Koran, in kostbaar leer gebonden, op perkament geschreven en beschilderd met de hand.³¹

> [There is Umar's European furniture, rocking chairs with fine upholstery, carved armchairs, tables with marble tops and curved legs, decorated mirrors, splendid, old cupboards, heavy, copper-bound iron chests, the European bed with gauzy curtains, and a small table heavy-laden with old newspapers. All this is defenceless prey to sarcastic astonishment, contempt, indiscretion, and violence. What can be looted is looted: *sirih* sets, a rug, a valuable cushion, a knife, and a beautiful, hand-painted, antique Koran written on sheepskin, bound in expensive leather.]

The clashing of European and East Indian culture is expressed in this description of objects assembled in the same space. European objects are not looted by the Dutch. For them only objects of the East are of importance; stealing those is a military act, but is also the appropriation of the East in a symbolic sense. Descriptions are never innocent, as we saw in Chapter 2 where the description of Van der Hooghen's room exactly reflects the character of its resident and the popular cultural taste of the period.

Hurgronje, the Dutch Arabist, and Teku Umar from Aceh, who temporarily comes over to the Dutch, are both parts of the contact zone, phenomena of transculturation, each other's reflections.

Another item in the novel's bibliography is that of the Aceh poet Dokarim's epic, the *Hikajat Prang Kompeuni*. By the writer's own account, this was the work on which she based her story. Székely-Lulofs saw the name of this poet by chance in the margin of a page in Hurgronje's book. Finding a native name in a Dutch study in the margin of a book on Dutch colonization I see as a metaphor: Hurgronje's book is one of the representatives of the empire of knowledge about the East. It takes a central place in this empire. An anonymous reader of the book scribbles Dokarim's name in the margin. It seems that this unknown reader of the Dutch empire, the centre, wanted to call attention to the native poet of the periphery. The Dutch writer's accidental meeting with the name of Dokarim creates the possibility for the bearer of the name to get into the centre. This can, however, only happen through the mediation of a writer from the centre who is already endowed with the power of writing. The way in which Székely-Lulofs 'uses' the Aceh poet's name is also remarkable:

> Hij heette Dokarim of Abdoelkarim. Ik verwierp Abdoelkarim; dat kon de naam zijn van een veedrijver of van een klerk of van een opzichter. Veel liever aanvaardde ik: Dokarim. Hij was een Atjehs dichter, maar aangezien het overgrote deel van het Atjehse volk niet kon lezen, reciteerde hij zijn heldendichten voor zijn publiek.[32]
>
> [His name was Dokarim or Abdulkarim. I rejected Abdulkarim; it could have been the name of a buckaroo or of a clerk or of a controller. I rather preferred Dokarim. He was an Aceh poet, but because most of the Aceh folk could not read he recited his heroic poems for his audience.]

Székely-Lulofs refuses one of the native poet's names, placing herself in the power position of those who give names to others. The name Abdulkarim is found to be much too popular, too simple; the writer's admiration is obviously not challenged by buckaroos, clerks, or controllers — typical serving functionaries of the colonial arena. Her personal sympathy is reflected in this; it is obviously much more on the side of the aristocracy than that of the lower social groups. Here in the introduction it is all about intellectual aristocracy, but in the novel itself, too, the aristocracy is a vital element of the world depicted.

Székely-Lulofs uses also other names of native poets in an unusual way in her bibliography. She assigns a work entitled *Hikajat Prang Sabi* to its Dutch translator, H. T. Damsté. The real author's name, Njaq Puteh, cannot be found either in the novel or in the bibliography. The title of Dokarim's poem is listed in the bibliography as headword, then comes the poet's name in the possessive form 'van Dokarim' (of Dokarim), and after that comes the translator's name, H. T. Damsté. Aceh poets' names are never placed in the first place in the bibliography, as they should be. Their works are only available in translation, so translators' names precede native authors' names. Authority/authorship — in both senses of the word — is not given to the colonized in a colonial context.

The Critical Reception of the Novel

On 1 July 1948 an advertisement was published in the communist newspaper *Waarheid* (*Truth*), where Székely-Lulofs's novel was recommended along with the books of Eva Curie, Alexej Tolstoy, and Theun de Vries. On 25 September in the same newspaper there appeared a laudatory review by someone called Amir. The reviewer emphasized that this work did not show the history of the Aceh war from a Dutch perspective, and also elaborated on the motives and human aspects of the 'enemy'. After this there came the synopsis of the plot. In the end, the reviewer referred to the jacket flap which warned the reader not to draw parallels between the Aceh war and the police actions taking place at the time when the book came out. This was not even theoretically possible, because when working on the novel the author could not possibly have foreseen the police actions that would take place later, at the end of the 1940s. The reviewer, however, did draw parallels on the basis of the text: what in the Aceh war was called 'the concentrated fortress ring' became during the police actions 'demarcation lines' which divided the two parties. Those native leaders who collaborated with the Dutch in the Aceh war had been decorated, as were those who did so during the police actions. Villages that revolted had been 'punished' as they were in the Aceh war and in the police actions, which actually meant extinction of the population of these villages. So the novel retained its contemporary relevance. That is why the reviewer drew the readers' attention to this work.

Since then, however, hardly anybody has reviewed the book. According to Peterson, one of the reasons for this was that the consequences of the Second World War and the police actions distracted the public's attention from the novel about the Aceh war.[33] Another reason could be, Peterson argues, that the novel was about natives and not about the Dutch. Another of the few reviews was an article written by C. J. Kelk in the literary journal *De Groene Amsterdammer* (*The Green Amsterdammer*).[34] Kelk praises the vivid rendering of the tropical landscape and that the writer succeeds in winning the reader emotionally. He resents, however, the fact that she wrote her work on the basis of someone else's documents.

When the second edition was published in 1985, the critical response was again sparse. Coos Versteeg in the *Haagsche Courant* (*The Hague Courier*) on 31 May 1985 attributed the book's lack of success to the circumstance that the writer confronted the Dutch with their own responsibility, and this made them ashamed of themselves. At the same time, he reproached her for not fully committing herself on the side of the Aceh people either.[35]

Rob Nieuwenhuys drew a parallel between the Second World War and the Aceh war in his review on 25 April 1985 in *Trouw* (*Faith*): 'Haar eigen verlangens naar vrijheid en zelfstandigheid, haar protest en haat tegen de Duitse bezetters vond ze in Tjoet Nja Din terug. Deze werd, om het fraai te zeggen, een 'identificatiemodel'. [She found her own desire for freedom and independence, her protest and hate for the German invaders in Tjoet Nja Din. Her figure became — to use a nice idiom — a 'model of identification'].[36] To my knowledge, the novel has not been analysed since that time. The silence around it may be due to two reasons. One is that this novel is the most radically critical of the violent military colonial politics of the Dutch in the author's oeuvre. The second reason can be related to the fact that she was a member of the Cultuurkamer, and the Dutch have never excused her for this.

The Rhetorical Context and Plot

The novel *Tjoet Nja Din* consists of eighteen chapters, the first of which is a kind of introduction. It explains the context of writing the novel. The plot elaborates on real, historical events in the form of a novel. The second and third chapters reflect on the history and on the social and power relations of Aceh. Only the fourth, fifth, and sixth chapters report on the history of the person Tjoet Nja Din. In the following chapters her life becomes more and more entangled with the different phases of the war and with her two husbands, Teku Lamgna and Teku Umar. In the meantime, the reader obtains insight into the complex situation of the three leading groups of Aceh society: the sultanate, the nobility and the religious leaders. Tjoet Nja Din, the relentless freedom fighter, really comes into focus only at the end of the novel when she is old, blind, and rheumatic. In the end she is exiled to Java, where she regains her sight (see Fig. 5.3). The end of the novel is ambivalent. It partly conveys the impression that the war ended with victory for the Dutch:

> Er worden wegen en bruggen gelegd, hospitalen ingericht. De markten zijn levendig, de Grote Moskee, door niemand meer Beitoe Rahman genoemd, wordt druk bezocht. Er bestaat geen Geconcentreerde Linie meer, Atjeh mèt zijn Onderhorigheden is in zijn geheel onder Nederlands oppergezag gebracht. De velden worden bewerkt, de belastingen vloeien in de schatkist, de oude Feodalen zijn bezoldigde Inlandse ambtenaren geworden.[37]

> [Roads and bridges are built, hospitals are equipped. Market places are lively, and the Big Mosque, which is never called Beitu Rahman any more, is visited by lots of people. There are no more Concentrated Rings, and Aceh and the territories administratively belonging to it are under Dutch rule. Fields are cultivated, taxes flow into the treasury as it were, and the old feudal masters became Native administrators.]

However, the outcome of the war seems to be less evident in the following passage:

> Maar de Generaal van Daalen, die een militair was, en die wist, dat ook, de troepen, waarmee van Heutsz dit land zo hard geslagen had, binnenkort naar Java zouden teruggaan; die wist, dat de priesters nog niét verslagen waren en dat de brand ten allen tijde opnieuw kon uitslaan, omdat wel de pacificatie weer werd ingevoerd, maar de Verzoening nog niet geboren was ... Van Daalen heeft het niet gewaagd Din temidden van haar volk te laten. Zij is door hem naar Java verbannen.[38]

Fig. 5.3. Group portrait with Cut Nyak Dhien after she was taken prisoner, 1905, Tropenmuseum Amsterdam. © Tropenmuseum, part of the National Museum of World Cultures

[General van Daalen, however, being a soldier, knew very well that those troops with which Van Heutsz had inflicted such a resounding defeat on this territory would soon return to Java; he knew that the priests had not been defeated yet and that the fire could flare up again any time, because although pacification had already been introduced, reconciliation has not yet been achieved ... Van Daalen did not dare to leave Din among her people. He preferred to exile her to Java.]

Thus doubt about victory is expressed and it is expressed as the last utterance in the novel. The real outcome of the war, therefore, remains ultimately inconclusive.

The Figures of Division

As already mentioned, the Dutch scholar Maaike Meijer has analysed Madelon Székely-Lulofs's novels *Rubber* and *Koelie* in detail from a post-colonial point of view.[39] She draws the conclusion that despite the good will on the surface both novels represent a colonial point of view because of their narrative techniques. Among these she discerns the so-called figures of division. She coins these inspired by Toni Morrison's essential study *Playing in the Dark* (1992).[40]

I shall apply Meijer's figures of division to the analysis of the novel *Tjoet Nja Din*, in order to decide whether or not this novel, which the writer herself considered her finest, represents an essentially colonial point of view despite its superficial good will. I shall examine the following figures of division:

(1). Tutelary narrative

(2). The arena of cruelty and non-civilization

(3). The lack of self-reflection of the natives

(4). Homogenization of human beings and landscape/environment, depersonalizing the native

I argue that these figures of division are undermined repeatedly in Székely-Lulofs's last novel. There is a critical distance between the narrative 'I' and the narrative 'we'. Identification of the narrative 'I' with her own people, the Dutch, who are the actual readers of the novel, becomes impossible. The critical distance mentioned above is due to irony, which is very often self-irony. Because of this irony, too, the anti-colonial point of view predominates. The novel is ambivalent.

1. Tutelary narrative

A narrative is called tutelary when a native subject can never really speak unless through the 'ventriloquism' of a (mostly) white narrator. In other words: because the native subject is never really allowed to speak, it is always the external narrator whose point of view determines the story. This is also true of *Tjoet Nja Din*. The eponymous heroine is not given the chance to speak until page 86. The narrator's text predominates over direct speech-texts. The novel is narrated by an 'I' who can be identified with the white European writer, Madelon Székely-Lulofs. She narrates the life story of an East Indian woman, daughter of an Aceh leader, who was one of the fiercest enemies of the Dutch. Tjoet Nja Din is the intended subject, but she is kept in the background in the novel. At the same time, she was the greatest figure in the fighting:

> Ik kan haar niet anders zien dan zó: de ongeslagen overwonnene, tot in de dood onze vijandin. Alleen zó ook kan ik haar liefhebben, met die liefde, die dezelfde mens eert in haar als ik zou willen eren in mijzelf.[41]

> [I cannot see her in another way than this: the invincible defeated, our enemy to the death. I can only love her like this, with the same love with which the same human being is respected in her as I would respect in myself.]

These sentences express ambivalence: although Tjoet Nja Din is the enemy of the nation to which the narrating 'I' belongs, the 'I' still wants to love her on the basis of their mutual trait, human quality. As if human quality could be independent of the historical and social context. This ambivalence determines the specific narration of the novel.

Although the story is narrated by a first-person narrator, this 'I' is not the main character, only a recording 'I', who guides herself by using other people's stories and rumour; she stands outside the plot. There are several expressions in the text like 'it is said that' or 'people say that'. These expressions also support the assumption that the narrating 'I' does not speak on the basis of her own experience or knowledge but on that of hearsay or of information from books. Although the narrating 'I' never allows Tjoet Nja Din to speak, sometimes she does allow Dokarim, the native poet who had written about the Aceh war:

> Ik moet nu Lezer, het woord geven aan Dokarim, want dit, wat hier in de Glitaroen-pas gebeurde — een verwarde, ja verraderlijk verwarde gebeurtenis! — geschiedde in de eigen tijd van de Atjehse dichter en hij weet het dus beter dan ik.[42]

> [Reader, I have to allow Dokarim to speak now, because everything that happened here in the Glitarun Pass — a chaotic, yes, a tellingly chaotic history! — happened in the Aceh poet's own time and therefore he knows it better than I.]

The story once sung by the native poet is transformed into a novel. Still, the narrator does not want to give the impression of an omniscient narrator — she distances her material, thus making her position relative.

The narrating 'I' focalizes as an external instance in the greater part of the story. As such she gives a picture of Aceh, of its population and of the Dutch army. In this impersonal role the narrative is at the most tutelary.

The 'I', however, has other forms, too: one of its synonyms is 'we' and its different grammatical forms. This 'we' occurs always in the meaning of 'we, the Dutch' or 'we, the people of The Compagnie' [The East Indian Company]. Because the 'I' is absent from most parts of the narrative, the emergence of 'we', of which the 'I' is part, always brings astonishment and estrangement in the reader. The sympathy of the narrating 'I' is in fact not on the side of 'we' but on the side of 'they', that is, the natives. Because the narrating 'I' counts herself an enemy of the natives in the form of 'we', there occurs some confusion, a kind of cognitive dissonance: who is the narrator actually? As already mentioned, this narrating 'I', who creates distance from herself, goes with another characteristic feature of the narration: irony. The colonizing enterprise becomes automatically ironized when the narrator uses the compulsory 'we' while her empathy is on the other side, with 'they'. This irony in the form of the estranging 'we' becomes criticism of 'we, the Dutch' against the Dutch East Indians. Some examples:

> Ik dacht na. Het epos van de Atjeh-oorlog! Gedicht door een Indonesiër. Niet door een Hollander, neen, door een Atjeher. Door een vertegenwoordiger van dat volk, dat wij als de 'Muzelmaanse barbaren' bestreden en onderwierpen met de leuze: 'Wij brengen hun de beschaving.'[43]
>
> [I thought about it. The epic of the Aceh war! A poem by an Indonesian. Not by a Dutchman but by an Acehian; the representative of a people against whom we fought as against 'Muslim barbarians' and conquered with the phrase: 'We bring them culture'.]

By putting 'Muslim barbarians' and 'We bring them culture' in inverted commas, the narrator distances herself from these colonizing phrases, mocking their alleged self-evidence.

When the reader learns in what subtle ways natives let other people into their village — a friend or a relative with their weapons, an armed Muslim who is otherwise a stranger, disarmed, while an enemy with whom they already had made peace is received by the chief of the village and his children saying 'See, I shall protect your life with my own sword and I'm greeting you with all my offspring!' — the narrator says: 'But we brought them culture. And we taught them by fire and sword how to salute and shake hands.' The conjunction 'but' changes these sentences into ironic comments. As the subtle system of greetings shows, the natives do have their own culture and etiquette, so they could easily manage without the culture inflicted on them by the Dutch.

Irony takes explicit shape also when the narrator is speaking about colonial politics or about the colonial enterprise. Some examples:

> Wij wilden nu zo snel mogelijk gaan regeren en onze van ouds beproefde Koloniale Orde in de plaats stellen van de anarchistische janboel der vroegere Atjehse Groten. Wij wilden wegen en bruggen bouwen, spoorlijnen aanleggen, de schurft, de malaria en de cholera gaan bestrijden en de schatten van het zo juist veroverde land, dat 'derhalve door recht van overwinning aan het Nederlands Indische Gouvernement behoorde', zodanig exploiteren, dat wij er behoorlijk van profiteerden, maar ook de Inheemse bevolking op een hoger levenspeil zouden brengen. Men kan tegen dergelijke aspiraties niet veel inbrengen, objectief gezien, is dit alles een loffelijk streven.[44]
>
> [We wanted to rule as quickly as possible and to place the long-established Colonial Order instead of the earlier Aceh Monarchs' anarchic disorder. We wanted to build roads and bridges, to establish railway lines, to conquer mange, malaria and cholera, and the treasures of the just captured country, that 'by right of conquest belonged to the Dutch Indian Government', we wanted to make use of it so as to get the maximum profit out of it, but also to raise the native population to a higher standard of living at the same time. We cannot fabricate too many protests against such aspirations; viewed objectively these are all honourable ambitions.]

Irony is the result of the double voice here too: the narrator speaks in the voice of the colonizing 'we', undermining every statement of this 'we' by means of the whole novel, which is one great protest against the above-mentioned aspirations. Somewhat further on we read the following:

> Inplaats van *onze* wegen en bruggen en spoorlijnen in zijn land te waarderen, inplaats van dankbaar te zijn, dat wij het oude, vuile krot van een moskee Longbata sloopten en met het puin er van het drassige terrein netjes ophoogden; inplaats van begrip te tonen voor onze liberale geste omtrent de cadeau gedane nieuwe Grote Moskee, waarmee wij toch duidelijk getoond hadden hun alleen maar te vuur en te zwaard onze Koloniale Orde te hebben willen opdringen en niet ééns onze Christelijke Ethiek,... kortom, in plaats van onze bedoelingen, die ondanks de door ons begane vernieling van hun huizen, erven en aanplanten, *goed* waren, te waarderen en te honoreren met loyale onderworpenheid, verloochenden de Atjehers hun afkeurenswaardige aard niet, maar toonden onmiddellijk, toen zij zagen, dat wij ons ontwapend hadden, hun trouweloosheid en valsheid.[45]
>
> [Instead of appreciating *our* roads, bridges, and railways in their country, instead of being thankful that we had pulled down their old, dirty ruin of a Longbata mosque and filled up the swampy moorland with the debris; instead of showing understanding towards the liberal gesture with which we had presented them with the Great Mosque and clearly showed them that we only wanted to impose the Colonial Order on them with fire and sword and not our Christian Ethics, ... in short, instead of appreciating and rewarding with obedient humility our aspirations, which were *good* in spite of our demolishing their houses, estates, and plantations, the Aceh people did not deny their contemptible nature, but as soon as they saw that we had disarmed ourselves, they immediately showed their disloyalty and falsity.]

This is again an excellent example of double speech: on the surface we hear the colonizer's voice; behind it, however, there is poignant irony. As a result, the truth of the long sentence becomes questionable. This is the writer's linguistic ingenuity: by making use of the classical rhetorical devices which were elaborated in the beginning of European culture by the Romans — devices of emphasis, long sentences, anaphoric structures, semicolons, suspension points, capital letters in the middle of a sentence — she illustrates the exhaustion of that very culture compared with another which also had its own traditions, its own rhetoric, even if these were of a totally different nature.

Tutelary narrative is ambivalent here. The sympathy of the 'I'-narrator towards the natives is given expression by the self-ironic, alienating use of 'we'. Focalization, however, stays with the 'I'-narrator throughout the narrative.

2. The arena of cruelty and non-civilization

This figure of division works also in an ambivalent way in the novel. Székely-Lulofs draws a detailed picture of the battles and conflicts between the natives and the Dutch on the one hand, and among the natives themselves on the other. We learn that in the beginning the Malay had moved from Central Sumatra to the North, where they settled on the west coast. The presence of gold caused several conflicts between the Muslims, the people of Menangkabau and Aceh, and the pagan Mantirs. The latter were the first inhabitants of the gold-rich territory, but were driven out. In this case, fighting for dominance of religion was related to that for the possession of gold. The 'I'-narrator takes the reader to the Aceh of a hundred years later, where there is a complicated system of possession of land and power. Those who actually have power — the sultans, that is, the Sagi-monarchs, the Ulubalang country squires and the Ulama religious leaders — are constantly at war with each other. The complicated relationships, continuous hostility and temporary alliances give the impression of a state of anarchy in which war against the Dutch is only one of the many wars among the natives. This picture, obviously taken from Hurgronje's book, suggests that there had been wars in Aceh from the earliest times, whether against the Dutch or not: it is a 'stage of cruelty and non-civilisation'.

The novel is, however, innovative compared to other colonial works because it emphasizes and focuses on the specific history of the native population. Most colonial works convey the impression that the colonized had not had their own history, their own economy, their own commerce or civilization before the colonizers came. In *Tjoet Nja Din* this is quite different. From time to time we read about the Portuguese who preceded the Dutch in the East Indies, about the native history before the Portuguese went there, and about the distinctive civilization of the East Indian archipelago. So there is a reference to an earlier matriarchal tradition which was still prevalent in Din's childhood. Daughters inherited their fathers' houses, where they could trade independently and where their husbands moved in. The house never became the property of the husband, but stayed in the possession of the wife. So in these regions building houses was the favourite play of girls, not of boys. This feature of the matriarchal tradition is very different from the European, patriarchal one, and it bears witness to a well-developed native civilization. The narrator sympathizes with the matriarchal tradition, and considers it proof of the existence of the native civilization.

The 'I'-narrator paints also a picture of the misogynistic, patriarchal tradition of the natives in the present. Accordingly twelve-year-old girls are given away in marriage by their fathers. We remember the case of Saïdjah and Adinda in *Max Havelaar*. Adinda's happiness is never questioned there: we the readers take it for granted because the narrator does not even mention this as a problem. Adinda was married off to Saïdjah just as Tjoet Nja Din was to Teku Lamgna. The 'I'-narrator in Székely-Lulofs's novel criticizes this practice implicitly, again by means of irony. She thinks as follows about the relationship between two persons who are forced by their parents to marry:

> Niets is zo moeilijk als van een mens te zeggen, of hij liefhad en gelukkig was. Maar Dokarim heeft gezegd van Tjoet Nja Din, dat zij de Tekoe Lamgna zeer

liefhad. Nu was Dokarim een dichter en onder de mensen zijn de dichters dié mensen, die het meest houden van de schone schijn. En schóner schijn dan de liefde bestaat er niet. Maar laat ons de dichter geloven en zeggen, dat zij Ibrahim van Lamgna liefhad en gelukkig was. En laat ons zeggen, dat ook de Tekoe Lamgna haar liefhad.[46]

[Nothing is more difficult than to find out whether a human being was really in love and happy. Dokarim, however, said of Tjoet Nja Din that she was very much in love with the Teku Lamgna. But Dokarim was a poet, and of all people poets are the ones who like to keep up appearances the most. And there is nothing to compare with love when keeping up appearances. But let's trust the poet and say that she was in love with Ibrahim of Lamgna and that she was happy. And let's say that the Teku Lamgna was also in love with her.]

Here it is the reference to Dokarim and to poets in general which creates distance and irony. The genuineness of love between two children who married because their parents forced them to is questioned subtly by the repetitive use of 'let's trust', 'let's say'. It also underlines the discrepancy between reality and representation.

The 'I'-narrator says the following about marriage based on the consent of fathers:

Bruid van een man, die zij totaal niet kent en die haar niet kent. Maar dat is zo de gewoonte en het verhindert niet, dat de bruiloft een vrolijk en verrukkelijk feest wordt, waaraan de hele kampong deel heeft.[47]

[Bride of a man whom she doesn't know at all and who doesn't know her either. But this is the custom, and it does not prevent the wedding being a happy and joyful celebration in which the whole village takes part.]

We readers never find out whether the bride herself also feels so happy and joyful. We never learn anything about the inner world of Tjoet Nja Din. We know her only from the outside. Still, doubt occurs about the happiness of the heroine in the dramatic conflict between the two quoted sentences. The narrator describes this custom from a European perspective as the arena of cruelty and non-civilization. In this case we cannot but agree.

3. The lack of self-reflection of the natives

Participants of the East Indian culture — Tjoet Nja Din in the first place — are depicted as puppets in the novel:

Zó met haar donkerrood beschilderde handen en voeten, in haar gouddoorweven zijden broek en van gouddraad stijf en nauwsluitend jakje, vol met gouden en diamanten juwelentooi, en verstard tot die voorgeschreven houding, zal de kleine Din geleken hebben op een prachtige, kostbare oosterse pop.[48]

[In this way, with her hands and feet painted dark red, in her silk pantaloons shot with gold, in her jacket stiff and tight with gold thread, decorated with lots of gold and diamond jewellery and holding herself in the required posture, little Din must have looked like a beautiful, precious Oriental puppet.]

Din never protests against those prescriptions and rules which downgrade her to the status of a puppet. She does not even think of objecting to the custom of arranged marriage. The consequence of this is that she gets a husband whom she does not know. And she does not revolt against the fact that husbands often have another, adult wife somewhere else. After sleeping together for the first time Din happily shows her mother the girdle she has been given by her husband. Din feels pain and shows resistance only when her country or her husband is in trouble. It seems as if she were not conscious of her humiliation as a woman. The privilege of thinking is also only given to men, not to women:

> Het is het geloof, dat in vrouwen en kinderen is en dat uit hun hart recht omhoog stijgt naar het Verlangde, zonder ééenmaal door nadenken of omzichtigheid te worden verstoord. Maar het geloof van de man gaat niet omhoog, maar rechtuit en dáár zijn de hinderlagen van overweging en berekening.[49]

> [It is faith which women and children have in them, and which rises straight from their hearts towards the Desired without the disturbance of thought or circumspection. The faith of men, however, does not go upwards, but goes straight ahead to where pondering and calculation set traps for them.]

Self-reflection is divided between the sexes, so this figure of division has a gender aspect rather than an ethnic one. The lack of female self-reflection leads us to the next figure of division.

4. Homogenization of human beings and landscape/environment, depersonalizing the native

Natives are often compared to animals; their physical aspects are underlined:

> (prins Mahoedoem Sati) was kort en krachtig gebouwd; onder zijn glanzende lichtbruine huid lagen de spierbundels zo lenig en bewegelijk als bij een jonge tijger; zijn glad haar glom blauwzwart in het zonlicht. Hij hield zijn gezicht gretig vooruit gestoken en zijn wijde neusgaten snoven de zilte zeelucht en de van het land aanwaaiende moerasdampen in, alsof hij het avontuur zelf wilde inademen en alvast herbergen in zijn lijf.[50]

> [(Prince Mahudum Sati) was small and robust; under his shiny, light brown skin his muscles were as flexible and brisk as those of a young tiger; his smooth hair glittered blue-black in the sunshine. He pushed his face forward eagerly, his broad nostrils drank in the salty air of the sea and the marsh gas coming from the land as if to drink in adventure and hide it in his body in advance.]

> Oemar stokt. Als een dier, dat in donker onraad speurt. Hij steekt zijn hoofd wat verder vooruit, zijn neusvleugels gesperd, zijn oren gespitst.[51]

> [Umar stops. Like an animal which senses danger in the dark. He pushes his head somewhat further forward, flaring his nostrils, pricking up his ears.]

> Maar [Tjoet Nja Din] is oud, kreupel en blind, en ze leeft, erger dan een hond, omdat zij niet over onderwerping horen wil.[52]

> [But (Tjoet Nja Din) is old, crippled and blind, and she lives a life even worse than a dog because she will not hear of subjugation.]

Homogenization of human beings and animals works as depersonalization.[53] It is notable that this type of depersonalization never arises in the case of white protagonists.

Another form of homogenization is that of between a human being and nature. The narrator gives a detailed description of the ceremonies which accompany Tjoet Nja Din's birth. One of the rituals is the so-called *Peutron*: the first time that a child is taken out into nature. This moment is narrated in the following way:

> Buitenshuis komen, betekent immers voor de Atjehse mens: uit zijn paalwoning afdalen om in aanraking te komen met de aarde. Met de aarde, die de Moeder is van alle leven en die haar schoot zóveel verbergt, wat de mens een eeuwig geheimenis blijft. Ontspruiten niet alle bomen en gewassen, goede èn slechte, aan deze aarde? Voeden niet mens en dier zich aan datgene, wat de aarde voortbrengt? En omvat zij niet het mysterie van de dood, dáárdoor, dat zij de afgestorvenen weer in zich opneemt en bewaart tot aan de jongste dag? Wie kent het magisch gebeuren, dat zich in alle stilte, diep in de aarde, voltrekt?[54]
>
> [Coming out from the house means for an Aceh person: to descend from his log-house in order to come into contact with the earth. With the earth, the Mother of all lives, whose womb hides a lot of things which remain eternal secrets for humans. Do not all trees and plants, good and bad alike, spring from this earth? Are not human beings and animals fed with what the soil produces? Does the earth not have all the mystery of death, taking the dead back into herself and guarding them to the last day? Who knows the magic that takes place in the greatest silence, deep down in the earth?]

This quotation describes the importance of coming out of the house from the perspective of the European narrator. From the second sentence, however, the reader cannot exactly say whether the significance of the ritual — merging with nature — is considered important by the narrator or whether we get only a description of how important it is for the natives. The use of free indirect speech is a sign of merging of the two perspectives: that of the narrator and the Aceh people. Somewhat later on it turns out that this habit is still not so general as was suggested at first. It concerns only women: 'Het is een plechtigheid, waarbij alleen maar vrouwen zijn gemoeid, geen man komt daaraan te pas, want de dingen der aarde en die der vrouw zijn evenredig en dus met elkaar in harmonie' [It is a ritual which concerns only women, no men are involved in it, because things of the earth and things of women are proportional, thus in harmony with each other.].[55] So first the Aceh inhabitant is isolated, later the Aceh woman. In the second part of the sentence it is again not quite clear whether it is the narrator or the Aceh people who function as the source of the statement. In any case, this does not alter the fact that human beings and nature are represented as if they were homogeneous. The object of the ritual described is Tjoet Nja Din, and this coincides with the main tendency of her depiction: not only does she stay in the background of the Aceh war, but she *is* the background herself, the land of Aceh which must be defended. She does not have the opportunity to act on her own initiative: this is reserved only for men around her. She is always in the company of the fighters, but never in the centre of events. The only exception is when she loses her husband. The only thing we read about her then is that she keeps on fighting against the Dutch for six years after this.

On the very last page of the novel Din is no longer only a part of Eastern mysticism, but an absolutely integral, independent personality. Again using the 'we'-form, the narrator acknowledges the equity of Tjoet Nja Din's hatred for the

Dutch colonizers:

> Maar wéten wij dan, welke gestalten en welke beelden haar herinnering bevolkten en welke dagdroom haar in zijn ban gevangen hield? Als wij één ogenblik ons naar haar overbuigen om die herinneringen met haar te delen, en wij denken aan Lamgna in de Glitaroen-pas, aan het verbrande Lampadang, aan de walmende Kloof van Beradin, aan Oemar's verborgen graf in het oerwoud langs de Meulabohstroom, en aan dat hartbeklemmende moment, waarop de paketboot naar Java zich losmaakte van de Atjehse wal ...
> Zullen wij dan niet tenminste de haat gunnen aan haar, die aan ons alles verloor, wat zij bezeten heeft en liefgehad?[56]
>
> [Do we really know then, which shapes and which pictures inhabited her memory and which daydream held her in its power? If we lean over to her for one moment in order to share her memories and we think about Lamgna in the Glitarun Pass, about the Lampadang, totally burnt down, about the smoking cove of Beradin, about Umar's hidden grave in the jungle on the bank of the Meulaboh river and about the heart-breaking moment, when the freighter moved off from the Aceh coast in the direction of Java...
> Shall we not at least give her the right to hate, she who lost everything because of us, everything she had had and loved?]

The acknowledgement of the right to hate relieves Din of her objectified existence for a moment. The 'we' are intruders in an autonomous world which has its own values and its own culture. These values, this culture are depicted metaphorically through the personality of Tjoet Nja Din.

Finally we can say that figures of division are also at work in this novel, but these are often balanced by other narrative techniques. Tutelary narrative is weakened by the ironic use of 'we'; beside the arena of cruelty and non-civilization, there occurs also the arena of humanity and civilization. Colonizing views are mixed up with rebelling views against colonialism. Taking the whole novel into consideration, the voice against colonialism seems to be the stronger.

At the beginning of this chapter I promised to give arguments for this statement by analysing the depiction of Van Heutsz. Well, Van Heutsz's name occurs nineteen times in the novel, the bibliographical items included. He is called 'winner' (p. 8), 'a cruel aggressor' (p.198), a *kaffir* [non-Muslim, pagan] general officer (p. 202), a soldier who respects nothing, the enemy of the Aceh people's hero Teku Umar:

> En dit is het begin van het einde, want van Heutsz is een andere tegenstander dan anderen. Hij volstaat niet met het verslaan en verjagen, hij ziet alleen heil in de vernietiging. En met voor ogen deze vernietiging van Oemar als de Volksheld, als drager van de idee der Onverzoenlijkheid, zet van Heutsz de rusteloze jacht in.[57]
>
> [This is the beginning of the end, because van Heutsz is a different kind of enemy than others. He is not satisfied with defeating and banishing, he sees salvation only in annihilation. His objective is the annihilation of Umar, the Folk Hero, and as bearer of Irreconcilability van Heutsz sets in motion a never-ending manhunt.]

The novel dispenses with everything Van Heutsz symbolized: Dutch colonial power, military aggression, the cruel extermination of the native population. It is partly for this reason that Willem Drees, former prime minister of the Netherlands, ordered this book to be removed from shop-windows during the 1948 police actions. Madelon Székely-Lulofs's novel *Tjoet Nja Din* patently opposed the ideology on which the police actions were based and launched by the Dutch government.

Notes to Chapter 5

1. Reinier Salverda, 'Beeld en tegenbeeld van het koloniale verleden', in *Rekenschap 1650–2000*, ed by D. Fokkema and F. Grijzenhout (Den Haag: Sdu Uitgevers, 2001), pp. 71–114 (p. 72).
2. Madelon Székely-Lulofs, *Rubber, roman uit Deli* (Amsterdam: Het Wereldvenster, 1931)
3. Madelon Székely-Lulofs, *Koeli* (Bussum: F.G. Kroonder, 1931)
4. On the contemporary reception of *Rubber* see Jaap Goedegebuure, '*Rubber*, een bestseller uit de jaren dertig', *Literatuur*, 1 (1984), 22–27.
5. Menno ter Braak, 'De roman als document. M. H. Székely-Lulofs: *De Andere Wereld*', *Het Vaderland*, 11 March 1934. On the contemporary reception of Székely-Lulofs see further Olf Praamstra and Gerard Termorshuizen, 'Inleiding', in Madelon Székely-Lulofs, *Doekoen* (Leiden: Koninklijk Instituut voor Taal- Land- en Volkenkunde, 2001), pp. 7–22 (p. 8).
6. Rob Nieuwenhuys, *Oost-Indische Spiegel. Wat Nederlandse schrijvers en dichters over Indonesië hebben geschreven vanaf de eerste jaren der Compagnie tot op heden* (Amsterdam: Querido, 1978).
7. Rudy Kousbroek, 'De boekhouders van de Nederlandse literatuur', *NRC/Handelsblad*, 8 July 1983; Rudy Kousbroek, *Het Oost-Indisch kampsyndroom* (Amsterdam: Meulenhoff, 1992); Olf Praamstra and Gábor Pusztai, 'Een "lasterlijk geschrijf", kritiek en (zelf)censuur in de Nederlands-Indische literatuur; de ontvangst van László Székely's *Van oerwoud tot plantage* (1935)', *Indische Letteren*, 12 (1997), 98–124; Olf Praamstra, 'Madelon Székely-Lulofs en het koloniale discours', *Indische Letteren*, 22 (2007), 209–39; Praamstra and Termorshuizen, 2001.
8. Kester Freriks, *Madelon: het verborgen leven van Madelon Székely-Lulofs* (Amsterdam: Conserve, 2005).
9. Frank Okker, *Tumult. Het levensverhaal van Madelon Székely-Lulofs* (Amsterdam: Atlas, 2008).
10. Maaike Meijer, *In tekst gevat: Inleiding tot een kritiek van representatie* (Amsterdam: Amsterdam Academic Archive, 1996), pp. 152–70.
11. Edward Said, *Orientalism* (New York: Vintage Books, 1979).
12. René Marres, 'Is de antikoloniale roman *Rubber* van Székely-Lulofs racistisch?', in René Marres, *Zogenaamde politieke incorrectheid in de Nederlandse literatuur, ideologiekritiek in analyse* (Leiden: International Forum voor Afrikaanse en Nederlandse Taal en Letteren, 1998), pp. 74–81.
13. Praamstra, pp. 209–39.
14. Quoted ibid., p. 231.
15. Madelon Székely-Lulofs, *De Hongertocht* (Amsterdam:Elsevier, 1936)
16. John Jansen van Galen, 'De vrouw achter rubber', *Haagse Post*, 13 July 1985.
17. Gábor Pusztai and Gerard Termorshuizen, 'De tweede man. Het huwelijk van Madelon Lulofs and László Székely', *Acta Neerlandica. Bijdragen tot de Neerlandistiek Debrecen*, 5 (2007), 49–62.
18. Van Galen.
19. Madelon Székely-Lulofs, *Tjoet Nja Din, De geschiedenis van een Atjehse vorstin* (Den Haag: Thomas & Eras, 1985), p. 10.
20. Cock van den Wijngaard, 'Madelon Székely-Lulofs (1899–1958)', *Bzzlletin* (1983), 110.
21. Ibid.
22. Franz Fanon writes about this phenomenon as follows: 'A white man addressing a Negro behaves exactly like an adult with a child and starts smirking, whispering, patronizing, cozening' (Franz Fanon, *Black Skin White Masks*, trans. by Charles Lam Markmann (London: Pluto Press, 2008), p. 19).
23. Wim van den Doel, *Zo ver de wereld strekt. De geschiedenis van Nederland overzee vanaf 1800* (Amsterdam: Prometheus, 2011), p. 341.
24. Wijngaard, p. 52; Madelon Székely-Lulofs, *Weet je nog wel ... een boek vol pluche en pleizier* (Den Haag: De Bezige Bij, 1957).
25. Salverda, p. 86.

26. Madelon Székely-Lulofs, 1985, p. 38.
27. Ibid., pp. 120–21.
28. Snouk Hurgronje was befriended with Ignac Goldziher, the Hungarian orientalist of Jewish heritage who also studied in Leiden. Hurgronje confessed to him in a letter that his conversion to Islam was not sincere but a necessary step to travel to Mecca. See further: http://www.newcivilisation.com/home/1605/ideas-philosophy/christiaan-snouck-hurgronje-history-of-orientalist-manipulation-of-islam/
29. The ring consisting of sixteen fortresses was built in 1884 by the Dutch in order to enclose those Aceh territories which were under Dutch authority keeping it free from the Aceh freedom fighters. Colonel Henry Demmeni, leader of the building works of the Fortress Ring met Teku Umar at this place, who offered himself as an ally for the Dutch.
30. Quoted by van den Doel, 2011, p. 119.
31. Székely-Lulofs, 1985, p. 200.
32. Ibid., p. 6.
33. Karin Peterson, 'Feit en fictie. De verbeelding van de Atjeh-oorlog in de romans van Madelon Székely-Lulofs', in *Atjeh: de verbeelding van een koloniale oorlog*, ed. by Liesbeth Dolk (Amsterdam: Bert Bakker, 2001), pp. 117–28.
34. J. C. Kelk, 'Historie contra heldendicht', *De Groene Amsterdammer*, 12 June 1948.
35. Versteeg, Coos, 'Een doodgezwegen roman herdrukt', *Haagsche Courant*, 31 May 1985.
36. Quoted by Peterson, p. 127.
37. Székely-Lulofs, 1985, p. 209.
38. Ibid., p. 214.
39. Meijer, pp. 152–70.
40. Toni Morrison, *Playing in the Dark: Whiteness and the Literary Imagination* (Cambridge, MA, and London: Harvard University Press, 1992).
41. Székely-Lulofs, 1985, p. 13.
42. Ibid., pp. 138–39.
43. Ibid., p. 6.
44. Ibid., pp. 152–53.
45. Ibid., p. 153.
46. Ibid., p. 75.
47. Ibid.
48. Ibid., p. 71.
49. Ibid., p. 198.
50. Ibid., pp. 15–16.
51. Ibid., p. 206 .
52. Ibid., p. 211.
53. Meijer, p. 159.
54. Székely-Lulofs, 1985, p. 48.
55. Ibid.
56. Ibid., p. 214.
57. Ibid., p. 203.

CHAPTER 6

The Subjugation of Female Subjectivity: A Feminist Reading of Karel van de Woestijne's 'De zwijnen van Kirkè'

In the following two chapters I concentrate on gender issues in works which have nothing to do with the theme of colonialism proper. However, as mentioned before, the notion of colonialism can be extended to all sorts of relations in which a person, a group, or a culture which has power subjugates another person, group, or culture which does not. The relation between colonizer and colonized is locked into a rigid hierarchy, just as those between men and women can be. This hierarchy is not only mimetic but also textual. In this sense gender criticism is a variation to and a part of colonial and post-colonial issues. The use of Susan Lanser's feminist narratology, therefore, is evident.

If a literary work inspires new questions and discussions even more than a hundred years after its first publication, it serves as evidence of its permanent value. This is exactly the case of the short story 'De zwijnen van Kirkè' (Circe's Swine) written by the Flemish writer Karel van de Woestijne (1878–1929). The following feminist analysis has been inspired by Hans Vandevoorde's article 'De onmacht die hem sarrend sloeg. Over Karel van de Woestijne' (The Pain of Powerlessness. On Karel van de Woestijne).[1] His article focuses on Karel van de Woestijne's idea of woman. Vandevoorde gives a careful picture of this idea based on Van de Woestijne's letters to his friend, the composer Lodewijk Ontrop, about some of his poems and the short story about Circe. The latter was usually called 'idiotic blather' by literary critics. In the reading of Hans Vandevoorde, however, this short story can be called 'the first Flemish feminist manifesto'.

In this chapter I argue that the text in question has deep roots in the ways of representation we are accustomed to in patriarchal society in spite of its benevolent ambition to depict the emancipated woman. There are certain patriarchal mechanisms of representation which isolate women. First, I present the traditional readings of the Circe motif. Then, having introduced Karel van de Woestijne, I analyse his Circe figure. I argue that Van de Woestijne's Circe representation is ambivalent; what is more, it is rather presented from a male-biased aspect. Under the surface structures of the Circe story there are also deep structures which I display by means of feminist narratology.[2]

The figure of Circe

Circe is the daughter of the sun-god Helios and the sea-goddess Perseis. She is a sorceress who can transform men into animals. She is the aunt of Medea, who has also has great power as a witch.

We know Circe basically from Homer's *Odyssey*. There she plays a crucial role both substantially and structurally. Odysseus arrives at the island of Aiaia together with his men. He sends them out to explore the island. When the companions enter Circe's house they are received cordially. They are also invited to drink a magic potion which, together with the touch of Circe's magic wand, changes them into swine. After this Odysseus and his men stay a whole year in Circe's palace until they feel homesick for Ithaca. Although Circe deprives Odysseus's comrades of their human shape by making them swine, she is the person who helps Odysseus substantially. Hermes had previously given Odysseus a herb with which he could resist Circe's magical power over him, and so he remains human. Circe falls in love with him and Odysseus accepts her love. When the time comes, Circe gives him good advice on how to reach his home in Ithaca. When they are lovers they are equals, and they stay equals also when they have to say goodbye. Circe is not possessive and Odysseus fully acknowledges her power.

Circe does not disappear after Homer. She becomes a motif in literary works from Alciato's emblems to Joyce's *Ulysses* and further on. She also appears and reappears in paintings throughout the centuries.

In later stories Circe became a frightening and cruel sorceress. Instead of the harmony and balance between the human values of men and women in Homer's work, there came polarization. Circe became the inscrutable, ferocious female, the other, the enemy of men, somebody who awoke anxiety and chaos. Polarization between men and women has always been closely connected with the social hierarchy of the sexes in and since Greek democracy. Women were subjected to men in every possible way. They had no place or voice in the political arena and were regarded as daughters, wives, and mothers but not as independent human beings in social and political life.

Every era and every culture makes use of mythological characters according to its own traditions and own needs. In the Middle Ages, for example, Odysseus is regarded as a Christian hero who resists the pagan debauchery of Circe by his own power.[3] The relationship between Circe and Odysseus is converted into the relationship between two cultural modes, namely that between paganism and Christendom. There appears a polarization of representation, reflecting a by no means neutral value system. The less developed, the old-fashioned, the regressive (in this case paganism) were connected to the feminine; the more developed, the new, the progressive (i.e. Christendom) to the masculine. It is notable that values that are regarded as positive are often associated with the masculine, and the negative ones with the feminine. Hélène Cixous argues that these value-charged binary oppositions are prevalent in almost all representations of men and women. Activity, culture, day, head, logos, ratio, human being are associated with maleness, whereas passivity, nature, night, body, pathos, emotions, and animal are more often than not identified with the female.[4]

As to visual representations of her, Circe was already depicted on antique Greek vases. Bram Dijkstra gives a detailed analysis of the Circe motif in painting at the end of the nineteenth and at the beginning of the twentieth century.[5] Circe's figure is represented by *fin-de-siècle* artists as a beautiful but dangerous female vampire: she is a sensual, strong lover who awakens both attraction and fear in men. This way of representation is a projection of men's own desire for and fear of women. Dijkstra lists several examples of this kind of representation of Circe in paintings by symbolist and Pre-Raphaelite artists such as Arthur Hacker, John Williams Waterhouse, Louis Chalon, and Félicien Rops.

The Outside Context

Karel van de Woestijne

Karel van de Woestijne (see Fig. 6.1) was a Flemish symbolist poet who belonged to the circle of Flanders's first full-fledged modern literary journal *Van Nu en Straks* (*On Today and Tomorrow*, 1896–1901). Beside poetry he also wrote prose works, essays, and journalism. He was well versed in contemporary symbolist literature and art, as well as in the history of Flemish and French Belgian literature from Ruusbroec to Maeterlinck. With his younger brother Gustave van de Woestijne he spent the years between 1900 and 1904 at the small picturesque village of Sint-Martens-Latem, some twenty kilometres from Ghent. He soon became a kind of spiritual leader of the art colony there. Later he worked as a correspondent of the eminent daily paper, the *Nieuwe Rotterdamsche Courant*. In 1921 he was appointed Professor of Dutch literature at the University of Ghent.

Among other things he was also immensely interested in classical mythology. He rewrote Homer's *Iliad* in Flemish prose in 1910 and he also published two volumes of poetry with the title *Interludiën* (*Interludes*, 1912–14) based on mythological themes.

In 1904 Van de Woestijne wrote the short story 'De zwijnen van Kirkè' which was first published in the Flemish journal *Vlaanderen* (*Flanders*) in 1905 and three years later republished in the volume *Janus met het dubbele voorhoofd* (*Janus with the Two Foreheads*), together with other pieces of his prose works. The author describes the circumstances in which the story was born in a humorous letter to the writer and journalist Emmanuel de Bom (1868–1953). He was staying at the resort of Blankenberge and his neighbour, who was otherwise a prawn fisherman, had two pigs in his sty. This served as an inspiration for Van de Woestijne.[6] To André de Ridder (1888–1961), another Flemish writer, poet, and literary critic he wrote about his new short story:

> Met de *Zwijnen van Kirkè* wou ik dit doen uitschijnen: de vrouw heeft de macht zuiver te beminnen, eene pure zieleliefde te koesteren. [...] de man echter, zoodra hij bij eene vrouw komt, schiet vol begeerte, hunkert naar vleeselijke communie en wordt [...] een zwijn. Dit alles komt hierop neer: de vrouwelijke liefde zuiver bedoeld, vindt geen weerklank in de mannelijke liefde.[7]

> [With *Circe's Swine* I wanted to shed light on the following: women have the power to have a chaste love, to cherish a pure love of the soul. [...] men, however, the moment they meet a woman, become full of desire, they long for

Fig. 6.1. Portrait of Karel van de Woestijne by Gustave van de Woestijne, 1910, drawing, 29,5 x 26,5 cm, Digitale Bibliotheek voor de Nederlandse Letteren

the communion of the flesh and they [...] become swine. All this results in the
following: female love intended as chaste does not find an echo in male love.]

The short story was written in the first year of Karel van de Woestijne's marriage, partly in St Amandsberg, on the outskirts of Ghent, partly in the seaside town of Blankenberge.

Karel van de Woestijne was not only one of the most important symbolist poets in Flemish literature, a typical interpreter of the weariness and *Weltschmerz* of the *fin-de-siècle*, but he was also a member of a new generation of Flemish writers and artists which criticized the anomalies of industrialized, capitalist society and dreamed about changing it. Ideas of socialism and anarchism were very popular in Belgium at the end of the nineteenth century and the beginning of the twentieth. Karel van de Woestijne also sympathized with these ideas when he was a contributor to the anarchist literary journal *Van Nu en Straks*. At the same time, disappointment with the new ideas soon came along as their fulfilment seemed much too far away and impossible. It was partly this disillusion which caused Van de Woestijne to become introverted and to retreat into his ivory tower. In interpreting the Circe story we should not ignore the seething social discontent, the desire to innovate, and the presence of new political ideas and movements. The centre of all these were Brussels and Ghent, the latter being the most important city for workers and socialists. Van de Woestijne's first creative period is also linked to Ghent until about 1906, when he moved to Brussels as the correspondent of the Netherlands daily newspaper *NRC*. By this time the Circe story had already been published for the first time. Supposedly, Van de Woestijne had also been following the ideas of the first feminist movement in Belgium.

The Ligue belge du droit des femmes (*The Belgian League of Women's Rights*) was founded in 1897 and organized international conferences in Brussels. From 1900 on several women's organizations were founded, modelled on the socialist trade unions. It was also in Ghent that these women's organizations united under the name of the *Gentse Federatie van Vrouwengroepen* (*The Ghent Federation of Women's Groups*). They cooperated with socialist men, but they wanted to deal with their own affairs themselves. Isabelle Gatti de Gamond founded the journal *Cahiers féministes* (*Feminists' Brochures*) in 1895 and in 1901 she became secretary general of the *Nationale Federatie van Socialistische Vrouwen* (*National Federation of Socialist Women*). This federation played a crucial role in the struggle for women's right to vote, which took place in a very complicated political arena at the end of the nineteenth century. Liberal and socialist men's organizations struggled together for men's general, single right to vote. They were reluctant, however, to extend this right to women because they were afraid that if it were, the number of Catholic voters would grow drastically. There was, that is to say, a prevalent opinion that women were under the influence of Catholic priests. That is why women's right to vote was not on the agenda of the men's socialist–liberal coalition, while socialists only encouraged socialist women's organizations to join their party. So it happened, and the women's movement itself also turned toward other aims of socialism such as founding trade unions and health insurance funds and not toward suffrage — although all this took place with several internal disagreements. Nevertheless, feminism as a social-political intellectual current was strongly present in Belgium at the end of the nineteenth century, and not only in Brussels but also in Flanders and especially in Ghent, in Karel van de Woestijne's immediate surroundings.

Karel van de Woestijne was one of the most outstanding figures of Flemish symbolism. The Belgian literary scholar Anne Marie Musschoot describes some specific characteristics of symbolism which are to be found in his work.[8] She emphasizes among others his atmospheric symbolism and the symbolic elaboration of his autobiography. How does the story of Circe fit into the symbolist context?

Van de Woestijne begins his story with Odysseus sitting around the table of Alcinous and Arete in the company of the Phaeacians. He is telling about his adventures with Circe on the island of Aiaia. This is the frame of the story — in the end we see him again finishing it in the same situation: sitting with Alcinous and Arete and the others. Odysseus's story here concentrates on the moment when Circe is sleeping on his knees after they have made love. Everything that had happened before — arriving at the island, sending his sailors to explore the island, Circe's transforming them into swine — is omitted and presumed to be known. Circe is sleeping and speaking in her sleep. This unconscious speech forms the essential part of the story. She is dreaming of the emancipation of women and she is formulating her wishes about a future when men and women are equal. Odysseus is listening to her, but he is tired in all senses: physically as well as spiritually. He does not react, he wants to leave the island. When Circe wakes up, they go to the sty where the sailors are human beings again. Circe lets them leave. In the end Odysseus confesses that he told this story because he had been impressed by the presence of Nausicaa, the daughter of Alcinous and Arete.

As Anne Marie Musschoot argues, symbolists had a preference for well-known stories, myths, and legends. They used these in order to project their personalities and the aesthetic and ethical problems of their time into them. Fairy tales, biblical and mythological stories, and the world of myths attracted symbolists partly because of their aesthetic beauty, partly because they were considered to be an escape from the apparently insoluble mental and social issues of the time. Several examples are at hand: *L'après-midi d'un faune* (*The Afternoon of a Faun*, 1875) by Mallarmé adapted by Claude Debussy in 1894; the mythical, dream-like, vague, mythological background of Maeterlinck's symbolist plays e.g. that of *Pelléas et Mélisande* (*Pelléas and Mélisande*, 1892); the role of Germanic mythology in Wagner's operas; or the *Moralités légendaires* (*Legendary Moralities*, 1887) by Laforgue. We can certainly interpret the use of themes from classical mythology by Van de Woestijne in this symbolist context of escapism, all the more so if we consider the problem of 'woman' at the end of the nineteenth century and the beginning of the twentieth, and the same problem in the life of the poet. It was the era in which a further polarization in representation took place: it was not only between man and woman, but developed further into a split between woman and woman. There was the 'good' woman, the saint, the mother, the virtuous, the chaste, and there was the 'evil' one: the vampire, the whore, the sensuous, the inscrutable. Circe had become the second long before the end of the nineteenth century. Just because she had this representational past her figure was easy prey for modern misogynist representation. Karel van de Woestijne was confronted personally with all the problems which defined the cultural climate of his time, among them the problem of woman. All the issues can be found in his own poetry and other writings: he saw woman as the embodiment of either good or evil, and he was engaged in solving this conflict with much suffering and internal struggle. His personality showed narcissist elements. He was extremely attached to his mother, and therefore developed a strange doubt and anxiety about his own love for his future wife. He was torn by the presumed clash between the chastity of Platonic love and sexuality. The disharmonious relationship between the sexes was an issue in his work. This explains many of the questions that are touched upon in his Circe story.

Another symbolist trait is the abstract, suggestive, and hermetic use of language. Symbolist poets did not regard intelligibility as their first priority. Meaning was not something to be grasped easily. This is surely valid for Karel van de Woestijne's text: it is obscure and hardly readable today because it makes use not only of archaic Dutch, but at the same time also of a very special local dialect and of several neologisms.

The motifs of evening, night, and sea are also popular in symbolist works. Van de Woestijne's story begins in the evening, and the absence of Helios is accentuated. Circe is here associated with the elements of water and darkness. Dream as such also formed a central motif in symbolist poetry. It is not only a theme but a structural part of the symbolist way of perception. In the story by Van de Woestijne Circe is dreaming and has a dream: both ways, literally and figuratively. The function of her dreaming is not only a plot, it is also structural. I shall come back to this later.

One of the most important features of symbolist art and literature is that the characters embody ideas. What is the idea behind Van de Woestijne's Circe? First of all she declares that although she is a goddess, she has empathy with the problems of human young girls. By that she actually means that she has something of a human being in herself. Her body might be divine, but her voice is human. That is what Odysseus in Homer's story also accentuates. Odysseus calls Circe a 'dread goddess of human voice' [deinē theos audēessa]. This aspect seemed to be of extreme importance to Karel Van de Woestijne. In his story the most important feature of Circe is that she speaks a human language that we, readers are presumed to understand.

Secondly, she states that she is not a learned person; at any rate she does not have the established knowledge that is only accessible to men. However, she does have another sort of knowledge that is different from that of men. Karel van de Woestijne is remarkably progressive here, drawing his readers' attention to the existence of a possible feminine way of thought, a feminine sort of knowledge, different from the established mainstream patriarchal modes of knowledge.

After stating her position she sums up her complaints and wishes. She argues that woman has always been subordinated to man, and that even being a mother is also dependent on the sanction of man. She wishes for herself and for all women to be equal to men, to be active in their relationship instead of passive. Women have always obeyed the laws of the animal world, she says. These laws push women into the role of the eternal debauchee. That is why they have to learn to be beautiful and attractive to men, instead of how to be equal partners to them. Women are themselves responsible for this situation: they have had too much patience, have never revolted. Circe encourages women to fulfil their ideals. According to her, it is the established order which again and again forces women to make swine out of men. The humbler, the more innocent the woman is, the more lascivious the man. She suggests that men should rid themselves of their egoistic love. Circe does not expect a quick change in the man–woman relationship, but she propagates change with full conviction.

On the basis of Circe's theses one can surely sense the idea of an exceptional feminist text *avant la lettre*. If we look at the narrative structure and style of the text, however, we come to a somewhat different conclusion.

Rhetorical Context and Plot

If we take a closer look at the structure of the narration, it turns out that the narrative strategies do not articulate Circe's emancipatory message. The reader can see and listen to Circe through two narrative instances. The first one is an extradiegetic narrator. In Lanser's terminology, he is a public narrator. His voice is that of the author which tells us about the well-known Odysseus. This voice, even if intended to be critical, cannot be, simply because it cannot ignore the positive values attached to and associated with Odysseus throughout the centuries: he is the clever hero, who after several dangerous adventures, returns to his wife in Ithaca. So the reader has this presupposition from the very beginning of the reading process.

In the first paragraph it is this narrator who presents us the scene with Odysseus sitting at the table of Alcinous and Arete. We do not know if this narrator is a man or a woman. The language used, however, indicates a masculine point of view. The extradiegetic narrator calls Arete 'humble'. This is not at all in accordance with the original story by Homer. In his portrait of Arete, as Yarnall convincingly argues, Homer emphasizes women's inclusion in society rather than their exclusion.[9] Arete — Greek for 'excellence' — is a woman who is making decisions of state on Phaeacia and is not at all 'humble'.

> Ze heeft een uiterst scherp verstand en een
> edel karakter
> en ze kan zelfs de geschillen oplossen van
> de mannen
> die ze sympathiek vindt.[10]
>
> [She lacks nothing in good sense and judgment —
> she can dissolve quarrels, even among men,
> whoever wins her sympathies.][11]

As the first female character in the story is described as 'humble' by Van de Woestijne's extradiegetic narrator, I conclude that this neutral omniscience looks through the eyes of a man. The adjective 'humble' attached to a woman is a stereotype. By the adjective 'humble' she is given the role of the passive receiver of the story, who keeps her mouth shut while the story is told by a man. She has no further role or profile in the story except bearing the two gendered adjectives 'humble' and 'chaste'. After the first paragraph the neutral omniscience gives the word to Odysseus. He is then an 'I as witness'-narrator and also the focalizer. He has the power of looking on and telling the story. When Circe is allowed to speak she is already doubly embedded in the discourse of two male narrators. The reader can only reach her through these male agents. She is the most distant character in the narrative space. Accordingly the chance for the reader to identify with her is minimal. Besides, she is only given the chance to deliver an unconscious monologue, but she does not have the chance to focalize. When she has finished her monologue Odysseus takes the word again. The story is finished by the neutral omniscient narrator.

What we have here is a matrix narrative and a hyponarrative.[12] The one who is telling the story and focalizing in the matrix narrative has power. The view of the character(s) in the matrix narrative defines the hyponarrative. In the Circe story by Karel van de Woestijne we see a very definite narrative hierarchical route: (1) first degree narrator: neutral omniscience (male) — (2) second degree narrator: I as witness: Odysseus (male) — (3) Circe (female) — (2) second degree narrator: I as witness: Odysseus (male) — (1) first degree narrator: neutral omniscience (male). She is looked at and listened to. Metaphorically speaking, she *is* (in) passive voice. The reader never sees her otherwise than through Odysseus's eyes, never hears her but through Odysseus's ears. Circe is not the one who is looking on, and her speech is banished to the realms of her unconscious, to her dream. She can give form to her integrity only unconsciously. She is closed up in her dream-world while Odysseus is an active character. Cixous's binary oppositions can easily be applied to them: Odysseus being awake throughout the whole story represents activity, awareness, day, logos, ratio, human being. Circe, who is asleep, stands for passivity, nature, night, pathos, emotions, animal. Van de Woestijne might have tried to undermine these oppositions by letting Circe speak and letting us hear her voice. Nevertheless, this all happens in her dream, so therefore the binary oppositions of the patriarchal value system remain in effect.

Stylistic Analysis

The adjectives reveal the implicit polarized values between the male and female characters. Odysseus has a very positive epitheton ornans: 'Odysseus-vol-listen' [Odysseus full of tricks]. Being tricky in Homer's vocabulary did not have any negative connotations. It meant having brains, creative power, being inventive. Karel van de Woestijne takes over this semantic field. Odysseus is a male character who is primarily attractive by virtue of his intellectual capacities. The adjectives Odysseus uses when speaking to female characters disclose another semantic field. Arete is not only called 'nederig' [humble] by the neutral omniscience but she is also addressed as 'kuisch' [chaste] by Odysseus. 'Humble' right at the beginning of the story and 'chaste' at the end form a gender-biased male view of Arete. Moreover, Nausicaa, Arete's daughter, becomes enclosed in a structure as 'Nausikaa der witte wangen die niet blozen moeten' [Nausicaa of the white cheeks that do not have to blush]. She is described by her bodily functions, which reflect her emotions. Nausicaa is again a female character who is verbally closed up in the world of her body and her emotions by a male character.

Circe's entrance in the story is preceded by a description of the time of day ('vochte nacht' = wet night) and of place ('te uitersten Westen-rijke van Okeanos' = at the uttermost western reaches of Ocean). Woman is associated again with water, the element of the unconscious, and with night, the element of sleep and dreams. While Odysseus is the cerebral hero, Circe is the threatening empire of the unknown. In the further parts of the text, too, in the descriptions that Odysseus gives of Circe, she has attributes that underline her stereotyped character. Everything to do with her is dark and mysterious, is placed somewhere deep down, is emotional and sensuous. Odysseus calls her the 'machtige en machtelooze Kirkè' [the powerful and powerless Circe]. This reflects the typically male *fin-de-siècle* projections: on the one hand, angst for the powerful and strong woman, and triumph over the powerless, chaste, and fragile woman on the other.

When Circe wakes up from her dream, Odysseus finds her ugly and abominable. He is afraid of her, her presence is disturbing. For Odysseus, the conscious Circe is no use: she may dream of women's emancipation, but in everyday life she must play her suppressed role. She is welcome when she takes care of men — she lifts the evil spell that made them swine — and she lets them go:

> Zij had goed begrepen. Zij had geen last zich haren droom te herinneren: ze kende hem sedert jaren van buiten. Met zuchten [...] liet zij de kleine boot vullen met vruchten en 't vleesch van reeën. Wijnen ontbraken niet, noch koeken van honig.[13]
>
> [She understood very well. It was not a problem for her to remember her dream: by this time she knew it by heart. Sighing [...] she ordered to fill the small boat with fruits and the flesh of deer. Wine was there too and honey cakes as well.]

Circe has only a dream and that dream has haunted her for a long time. Dreaming and unconscious speech have had no result as yet. Circe's speech even has characteristic feminine elements. She begins it with a topos of modesty: 'neem me niet kwalijk, maar ...' [don't be angry, but ...]. She thinks she must apologize in advance for what she is going to say. Here is another example of the topos of modesty in her speech: 'Ja! — en vergeef me dat ik, langzamerhand, eenigszins vergeet wel-voeglijkheden en een klaeren blik op de logiek der gezette redekunde' [Yes! — and please forgive me that I am slowly forgetting proper expressions and a clear view on the logic of the required rhetoric.].[14] The next steps she should take would be awakening, renewal of rhetoric, and turning words into actions. In Van de Woestijne's story Circe is not able to realize any of these. Her femaleness does not change into performativity; revolt is only present in her unconscious.

A First Feminist Manifesto?

Hans Vandevoorde calls Van de Woestijne's story about Circe the 'First Feminist Manifesto' in Flemish literature. He argues:

> Men merkt dat het beeld van de vrouw bij Van de Woestijne niet zo scherp schematisch te stellen is, in de zin van: de vrouw staat voor het dierlijke, de man voor het spirituele. Kirkè heeft hier wel degelijk een sterk geestelijke dimensie. Zij wordt bijvoorbeeld geassocieerd met zuiverheid, met trouw.[15]

[One can see that the image of woman in Van de Woestijne is not so sharply schematic in the sense that woman stands for animalism while man stands for spiritualism. Circe has here a strong spiritual dimension. She is associated, for example, with chastity, with fidelity.]

'Chastity' and 'fidelity' are in fact old clichés of traditional female characteristics and beside their 'spiritual dimension', if any, they also have sexual connotations. Writers at the end of the nineteenth century saw women in an ambivalent way: they were either sexual animals or inaccessible virgins, either whores or Holy Mothers. Both perspectives were constructions and gender-biased projections made by men.

Vandevoorde argues further that it is the content of the story which makes it so modern: first, because Circe expresses her unconscious wishes in her dream and in this respect the story is a precursor of surrealism; second, because of the emancipatory content of her unconscious monologue. Vandevoorde may be right here, but he overlooks the narratological structure of the text. In a feminist narratological reading, the circumstances that Circe is seen through the eyes of two men, and that she shares her deepest thoughts only in her dream are of structural importance. I do agree with Vandevoorde that Van de Woestijne depicts Circe in a more nuanced way than other writers do at the time. It is also true that Van de Woestijne makes use of a kind of *écriture féminine avant la lettre* and that makes his text very modern. However, I hope I have demonstrated convincingly that Circe maintains her ambivalent character also with Van de Woestijne: on the one hand she is sensual, animalistic; on the other hand she is ethereal, spiritual. Her dream leads to the realm of the intellect, but dreams also represent the world of instincts. Circe is also the opposite pole to the always thinking, always clever and intellectual Odysseus in this story.

Therefore I find Vandevoorde's statement about the first feminist manifesto something of an exaggeration. Circe's thoughts might be convincing and progressive, but the narrative structure of the story depicts those thoughts embedded in a masculine speculative pattern. Circe is closed up in her dreamworld for the time being, and she must wait a long time to realize it. She is presented as a woman aspiring to emancipation, who proclaims equality between man and woman. This emancipatory idea has, however, no place either in Van de Woestijne's social reality, or in this short story. Although Circe seems to be an emancipated woman, she has not achieved that status yet.

Van de Woestijne's sensitivity to women's problems is incontestable. How he gave form to this sensitivity is ambivalent.

Notes to Chapter 6

1. Hans Vandevoorde, 'De onmacht die hem sarrend sloeg. Over Karel van de Woestijne', in *Brussel en het fin-de-siècle. 100 jaar Van Nu en Straks*, ed. by Frank de Crits (Antwerp and Baarn: Houtekiet, 1993), pp. 105–16.
2. Susan S. Lanser, 'Towards a Feminist Narratology', in *Feminisms: An Anthology of Literary Theory and Criticism*, ed. by R. R. Warhol and D. Price Herndl (New Brunswick, NJ: Rutgers University Press, 1991), pp. 674–93.
3. Eric M. Moorman and Wilfried Utterhoeve, *Van Achilleus tot Zeus. Thema's uit de klassieke mythologie in literatuur, muziek, beeldende kunst en theater* (Nijmegen: Sun, 1987), pp. 172–73.

4. Hélène Cixous and Catherine Clément, *The Newly Born Woman*, trans. by Betsy Wing (Minneapolis and Manchester: University of Minnesota Press, 1986), pp. 63–64, 83–88, 91–97.
5. Bram Dijkstra, *Idols of Perversity: Fantasies of the Feminine Evil in the Fin-de-siècle Culture* (Oxford: Oxford University Press, 1986), pp. 322–26.
6. *Niks geniaal vandaag. De briefwisseling tussen Karel van de Woestijne en Emmanuel de Bom*, ed. by Bert van Raemdonck (Kapellen: Pelckmans, 2010).
7. Karel van de Woestijne, *Verzameld Werk*, III: *Verhalen en parabelen* (Bussum: C. A. J. van Dishoeck, 1947), p. 992.
8. Anne Marie Musschoot, 'Karel van de Woestijne en het symbolisme', in *Op voet van gelijkheid. Opstellen van Anne Marie Musschoot*, ed. by Yves T' Sjoen and Hans Vandevoorde (Gent: Studia Germanica Gandensia, 1994), pp. 104–24.
9. Judith Yarnall, *Transformations of Circe: The History of an Enchantress* (Urbana and Chicago: University of Illinois Press, 1994), p. 64.
10. Homerus, *Odyssee*, trans. by Imme Dros (Amsterdam: Athenaeum, 1996), p. 115.
11. Homer, *The Odyssey*, trans. by Robert Fagles (London: Penguin Books, 1997), <http://www.ahshistory.com/wp-content/uploads/2013/04/Homer-Odyssey.pdf>.
12. Mieke Bal, 'Notes on Narrative Embedding', *Poetics Today*, 2.2 (1981), 41–59.
13. Van de Woestijne, p. 136.
14. Ibid., p. 133.
15. Vandevoorde, p. 14.

CHAPTER 7

Beatrijs and her Younger Sisters: Narrative Structures in Fictions of Female Development

In this last chapter I focus on structural patterns in literary works which create and re-create the subjugation of women by men. I examine narratives of female development where substantial repetitions of certain structural patterns are most manifest. How subjugation of women by men recurs in these narratives of female development throughout the centuries is the topic of this summarizing and concluding chapter.

Development is a relative concept manifesting itself in aspects of social class, history, and gender, argue the editors of the volume *The Voyage In*.[1] They state that because of its formal complexity it is the genre of the novel which is most able to depict a personality's individual development. The desire to deal with all aspects of such a development organized in a coherent narrative created the genre of the novel of development, the so-called *Bildungsroman*.

According to traditional views, the novel of development was born in the time of the Enlightenment and in Germany. Goethe's *Wilhelm Meister's Apprenticeship* (1795–96) is considered the first example of the genre. Reception research after the Second World War, however, legitimated a pragmatic study of the novel of development, and its origin in the eighteenth century has been questioned.[2] Definitions of the genre emphasize the interplay of psychological and social factors and the individual's complex relation to society. Abel, Hirsch, and Langland find it remarkable that the protagonist's sex is not an essential category in these definitions. However, being a man or a woman is a crucial element for all aspects of the novel of development, be it the narrative structure, the inherent psychology, or the depiction of social ambitions and imperatives. Neither descriptions nor narrative structures are 'innocent'. Their sexualized characters are related to ideologies.

Crucial considerations in studying narrative structures of fictions of female development are the subject and object positions, the performative and passive gender roles, the plot and the alternative endings.

Subject and object positions have two aspects: a social and a narrative one. The social aspect indicates to what extent the individual can realize her own ideas or herself in the given social circumstances, how much ground she can gain for her goals, to what extent she can live her life in an active way in accordance with her independent decisions, and to what extent she is forced to make compromises while realizing herself. The narrative aspect shows the ways in which the female protagonist is depicted in the literary text. Does she have the power of focalization and narration, or is her story told by others, be it from her own perspective or from someone else's?

Nancy K. Miller has convincingly argued that female protagonists in eighteenth-century English and French novels have two alternatives: marriage in which they are in an object position, or death, which is identical with the total failure of an attempt to reach a subject position.[3] Miller uses Greimas's term 'euphoric text' for stories where the female protagonist becomes integrated into society, when she rises from 'nothing' and achieves 'everything' by marriage. The other type of story, that in which the female protagonist dies in her youth, moving from 'everything' to 'nothing', is called a dysphoric text.

Female narratives of development, as Miller argues, can be traditional — the object position of the female protagonist gets internalized — but female protagonists can also revolt against their object position and may try to achieve a subject position. In this case the notion of gender is interpreted as performative, as activity and not only as a socially predestined way of being.

As far as plot concerned, Abel, Hirsch, and Langland distinguish two models. The first is chronological and shows the years of apprenticeship as in male fictions of development, in which the story begins with childhood and goes on until maturity with all the conflicts involved. The other model is that of the awakening; it begins with marriage and motherhood and shows a fragmented structure. Tensions are organized in surface and submerged plots. Abel, Hirsch, and Langland also suppose a special pre-oedipal mother–daughter boundary in fictions of female development.[4]

Rachel Blau DuPlessis, an American feminist researcher, introduced the term 'writing beyond the ending'.[5] She propagates an open ending for love stories. This is because emancipatory movements and the freedom that women have attained nowadays make it possible for female protagonists also to have other perspectives than marriage or death.

Let us return to the origins of the novel of development. As Mikhail Bakhtin showed, some aspects of the novel of development can already be found in medieval parables, legends, and folk tales.[6] In these genres, too, there is only one protagonist, whose life is at the focus of the story. They differ from later novels of development mainly in that they do not give a full picture of the protagonist; only one aspect of his or her personality is underlined. They are like posters and have a simplified character, which is why the protagonists' life can be understood as an example, a moral lesson for the public.[7]

I consider the medieval Dutch Maria-legend, the *Beatrijs* (the verse version of which comes from the last quarter of the fourteenth century) (see Fig. 7.1), a story of development. It focuses on the life of a single person, and the tense relation between the individual's dreams and social expectations plays a crucial role. I agree with Abel, Hirsch, and Langland that aspects of gender are unavoidable at all phases of

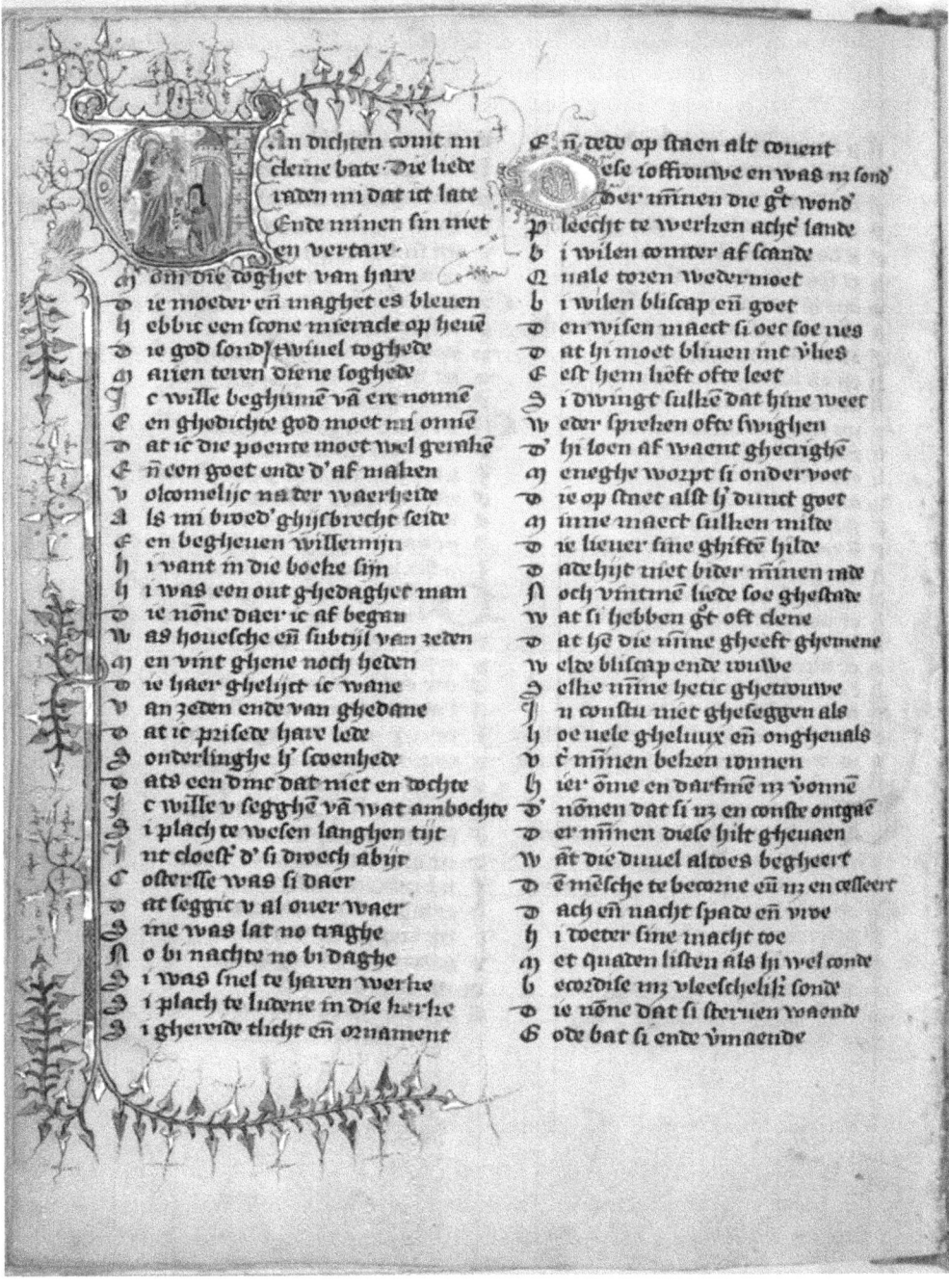

Fig. 7.1. The first page from the c.1374 Manuscript of the *Beatrijs*

development. Men and women have never had identical options in society. While men could mostly enjoy some kind of formal education, women were excluded from it. Women in nineteenth-century novels could seldom leave their homes to live independently in some big city. Even if they did this, they could not go out and discover their broader surroundings. They only exchanged one living room for another. While several amatory experiences were considered necessary for the emotional and moral development of men, women were literally and figuratively excluded from society after their first love affair unless they married.[8]

These are the considerations on the grounds of which I relate *Beatrijs* to later female stories of development. Their narrative structures and characteristic features will be examined. I shall put the following questions: to what extent does gender play a role in the work and in its narrative structure? Does being female have a crucial importance, and if so, do we have to assign a special meaning to this?

The Outside Context

The Genre of 'Beatrijs'

Beatrijs belongs to the genre of Mary miracles. These are rooted in the medieval Mary cult which led to the birth of several Mary legends from the twelfth century on. In the thirteenth century these texts were collected and noted down in Latin. The story of Beatrijs was first found also in the thirteenth century, noted down in prose by Caesarius of Heisterbach, a Cistercian abbot. Later a poet put the story into verse in Middle Dutch. While the prose version was intended for use as a sermon, the poem was not. One of the religious messages of *Beatrijs* is that we are weak against the power of evil, but if we stay true to Mary and pray to her regularly she will bring us God's mercy and absolution from worldly shame. The motif of confession in the end added a new element to the didactic message of *Beatrijs*, saying that Mary's mercy is not enough, you must also confess. Beatrijs and her lover must live according to the religious and secular norms and values of their time alike. The secular message was to keep your good reputation if you belonged to the nobility as Beatrijs and her lover did. As a didactic literary work, *Beatrijs* was adjusted to the special interests of the public, not only showing how noble persons should behave, but also reflecting on the religious expectations of the time by showing the obligation to confess.[9]

Rhetorical Context and Plot: 'Beatrijs' as a Narrative of Female Development

Beatrijs is about a young nun. She is only twelve years old and comes from an aristocratic family. Falling in love with a similarly young nobleman, Beatrijs cannot resist her love and leaves the cloister to join her young man. They marry and two sons are born. After seven years they run out of money, Beatrijs's partner leaves the family, and she has to prostitute herself in order to earn enough for her sons and herself. She lives another seven years in sin. Later she repents of what she has done and decides to go back to the cloister. On the way back she puts her two sons into the care of an elderly widow. An abbess sends money to the widow in order to help bring up the boys. When Beatrijs enters the cloister, she realizes that her absence has not been noticed, because the Virgin Mary has taken her place there. After this she makes a confession and goes on living as a nun.

Of course, we can read this story with other connotations in mind: for example, when secular love takes possession of Beatrijs so much that she exchanges the security of the cloister for the uncertain life outside its walls. This topos can be found in several fairy tales as well: Little Red Riding Hood goes out to the forest from her safe home only to meet the wolf there. According to Bruno Bettelheim, the mythical forest in which characters in fairy tales become lost is a symbol for the outside world, where the little child becomes adolescent through all kinds of dangerous adventures.[10] In other words, the forest is a school in which the child grows up to be an adult. This forest or school can be identified in *Beatrijs* as the field, and later on the town where Beatrijs and her lover arrive. The number seven — repeatedly mentioned in the story — stands not only for the biblical time of the lean kine and the seven years of plenteousness. The number seven occurs also in fairy tales, as, for example, the seven dwarfs, the seven-league boots, or the seven-headed dragon. Beatrijs's vicissitudes — she has to live in poverty, her lover leaves her behind with their two small children, she must prostitute herself in order to make ends meet — also interrelate with the narrative structure of fairy tales in which the protagonist must first touch bottom and go through several trials in order to develop him- or herself later.

After her vicissitudes Beatrijs returns to the cloister. First she finds solidarity with a widow with whom she leaves her children, then with the abbess who sends money for the education of the children. As it turns out Mary also had stood behind her all the time: she replaced her in the cloister, so that nobody noticed Beatrijs's absence. These characters form a network of a special female solidarity; they don't condemn, but help her.

If we read the story in its historical context, we may consider its ending euphoric: Beatrijs's life in the cloister was a real alternative for women's social integration and career in the Middle Ages. By confession her good reputation is regained as well. When we read it from our present time in a modern way, however, the text seems rather dysphoric. Beatrijs's return to the cloister means her exclusion from secular life: her chances to act, her secular ambitions, even her role as a mother, are ended.

Beatrijs's path is circular, from cloister back to cloister. She goes out to the outside world only temporarily, in order to return to the cloister and back to her own inner world — a 'voyage in', to quote the title of the volume I already mentioned, which reverses the title of Virginia Woolf's first novel *The Voyage Out* (1915).

This narrative pattern recurs also in later female narratives of development with, of course, the necessary changes.

Circular Paths of Life in Later Stories: the Eighteenth Century

The Outside Context

The first signs of modern, bourgeois fiction can be traced back to the eighteenth century, just as in England. It is a period of conflict between the regents and the burghers. The party of the Patriots — sympathizers with the Republican form of state — was formed itself from the middle class as well as from some members of the country gentry and the enlightened regents.

To this spiritual elite belonged Betje Wolff-Bekker (1738–1804) and Aagje Deken (1741–1804). Betje Wolff was born into an orthodox Protestant family of merchants. However, she enjoyed a modern education. She was almost seventeen years old when she ran away with a young ensign. This adventure lasted only one night: a relationship with as poor a man as the ensign was impossible. They were both put under the control of the local church council. Betje managed to escape her family and surroundings by marrying a pastor, Adriaan Wolff, thirty years her senior. She called this a 'philosophical marriage' where she perhaps did not find emotional satisfaction but did find compensation in friendship and literature. Before her marriage she read a lot of contemporary literature. When she was sixteen, she was portrayed with Pope's *Essay on Man* in her hand. Living with her husband she began to publish her own work, in which she criticized the stubborn and narrow-minded Protestant orthodoxy. She made a lot of friends but also a lot of enemies, because of her sharp satirical works.

As to Aagje Deken (1741–1804), she became an orphan when she was four years old and was brought up in an orphanage in Amsterdam. She served as a companion to elderly women. Once she worked in a family where she became friends with the daughter, and with her wrote and published poems. Her attention was aroused by the critical works of Betje Wolff. She wrote her a letter in which she expressed her disapproval in a sympathetic way. Betje answered her immediately and they became lifelong friends (see Fig. 7.2).

After the death of Betje's husband in 1777 they went to live together in De Rijp, a village in North Holland. Their main topic was education. Education was supposed to enlighten readers and to develop love for the fatherland. This should create national solidarity, which was fruitful for the economy and the culture of the country. When Aagje received an inheritance they were able to buy a modest house in Beverwijk. Here they reached the zenith of their oeuvre: in 1782 they published the epistolary novel *De Historie van mejuffrouw Sara Burgerhart* (*The History of Miss Sara Burgerhart*), the main topic of which was the education of young women so that they become good wives and mothers. Encouraged by the great success of this novel, they wrote an even longer epistolary novel, *Historie van den heer Willem Leevend* (*The History of Willem Leevend*, 1784–1785). Here they demonstrated the triumph of biblical Christianity over unbelief.

As a result of the conflict between Patriots and Orangists (the supporters of the Monarchy) in 1787, the two writers fled from Holland to France. Ten years later they returned, old and poor, to The Hague. They tried to live by the pen, but without much success. Publishers did not pay very well, and Betje and Aagje lost

Fig. 7.2. The portrait of Aagje Deken en Betje Wolff by A. Cardon and W. Neering 1784, etching, Digitale Bibliotheek voor de Nederlandse Letteren

their public. Their third novel, written in France, *Historie van mejuffrouw Cornelia Wildschut* (*The History of Miss Cornelia Wildschut*, 1793–96) in six volumes did not become popular either. The most important work of their period in The Hague was their pseudo-autobiography, *Geschrift eener bejaarde vrouw* (*Writings of an Elderly Woman*, 1802). They also published several poems, both separately and together.

Rhetorical Context and Plot

The novel *Sara Burgerhart* radiates the same serene Christianity as the works of the popular Spinozist philosophers Pontiaan van Hattem, F. van Leenhof, Jacob Bril, Marinus Boom, or Willem Deurhof, who tried to harmonize the morals of Christ with the postulates of everyday life. They preferred the joys of life to sombre devotion. Their popular Spinozism formulated a democratic-rationalistic credo which became the most characteristic feature of the rising bourgeoisie.

The authors never denied that they had a model: Richardson. They could read his *Clarissa* in the translation by a Baptist pastor, Johannes Stinstra, who had been suspended because of accusations of Socinian heresy. They were proud, however, that their novel was not a translation but a completely original work (see Fig. 7.3).

Wolff and Deken continue the tradition of theoretical introductions. In the introduction to the second edition of their novel they formulate the postulates of realism: there are strict laws of character drawing, the events must seem probable. They draw the line between their work and the hitherto accepted fashionable romance genres.

The authors delineate their new public: that of young women. As mentioned above, their subject matter is the appropriate education of young ladies. While showing this they succeed also in depicting eighteenth-century Dutch everyday life in its rich variety and liveliness. The motto of the novel sums up concisely its characteristic rationalism advising moderation: rigid strictness and limitless libertinism can both eliminate morals. This jovial middle-course philosophy gives an irresistible charm and serenity to the novel but at the same time deprives it of the dramatic depth and dynamism so characteristic of the story of Richardson's protagonist, Clarissa.

The form of the novel, too, follows its English predecessor: it is an epistolary novel. The letter as a form of fiction is a semi-private space in which women's voices are articulated. Writing letters in epistolary novels constitutes the plot endowing their writers — mostly women — with subjectivity. The middle class defines itself for the first time in Dutch literature. Sara chooses between two worlds: instead of the narrow-minded, Calvinistic, ostentatiously parading, stupid circle of her guardian, Suzanna Hofland, she decides to attach herself to the enlightened, liberal middle-class milieu at the boarding-school of Mrs Spilgoed. The novel shows her route, with all its difficulties, leading from a world of hypocrites to a different one as she directs herself towards the safe haven of marriage. The authors also make it clear that they postulate love as a positive value only in so far as it leads to an appropriate marriage. Nevertheless, Sara longs for a free life. She would not escape at just any price to the bondage of marriage from her narrow-minded, covetous guardian. In Madame Spilgoed's house, in the circle of young ladies, she absorbs not only

FIG. 7.3. The title page of the eighth edition of *Sara Burgerhart* 1891, VU University Library, Amsterdam, shelfmark XU.04474.-

music, literature, and theatre but also a rich fabric of human relations. A sober freedom within the compass of sensible rules is realized here. The equilibrium between rules and libertinism is a delicate one: it inclines easily towards libertinism. The storm of physical love has almost fatal consequences, but Sara is rescued in time from the claws of the dubious Mr R. and so she can return to her arcadian idyll at the boarding-school. However, wise restraint is obligatory not only on one side. The Lutheran priest Edeling must reconcile himself to the marriage of his son Hendrik to the reformed Sara. This is the greatest victory common sense could ever gain in a society like the Dutch, which has always been very much divided. Therefore — though according to one of the best analysts of the novel, P. J. Buijnsters, marriage has the highest value in the novel — the apologia of religious tolerance is one of its most essential messages.[11] Neither boundless freedom without rules or limits, nor petty-minded freedom can be considered ideal.

While Clarissa stands in opposition to the universal order of nobility, Sara's way leads out from a hostile world to a different one. The social ideal propagated by the authors can be seen in the depiction of social groups and spiritual trends which articulate themselves in a coordinated way, side by side, rather than in sharp opposition to one another. Descriptive elements and reflective essay-like, instructive passages predominate.

The novel *Sara Burgerhart* can be considered something new compared to *Clarissa*: it describes the relationship of not only four but twenty-four correspondents. Therefore the narrative perspective changes constantly, and so there unfolds a wider tableau of points of views and opinions. True, this polyphony reduces the dramatic character of the novel a great deal. But *Sara Burgerhart* has done its duty perfectly: it demonstrates the coexistence of social and religious groups, the fact that there exists a harmony in variety. It is no accident that Sara is rescued from the trap of Mr R. by the daughter of the gardener, the Catholic Klaartje, with the help of Pieter, the son of a peasant woman. In this way that very layer is also represented whose members have been 'forgotten' by the patriots, and who are exploited and are always losers: their social situation will only be taken into consideration in literature at the end of the nineteenth century. It is remarkable that precisely this lowest layer is helping the representatives of the middle class who are striving to assert themselves politically, legally, and economically.[12]

Sara Burgerhart as a Narrative of Female Development

As mentioned above, the novel *Sara Burgerhart* shows us the growing-up of a twenty-year-old orphan girl. By the end of the novel she becomes a young woman and a wife. The narrative structure of this novel does not fit into the dual pattern of Abel, Hirsch, and Langland. Neither the years of 'apprenticeship' nor those of 'awakening' are depicted. Her story begins at a rather late point: her education is not in the hands of her parents, who die right at the beginning. One of her guardians is Suzanne Hofland; the other is Abraham Blankaart, who lives in Paris and writes his letters to Sara from there. A third person who later becomes responsible for her education is Mrs Spilgoed, the head of a girls' boarding school. The story ends with Sara's marriage. How she experiences marriage, we never discover.

At the opening of the story, however, we find a strong mother–daughter bonding: Sara nursed her dying mother for a long time. Sara speaks of her with intense emotion after her death.

Like Beatrijs, Sara also escapes her surroundings. The absence of parents gives the protagonists a special freedom of action. Sara's motivation to escape — unlike Beatrijs's — is not love, but her impossible situation at the house of the hypocritical and cruel Suzanne Hofland. Like Beatrijs, Sara also longs for freedom where her own priorities can prevail. After a relatively calm phase in her life there comes a period of trial in the adventure with Mr R. The Hortus Medicus where Sara and Mr R. meet can be considered as a new version of the rose-bush under which Beatrijs sees her lover.

When Sara understands that her 'adventure' with Mr. R. makes her prospects in society impossible, necessity makes her find the 'solution': she marries her upright suitor, Hendrik Edeling. This solution is preceded by penitence: while Beatrijs confesses her sinful life after returning to the cloister, Sara confesses before her marriage, as she herself says: 'Ik zal boete doen: ik zal mijn dwaasheid afwisselen tegen de volkomenste geleidelijkheid aan uw vermaningen, ik zal mezelve zover zien op te heffen, dat uw vermaningen in goedkeuringen zullen veranderen' [I shall do penance: I shall change my mad deviations for your warnings which I shall absolutely follow; I want to lift myself up to such heights so that your warnings will change to acknowledgements].[13] The question whether her marriage to Hendrik Edeling is also a form of penitence remains unanswered.

Hendrik Edeling, the future fiancé, fits Sara's letter about Mr R. into his own letter to a friend (Letter 139). This is a striking example of textual subjugation. As in the case of Circe, this time Sara's utterance is similarly embedded by a male protagonist in his own text addressed to another man; Sara's crucial letter does not appear in its own right.

Sara's letter can be considered a confession in spite of her Protestant background. There are several similar 'confessions' in Dutch literature, for example in Marcellus Emants's novel *Een nagelaten bekentenis* (*A Posthumous Confession*) of 1894. J. J. Oversteegen, a Dutch scholar, wrote:

> Het grootste deel van de Nederlandse natie gaat sinds de zestiende eeuw niet meer te biecht. Misschien komt het daardoor wel (en door het forse accent dat het calvinisme op het schuldgevoel heeft gelegd), dat onze literatuur zo opvallend rijk is aan auteurs met een neiging tot bekentenissen. Men zou dus zeggen, wie een authentiek Nederlands verhaal wil schrijven, kan niet beter doen dan er letterlijk de biecht van een personage van te maken, over de zonden der vaderen en de eigen slechtheid. Dat heeft Emants gedaan, vreemd genoeg zonder veel concurrentie.[14]

> [The greatest part of the Dutch nation has not gone to confession since the sixteenth century. Perhaps this is the reason (and the strong accent which Calvinism puts on guilty conscience) why our literature is so rich in authors who have had a bent for confession. One could say, if somebody intended to write an authentic Dutch story, the best way to do this is to put down the protagonist's confessions about the sins of his forefathers and about his own wickedness. Emants did this, strangely enough without much competition.]

This quotation is a good example of a characteristic of the 'merlynists' which the Dutch feminist literary scholar Maaike Meijer has called 'manziekte' (man-illness).[15] Oversteegen speaks about the sins of forefathers and the wickedness of a male protagonist. In the context of *Een nagelaten bekentenis* this statement implies male authors who write about male characters, male sins, and male wickedness. In stories about female development, however, there are also confessions made by women. This is also the case with Sara's embedded letter. There will be female confessions also in further novels which I shall analyse in this chapter.

Sara becomes 'The Angel of the House'.[16] The novel has a euphoric ending. Marriage was the norm and frame in which women could unfold their capacities as wives and mothers in the eighteenth century. The innovative character of the novel lies in the acknowledgment of social positions such as being daughters, wives, and mothers which came to be considered not less valuable than those of men working outside their homes, who sometimes fought in wars or took part in public affairs. Sara's life, however, remained restricted: she could achieve everything inside her house, but life and spaces outside her house remained closed to her. Her emotional adventure with Mr R., to whom she evidently feels attracted, is terminated so that Sara can arrive at the safe haven of marriage. If Beatrijs's predestined path led from cloister back to cloister, Sara's predestined path led from the absence of a loving family to a realized family. The circle is closed here too. Obeying sexual urges would break the (wedding) ring, to use Swinnen's striking expression. Other alternatives of female lifestyles, such as that of the learned woman, are ridiculed by the authors themselves. The cloister and a reasonable marriage — both institutions ideologically strictly charged — were meant to settle norms for women of noble or bourgeois origin. Sara's happiness therefore also depends on her guilty conscience: she only realizes that she should marry Hendrik Edeling after she has been seduced by R.

Female solidarity plays a crucial role also in this story: Mrs Spilgoed, Letje Brunier, the circle of young girl-friends, Anna Willis, and the gardener's Catholic daughter who helps Sara to escape Mr R., all help Sara to reflect on herself and to find her own way in life.

In the Nineteenth Century

The Outside Context

Nineteenth-century liberalism resulted in the founding of political organizations with different orientations. Because of the growth of the population and especially the development of the industrial proletariat, it became necessary for the diverse social groups to be able to make their own voice heard, a condition of their social emancipation. Ideological organizations were established, the so-called pillars which formed the basis of the political system in the Netherlands. These were the orthodox Protestant, the Catholic and the social democratic groups. In addition to these there came also organizations which declared themselves neutral or general.

The growing participation of the broad layers of the population in political and social discourse was stimulated by the mass press. Trade unions and political parties achieved a central place. As a result several social acts came into existence around the turn of the century. These were aimed at the diligent, thrifty, and trained workers rather than the proletariat. Men were given suffrage in 1917, while universal suffrage was introduced in 1919.

The end of the nineteenth century brought many innovations in Europe. This concerned both the humanities and the natural sciences, in which an analytical view of the world increasingly gained ground. While Sigmund Freud (1856–1939) analysed the human psyche and contended that sexual desire was the most important motivation of human life, Karl Marx (1818–83) and Friedrich Engels (1820–95) studied economy and society in a similarly analytical way. Charles Darwin (1809–82) offered an alternative to the traditional Christian world-view with his evolution theory, and Hippolyte Taine (1828–93) argued that human beings were determined by three factors: race, circumstances (*milieu*), and time (*moment*).

The Middle Ages 'came into fashion' at the end of the nineteenth century in the Netherlands as in the rest of Europe. A special nostalgia was felt for a sincere and naive religiosity, small communities, handicrafts, and a would-be unreflective life style. These idealized Middle Ages had, of course, not much to do with the historical facts. They were a construction, just like illusions of other periods of the past.[17] After the aristocratic individualism of the 1880s there came an intellectual turn which took shape in the abstractions of community, idea, and faith. This is the period of applied arts, *Gesamtkunstwerk*, and an emotional and romantic Catholicism. The representation of women shows a special divide: they are either saints or prostitutes.[18]

The life and work of Frederik van Eeden (1860–1932) (see Fig. 7.4) represents the manifold clashes of different ideas at the end of the nineteenth and the beginning of the twentieth centuries. He studied medicine in Amsterdam, but he developed a scepticism against positivist-based science. Like Freud, his interest turned to the psyche and the realm of dreams. One of his statements was that the psyche was determined not only by genetic but also by social factors such as wealth versus poverty, social classes, parents, friends, peer-groups, and education. Van Eeden was the first psychiatrist, together with his colleague Albert Willem van Renthergem, to open a consulting-room for psychotherapy in the Netherlands. His novel *Van de koele meren des doods*, 1900 (*Deeps of Deliverance*, 1974), was accused by some readers of being a mere case study of a hysterical patient.

His findings about the decisive impact of social background on his patients' psyche brought him to his other field of interest: social reform. He contended that work was essential for psychological health and that many problems were caused by idleness. All layers of society, even the well-to-do, should do some kind of work in order to be healthy and to build a healthy society. People should form working communities. Impressed by the book of the American writer, philosopher, and abolitionist Henry David Thoreau, *Walden or Life in the Woods* (1854), he founded a community colony with the same name near Bussum. Colonists were expected to live there in small huts, to grow and produce food so that they could support themselves. The deeper sense of community and work should follow automatically. This idealistic enterprise went bankrupt definitively in 1907. Expertise and money

FIG. 7.4. Portrait of Frederik van Eeden by Jan Veth, etching
Digitale Bibliotheek van de Nederlandse Letterkunde

were both missing. In his novel, however, the ethical imperative to work as a cure for all kinds of psychological maladies is a conspicuous element and constitutes one of the most essential messages. *Van de koele meren des doods* (to be discussed below) was also written during his stay at Walden (see Fig. 7.5).[19]

Another idealistic dream of Van Eeden's was to create world peace by cooperation among prominent intellectuals such as Martin Buber, Upton Sinclair, Walther Rathenau, Gustav Landauer, Romain Rolland, and Sigmund Freud. He tried to convince these people about his plans in several letters, but the First World War refuted all his intentions and dreams.

When his quest to reform his life failed both in psychological and in social respects, he turned to religion and transcendence. Like his experiments with the human psyche and with social circumstances, his conversion to Catholicism was also triggered by the urge to change, by his very serious, ethical frame of mind. His whole life was characterized by searching for a better life, a better society, a better human being. He was extremely sensitive to the main problems of his time: the conscious versus the subconscious, the healthy versus the sick, the poor versus the rich, peace versus war, suppression versus confession, nature versus culture, countryside versus urban life.

Rhetorical Context and Plot

Hedwig Marga de Fontayne, protagonist of *De koele meren des doods*, is a scion of an upper-middle-class family. Her mother dies when she is very young, and her father becomes an alcoholic. Hedwig marries not the boy she loves, Johan, but Gerard, a dull notary who has problems with his own sexuality. At this point she is seriously reproached by Joob, a poor man, who tells her of the consequences of an idle life and the blessed impact of work on the human psyche. Her marriage with Gerard stays asexual and breaks down. When she leaves her husband for Ritsaert, an attractive pianist, she is expelled by her own social class. She experiences passionate love with Ritsaert, but the birth of their child puts an end to the unlawful relationship. Ritsaert feels himself hindered in his career and his love is extinguished. The baby dies. At that time Hedwig's decline begins: she becomes more and more deprived socially and financially until she turns to prostitution and becomes a morphine addict. At a certain point she is brought to a hospital where she is cured not by doctors but by Sister Paula, a nun who draws her attention to the realms of transcendence and selflessness. Finally she finds the aim of her life among poor peasants, moves in with them, and does the work of simple people in the fields. She dies at the age of thirty-three.

Van de koele meren des doods is a novel which shows the synthesis of all the psychological, medical, emancipatory, spiritual, and social problems of the *fin-de-siècle*.[20] Like that of Beatrijs, Hedwig Marga de Fontayne's life-path is also circular: from the safe bourgeois home of her parents she returns to the Harmsens' farm. This may be a new home, but geographically it lies in the near neighbourhood of her old home, far away from the outside world.[21] In the meantime she has more than one love affair, but they all run aground. Like Beatrijs's, Hedwig's story also

Fig. 7.5. Cover of the first edition of the *Van de koele meren des doods*, 1900, Leiden University Libraries 22544 D 40 001

has the motif of 'awakening': her unsuccessful relationships trigger a process of self-reflection and the need to change her life. As mentioned above, the man by whom Hedwig has a child leaves her and the child dies shortly afterwards. In order to live and earn money independently Hedwig becomes a prostitute. Like Beatrijs, Hedwig also 'confesses' her sins, this time in the form of a diary. The fragments of the diary form a *corpus alienum* in the otherwise third-person omniscient narrative because of their first-person singular point of view, which endows her — also by the act of writing — with a subject position. Writing becomes plot. It is a semi-private narration as it is embedded in the public narration of the narrator. The diary, although it is a fictional one as in this novel, is one of the few genres by which women could let their voice be heard at the end of the nineteenth century. The diary is here also a precursor of modernism, switching the code of writing from realistic prose into a subjective, almost expressionist female narrative, sometimes even coming close to stream-of-consciousness techniques.

Hedwig also imposes penitence on herself: she does agricultural work among peasants. This means that, like Beatrijs, she too is able to develop only one aspect of her personality, the spiritual. Love, sexuality, *and* work all together do not belong to her possibilities, as if there was no escape from 'race, milieu, moment'.

This novel also shows us female solidarity: Hedwig's mother who dies early just like Sara's mother, and with whom Hedwig has a very strong relationship, Sister Paula who is a kind of surrogate-mother to Hedwig, and the ideas of the seventeenth-century French philosopher and quietist writer, Madame Guyon, build up this special network of female relationships. It is worth mentioning that it is not Joob's — a man's — virile world of ideas full of outer imperatives which really helps Hedwig but that of two women, Sister Paula and Madame Guyon.

The contrast between spiritual values and sexuality plays an essential role, as with Beatrijs.[22] Both stories are organized around the dichotomy of the idealized countryside and the guilty city. Community — the cloister for Beatrijs, the circle of girlfriends for Sara, and the Harmsen family for Hedwig — solves the heroines' problems only partially. Full development of their personality is not attainable.

At the end of the novel Hedwig finds happiness with the Harmsen family, but she dies at the age of thirty-three. Although she succeeds in reaching a subject-position by deliberately opting for a lower social status, in which by working in the fields she can exchange her passive life for an active one, the end is still dysphoric. The heroine has no opportunity to exercise her rights as an independent, free woman in a new social context. Her only alternative is death.

In the Twentieth Century

Another Dutch example of a narrative of female development is Carry van Bruggen's (1881–1932) novel *Eva* (1927) (see Figs 7.6 and 7.7). The life and work of Carry van Bruggen has been convincingly discussed and analysed from a feminist point of view by Jane Fenoulhet.[23] As a woman, an autodidact, a Jew, and belonging to the lower middle class, in her work she negotiated being an outsider and being different. *Eva* is the name of the protagonist who is in search of happiness. She becomes a teacher and has several girlfriends, among them Andy, who is disappointed in men. Andy finds that Eva is more like a boy than a girl. To her Eva seems the ideal boy, so she kisses her at a certain moment. Eva gets frightened because she finds that such things should not happen. Eva meets her future husband, Ben, at a discussion of socialism at a friend's house. She has two children by him, but has no pleasure sleeping and living with him. Her marriage is unhappy. After divorcing Ben she meets Marius, to whom she feels very attracted. They kiss at the seaside. Eva never sees him again, but she is satisfied because she knows that the final aim of all wisdom is to face death calmly. Like Van Eeden, Carry van Bruggen also brought social, psychological, and gender problems together in her novel. Like Van Eeden's novel, *Eva* also was written in the context of the first feminist wave.[24] Carry van Bruggen, however, had an ambivalent relationship with feminism. The novel, however, should not be read without paying attention to this context. The central theme is the 'thinking woman' who tries to get rid of the social stereotypes of men and women. The title of the novel can be read as a reference to the biblical Eve, the antithesis of Mary, who is punished for her thirst for knowledge. Like Van Eeden's novel, too, Van Bruggen's story is about a protagonist in search of a *modus vivendi*, about the conflict between intellect and sexuality. Like Van Eeden's novel this work also contains the motif of awakening. However, what with Frederik van Eeden was a faint beginning in the diary fragments of Hedwig becomes in *Eva* the constituent narrative technique: the structural application of the stream of consciousness makes the story a fragmented narrative. No letter, no diary is needed anymore. It is a full-fledged, emancipated public narration written by a woman about a woman in its own right.

There are even some explicit references to Frederik van Eeden in the novel, although not to *Van de koele meren des doods* analysed above but to his *Johannes Viator* (1892). Eva changes Viator's philosophy like this: 'Niet de liefde maakt het lijfsverlangen goed. Het lijfsverlangen maakt de liefde goed' [It is not love which is a proof of carnal desire. It is carnal desire which is a proof of love]. Eva thinks for a while that she has found her internal balance. Most scholars share this opinion.[25] The last paragraph and the last chapter of the novel, however, provide evidence of the opposite. The happiness caused by the new philosophy of life quoted above is only temporary. Eva, who has divorced her husband in the meantime, must return to everyday life, in which she has to look after her two children. The long final paragraph of the novel about summer changing into autumn, then autumn into winter, has symbolic force: it symbolizes circularity. Enthusiasm during summer time, finding the philosophy of life lasted only for a short moment. Winter, with which the novel began, comes back in the end. The decisive philosophy of life

FIG. 7.6. Portrait of Carry van Bruggen by Annie de Meester, drawing, 1915, Digitale Bibliotheek voor de Nederlandse Letteren

Fig. 7.7. The cover of the first edition of *Eva*, 1927
Leiden University Libraries, MTRB 5 E 001

changes into the quotation from Montaigne: 'en het einddoel van alle wijsheid is het rustig tegemoetzien van de dood'[26] [and the final aim of all wisdom is to face death calmly]. Although Eva succeeds in getting rid of several social expectations towards women, her internal voyage cannot be considered a 'voyage out'. Like Beatrijs, she also is left alone with two children. Eva's 'voyage' too is circular: it begins and ends with Yom Kippur when remembering and confessing our sins have a central role. The first chapter is built up of the same elements as the last one: it lasts from sunset to sunset like Yom Kippur; the 'thousand birds and promises', Kol Nidrei, the stable boy, the closed doors, water and several other elements return as well. Sentences in the last chapter such as 'Er zijn dingen in de verten, in de verste verten, die je alleen onderscheidt met een naar binnen gekeerde blik'[27] [There are things far away, the farthest away, which you can only discern with an inward eye] imply that the female eye is only an eye looking inward even in this emancipatory novel. There is perspective for Eva only in her internal world, not outside. Love and sexuality are not connected to self-fulfilling work here either. Like Beatrijs, Eva too looks for happiness in transcendence, not in real life. That is why we find several implicit references to God in the text: 'In glanzende golvingen zichtbaar wandelt de wind de akkers over, over de toppen der doorgloeide aren wandelt de wind naar mij toe'[28] [In glittering waves visible, above the fields, above the top of the dry corns the wind is walking towards me]. Or: 'Waar de zomerwind wandelde over de toppen van het koren' [Where the summer wind walked above the tops of the wheat].[29] This presence of God, however, is not a sign encouraging performativity as in the Bible, where the sound of God's going in the tops of the mulberry trees warns David to fight against the Philistines.[30] It is rather a sign of resignation, contemplation, of sheer existence. Contemplation on time passing by appears in both the first and the last chapter: 'Zij zaten in die verre eeuwen aan hun verre zeeën en wij zitten in deze eeuw aan onze zee en alles is en blijft tot in eeuwigheid enerlei, mensen en hun roerselen, zeeën en hun bewegingen' [They sat there in centuries long past on the shores of distant seas, and we sit in this century on the shore of our sea, and everything is always the same, and remains the same, people and their emotions, seas and movements of seas as well].[31] We can say that the character of the female protagonist is rather contemplative than performative.

The novel *Eva* has an open ending in contrast to the works of female development discussed thus far. It is neither euphoric nor dysphoric. Eva does not marry again nor does she die. We do not know how her life is to be later on.

In the Twenty-first Century

The 2003 novel *Een schitterend gebrek* (*In Lucia's Eyes*, 2005) by Arthur Japin (born 1956) can again be considered as a type of awakening novel with a fragmented structure (see Figs 7.8 and 7.9).[32] Japin, as our contemporary in our postmodern and post-colonial time, often explores the problems of centre and periphery and the questions of how to comply with social, ethnic, and sexual borders and how these borders can be eventually crossed/transgressed. In addition, *Een schitterend gebrek* tackles borderline positions as its protagonist is a prostitute living for a while on the periphery of society.

Fig. 7.8. Portrait of Arthur Japin © Corbino

FIG. 7.9. Cover of *Een schitterend gebrek* © Steven van der Gouw. Henry Morland, De Arbeiderspers Amsterdam

Lucia is Casanova's first lover. She tells her own story. She holds her narrative subject position throughout the whole text. At the very end of the novel, however, it turns out that the story is actually a long confession in the form of a letter written by Lucia to her first child. This confession does not appear to be embedded in another story as in the case of Sara, nor is it written because of guilty feelings as in the case of Hedwig. Lucia is a first-person singular narrator and as such endows herself with a new name — Galathée de Pompignac — and with this new name also a new personality. Her growing-up is not described in chronological order. The story jumps from the present into the past, then from the past into the present; her idyllic childhood with her kindly parents in Pasiano is interrupted by her adventures in Italy, Amsterdam, and Paris until she leaves for America. Lucia is a female counterpart of Casanova. She takes both an external and an internal voyage. Geographically this voyage leads her from Italy to Holland, and from Holland to America, the land of freedom. She arrives intellectually as well as emotionally but she has to pay a huge price.

As a result of the smallpox which she catches from her private tutor, De Pompignac, at the age of fourteen she is permanently disfigured. This again reminds us of the way in which Eve is punished in the Bible for wanting to have knowledge. From that point on, cognitive knowledge and emotions are discussed as the dichotomy of female existence. Lucia is given such an intensive education that she can come up as an adequate wife of the promising young man Giacomo Casanova. For that she must pay a high price: she becomes literally stigmatized for her whole life. Knowledge and love were incompatible factors for women according to the social norms of that time. When Lucia catches smallpox, she decides to leave her lover Giacomo, so that he would not be obliged to live his life with a disfigured wife. Casanova's career would be jeopardized by her appalling looks. The sacrifice she decides to make in renouncing her future husband is forced upon her by the conventions of the time: external appearances define everything for women; knowledge and internal values which could make her a subject in society don't count. Lucia escapes from Pasiano and her awakening and independent life begin. The mirror is a leitmotif of the plot: it is a means of critical (self-)reflection. When she decides to wear a veil for the rest of her life, this is a performative act of gender by which she puts herself in a social and narrative subject position. Her personality is not formed by the gaze of others — primarily of men — but by her own. This way she is the one who has the power of looking; all the others are deprived of looking at her. The veil can be thus interpreted as a sign of negation of all kinds of interpellation directed to her by society. The concept of interpellation was further worked out by Louis Althusser, based on the ideas of Jacques Lacan. According to Lacan, babies younger than eighteen months think that their reflection in a mirror is their real self (misrecognition).[33] Elaborating on this idea, Althusser argued that we can speak of a similar delusion in the case of grown-up individuals. Society interpellates, challenges its individuals, as it were, to recognize their real selves in identities offered them by social formations as civilians, consumers, electors, etc., while these identities are only different roles which mislead individuals about the real nature of their identity.[34] Lucia's disfigurement is an inevitable condition for her to realize that her undistorted face would also be distorted by what society expects from women. By the act of veiling her face she resists this practice, and by making her real self invisible she renders visible its most specific feature, its integrity.

After several attempts to find work, Lucia is forced to become a prostitute. But even as a prostitute she keeps her social and narrative subject position and the performative character of her female existence. Having a subject position, however, does not mean automatically the realization of the self. Nor does it mean that Lucia does not suffer as a prostitute. Her story gives several examples of female solidarity: countess Montereale, Mrs Morandi Manzolini and her feminist circle, Zélide, Danae and Giovanna all help her in their own way. In the end Lucia still accepts an object position. Although she chooses the free world of America against Holland she does this as the wife of an American merchant, Jamieson, with whom she is not in love. She gives birth to four children, the first of them being probably the child of Giacomo. She disappears from her own story as wife and mother together with the chances of an independent female existence. At the end of the novel the narration turns out to be Lucia's written confession addressed to her children. This is a return to the semi-private narration of women, but it is no longer embedded in a male narration. There is no 'writing beyond the ending' in spite of the fact that the story itself offers the possibility of this.

★ ★ ★ ★ ★

While analysing narratives of female development I have used the concept of gender as a structural category. This made it possible to draw conclusions from both a thematic and a structural point of view.

The question whether *Beatrijs* is one of the first works in the Dutch tradition of fictions of female development can be answered positively. In the novels analysed above we hear an echo of *Beatrijs*. 'Echo' as a term is used by Odile Heynders following the Russian writer Joseph Brodsky.[35] It refers to a reading experience when the reader hears the echo of earlier works in later literary utterances. This way a continuum is established. It must be emphasized that this echo is not (always) an inherent phenomenon between two or more works. It is rather 'discovered' by the reader, as it were. The lines I have drawn from *Beatrijs* to later literary works are my subjective lines, interrelations established by myself. On what grounds have I established these interrelations?

In most of the stories of female development the heroine's 'voyage' was not chronological or linear, but circular (Beatrijs, Sara, Hedwig, Eva). This means that in the end they arrive at the place from where they began searching for happiness, but after all kinds of vicissitudes they arrive at an intellectually higher level (Beatrijs, Sara, Hedwig, Eva). In the case of Lucia, awakening makes a return of the heroine to her point of departure impossible, but the harmony of real self-fulfilment, love, family life, and work cannot be realized just as in the cases of the other heroines.

The more time progresses, the stronger the heroines' social and narrative subject position becomes. While Beatrijs's story is told by an external narrator and Beatrijs herself only speaks in dialogues, Lucia's story and her reflections are narrated in the first-person singular. Sara can focalize directly as a result of the genre of the epistolary novel; Hedwig does the same in her diary. The power of focalization and having one's own voice do not automatically lead to the occupation of a social subject position. None of the stories offer harmony between love and intellectual life for women.

The heroines' voyage is not a 'voyage out' but a 'voyage in'. This is the reason why the motif of confession is a recurring form. Confessions are often inspired by guilty feelings in the form of letters, diaries, or oral confessions. Sometimes they are just stories written for another person. Sometimes they are embedded in men's stories. Sometimes they appear directly. In all cases they are manifestations of female self-reflection.

Real self-fulfilment by the heroines is not realized in these narratives. Innovative ideas about the social position of woman, however, are prominent in all of them. In *Sara Burgerhart* we see a new-born appreciation of such women's tasks as being a wife and a mother, in *Van de koele meren des doods* we read about the importance of work for women as a possible means of self-fulfilment, in *Eva* there is an independent way of female thinking, and finally in Japin's novel gender becomes performative — all of them signs of innovative ideas on the emancipation of women.

A further question is whether we see *Beatrijs* in a new light after we 'have recognized' this literary work in later novels. The answer is positive again. Not only do we hear the echo of *Beatrijs* in later works, but paradoxically enough *Beatrijs* also echoes later works. This is a wonderful dynamic of literature. In order to explain this phenomenon I refer to Heynders again. She argues:

> Maar de corresponderende lectuur zoals ik mij haar voorstel, zinspeelt op meer dan analogie of symbolische overeenkomst. Het gaat er ook om hoe het ene werk in beweging komt door het andere, hoe er ander licht op valt, zaken in breder verband zichtbaar worden. De context van het te lezen gedicht of oeuvre wordt als het ware verruimd of verschoven door er werk van een andere dichter naast te plaatsen of zelfs in te schuiven, zodanig dat de compositie van het gedicht of het imago van het dichterschap ineens een andere indruk gaat wekken. Andere betekenisnuances kunnen zich dan openbaren.[36]

> [But corresponding reading, as I imagine it, refers to more than analogy or symbolic coincidence. The point is also how a work is brought into motion by another, how we see it then in another light, how things are seen in a broader context. The context of a poem or an oeuvre which we are going to read becomes broader or shifted by putting another poet's work next to it or even inserting one into the other so that the composition of the poem or the imago of being a poet suddenly gives another impression. Other nuances of meaning can appear.]

What Heynders describes here can be applied to other genres too, such as the Mary miracle *Beatrijs* or the novel. Reading later works sheds another light on our image of *Beatrijs*. Her story is no longer seen as a Mary miracle or an example, but as a narrative of a typical female development. The modern reader brings her up to date. All the more so, because modern readers usually read 'backwards', as it were, from their present time, with their modern eyes. They seldom read in a historical way.

As opposed to the historical way of reading, when Beatrijs's return, her confession, and penitence are considered as the salvation of all sins and a catharsis, the modern reader feels sympathy for her fate instead. We recognize the 'voyage-in' element in her life-path. Because of the 600 years between the first appearance of *Beatrijs* and literary works of modern times, the reader of today sees the human being in Beatrijs not as a sinner but rather a victim of the social norms and values of her time. We do not read it as a story with a lesson. Modern readers dare to put other questions about her actions. These questions are not about her secular love affair, her prostitution, or her begging. They are rather about her leaving her two children behind at the house of the widow in order to return to the cloister at any price. This is not intended to be a moral reproach on my part. It is only a reflection in the light of norms and values of modern times.

Thanks to all these deliberations, *Beatrijs* can move even the reader of today, who has a whole repertoire of later literary works in his or her mind from *Sara Burgerhart* via *Van de koele meren des doods* and *Eva* to *Een schitterend gebrek*. When we read a literary work of the Middle Ages, we read it in our own time, the norms and values of which play an essential role in the interpretation of old literature. *Beatrijs* may be situated in its historical context and read in a historical way by scholars of the Middle Ages, but for the modern reader, however, who is responsive to gender issues and is not a medieval scholar, Beatrijs comes across as a young, modern woman oppressed by social regulations. That she can move us even today is partly because of her 'younger sisters' who, in turn, have her to thank for their existence.

Notes to Chapter 7

1. E. Abel, M. Hirsch, and E. Langland, 'Introduction', in *The Voyage In: Fictions of Female Development* (Hanover, NH and London: University Press of New England, 1983), pp. 3–19.
2. Aagje Swinnen, *Het slot ontvlucht. De 'vrouwelijke' Bildungsroman in de Nederlandse literatuur* (Amsterdam: Amsterdam University Press, 2006), p. 14.
3. Nancy K. Miller, *The Heroine's Text: Readings in the French and English Novel, 1722–1782* (New York: Columbia University Press, 1980), pp. 18–19.
4. Abel, Hirsch, and Langland, 'Introduction', pp. 9–12.
5. Rachel Blau DuPlessis, *Writing beyond the Ending: Narrative Strategies of Twentieth-Century Women Writers* (Bloomington: Indiana University Press, 1985).
6. Mikhail M. Bakhtin, 'The Bildungsroman and its Significance in the History of Realism: Toward a Historical Typology of the Novel', in *Speech Genres and Other Late Essays*, ed. by Caryl Emerson and Michael Holquist (Austin: University of Texas Press, 1986), pp. 10–59.
7. These genres also differ from each other: parables give us a moral or philosophical lesson through a concrete story, while legends use also supernatural elements for their message. Folk tales are a combination of the two, while space and time remain abstract.
8. Abel, Hirsch, Langland, 'Introduction', p. 8.
9. This summary follows the 'Inleiding' of F. Lulofs to *Beatrijs* (Leiden: Martinus Nijhoff, 1983), pp. 7–24.
10. Bruno Bettelheim, *The Uses of Enchantment: The Meaning and Importance of Fairy Tales* (New York: Knopf, 1976).
11. P. J. Buijnsters, 'Sara Burgerhart en de ontwikkeling van de Nederlandse roman in de 18e eeuw', in *Nederlandse literatuur van de achttiende eeuw* (Utrecht: HES Uitgevers, 1984), pp. 199–222.
12. See Judit Gera, 'Stages in the Development of Dutch Fiction', *Neohelicon*, 18.1 (1991), 225–38.
13. Deken and Betje Wolff, *De historie van mejuffrouw Sara Burgerhart* (Amsterdam: Wereldbibliotheek, n.d.), p. 262.
14. J. J. Oversteegen, 'Uit de donkere dagen van voor Freud', in *De Novembristen van Merlyn. Een literatuuropvatting in theorie en praktijk* (Utrecht: HES Uitgevers, 1983), p. 126.

15. The journal *Merlyn* (1962–66) introduced structuralism in the Netherlands. It can be seen as the Dutch forum of New Criticism. One of its most important editors and contributors was Jaap. J. Oversteegen. There were no women among the editors and contributors, who confined their criticism to male authors, and simply ignored questions of gender.
16. This was the title of the English poet Coventry Patmore's poem of 1854, rewritten in 1862, in which he writes about the Victorian ideal of woman. It was this poem that Virginia Woolf quoted in 1931, and said that the task of the female writer was to kill the angel of the house.
17. See Jacqueline Bel, 'De mystiek in de Nederlandse letterkunde rond de eeuwwisseling', *Forum der Letteren* (1986), 81–91.
18. Bram Dijkstra, *Idols of Perversity: Fantasies of the Feminine Evil in the Fin-de-siècle Culture* (Oxford: Oxford University Press, 1986).
19. Frederik van Eeden, *Van de koele meren des doods* (Amsterdam: Salamander, 1983); *Deeps of Deliverance*, trans. by Margaret Robinson (London: Fisher Unwin, 1902).
20. Judit Gera, 'Frederik van Eeden Van de koele meren des doods című regénye mint a holland századvég problémáinak művészi szintézise' (Frederik van Eeden's Novel *Deeps of Deliverance* as the Artistic Synthesis of the Dutch Fin-de-Siècle) (unpublished doctoral thesis, Eötvös Loránd University, Budapest, 1991).
21. Judit Gera, 'Frederik van Eeden: Feminist of Antifeminist', *Mededelingen van het Frederik van Eeden Genootschap*, 44 (1999), 20–27.
22. Jan Fontijn, *Tweespalt: Het leven van Frederik van Eeden tot 1901* (Amsterdam: Querido, 1990).
23. Jane Fenoulhet, 'The Individual Asserts Herself', in *Making the Personal Political: Dutch Women Writers 1919–1970* (London: Modern Humanities Research Association and Maney Publishing, 2007), pp. 40–61.
24. C. M. Meijers, 'Intree in de maatschappij', in *Van moeder op dochter: De maatschappelijke positie van de vrouw in Nederland vanaf de Franse tijd*, ed. by W. H. Posthumus-van der Groot and others (Nijmegen: SUN, 1968), pp. 109–218.
25. For example J. M. J. Sicking, *Overgave en Verzet: De levens- en wereldbeschouwing van Carry van Bruggen* (Groningen: Passage, 1993).
26. Carry van Bruggen, *Eva* (Amsterdam: Querido, 1993), p. 188.
27. Ibid., p. 154.
28. Ibid., p. 162.
29. Ibid., p. 188.
30. 2 Samuel 5:24 The King James Bible.
31. Van Bruggen, p. 174.
32. Arthur Japin, *Een schitterend gebrek* (Amsterdam: De Arbeiderspers, 2003); *In Lucia's Eyes*, trans. by David Colmer (London: Chatto & Windus, 2005).
33. Jacques Lacan, *The Language of the Self: The Function of Language in Psychoanalysis*, trans. and ed. by Anthony Wilden (Baltimore: Johns Hopkins Press, 1968).
34. Ian Buchanan, *A Dictionary of Critical Theory* (Oxford: Oxford University Press, 2010), p. 322.
35. Odile Heynders, *Correspondenties. Gedichten lezen met gedichten* (Amsterdam: Amsterdam University Press, 2006).
36. Ibid., p. 20.

BIBLIOGRAPHY

ABEL, E., M. HIRSCH, and E. LANGLAND, eds, *The Voyage In: Fictions of Female Development* (Hanover and London: University Press of New England, 1983)
ALPERS, SVETLANA, *The Art of Describing: Dutch Art in the Seventeenth Century* (Chicago: University of Chicago Press, 1984)
ALPHEN, E. VAN, *Bang voor schennis? Inleiding in de ideologiekritiek* (Utrecht: Hes, 1987)
BAKHTIN, MIKHAIL M., 'The Bildungsroman and its Significance in the History of Realism: Toward a Historical Typology of the Novel', in *Speech Genres and Other Late Essays*, ed. by Caryl Emerson and Michael Holquist (Austin: University of Texas Press, 1986). pp. 10–59
BAL, MIEKE, 'Notes on Narrative Embedding', *Poetics Today*, 2.2 (1981), 41–59
—— 'Reading as Empowerment: Teaching the Bible from a Feminist Perspective', in *Teaching the Bible as Literature in Translation*, ed. by Barry N. Olhsen and Yael S. Feldman (New York: Modern Language Association of America, 1989), pp. 87–92
—— *De theorie van vertellen en verhalen. Inleiding in de narratologie* (Muiderberg: Coutinho), 1990)
—— *Narratology: Introduction to the Theory of Narrative* (Toronto: University of Toronto Press 1997)
BALAKIAN, ANNA, 'The Unfamiliar Literatures', in *The Snowflake on the Belfry: Dogma and Disquietude in the Critical Arena* (Bloomington and Indianapolis: Indiana University Press, 1994), pp. 236–40
BANK, J and BUUREN, M. VAN, *1900· Hoogtij van burgerlijke cultuur* (Den Haag: Sdu, 2000)
BAREND-VAN HAEFTEN, MARIJKE, 'Van scheepsjournaal tot reisverhaal: een kennismaking met zeventiende-eeuwse reisteksten', *Literatuur*, 7 (1990), 222–28
BASTET, F. L., *Louis Couperus: Een biografie* (Amsterdam: Querido, 1987)
Beatrijs: Een Middeleeuws Maria-Mirakel, ed. and introduced by Theo Meder (Amsterdam: Prometheus/Bakker, 1995)
BEEKMAN, E. M., *Troubled Pleasures: Dutch Colonial Literature from the East Indies 1600–1950* (Oxford: Clarendon Press, 1996)
BEETS, N., *De bevrijding der slaven. Redevoering gehouden in openbare vergaderingen van de Nederlandsche Maatschappy ter bevordering van de afschaffing der slaverny* (Haarlem: Bohn, 1856)
—— *Camera Obscura en verspreide stukken* (Utrecht and Antwerp: Veen, 1982)
—— *Camera Obscura*, ed. by Willem van den Berg, Henk Eijssens, Joost Kloek, and Peter van Zonneveld (Amsterdam:Athenaeum–Polak & Van Gennep, 1998)
BEL, JACQUELINE, *Nederlandse literatuur in het fin-de-siècle: een receptie-historisch overzicht van het proza tussen 1885 en 1900* (Amsterdam: Amsterdam University Press, 1993)
—— 'Mansfield Park versus de Camera Obscura. "De familie Kegge" als koloniaal verhaal', in *Literatuurwetenschap tussen betrokkenheid en distantie*, ed. by Liesbeth Korthals Altes and Dick Schram (Assen: Van Gorcum, 2000), pp. 375–86
—— 'De mystiek in de Nederlandse letterkunde rond de eeuwwisseling', *Forum der Letteren* (1986), 81–91
BETTELHEIM, BRUNO, *The Uses of Enchantment: The Meaning and Importance of Fairy Tales* (New York: Knopf, 1976)

BHABHA, HOMI K., *The Location of Culture* (London: Routledge, 1994)
BLAU DUPLESSIS, RACHEL, *Writing beyond the Ending: Narrative Strategies of Twentieth-Century Women Writers* (Bloomington: Indiana University Press, 1985)
BÓKAY, ANTAL, *Bevezetés az irodalomtudományba* (Budapest: Osiris, 2006)
BONTEKOE, *Memorable Description of the East Indian Voyage: 1618–25*, trans. by C. B. Bodde-Hodgkinson and Pieter Geyl, with an Introduction and Notes by Pieter Geyl (New York: Robert M. McBride & Company 1929)
BOOTH, WAYNE, *The Rhetoric of Fiction* (Chicago: University of Chicago Press, 1961)
BORK, G. J. VAN, 'Enkele sociale aspecten van "de familie Kegge"', *Spektator*, 4 (1974–75), 284–88
BOSTOEN, KAREL, 'Held in een bloedstollend drama', in *Bontekoe. De schipper, het journaal, de scheepsjongens*, ed. by K. Bostoen and others (Amsterdam and Zutphen: Walburg Pers, 1996), pp. 41–52
BOVEN, ERICA VAN, *Een hoofdstuk apart. 'Vrouwenromans' in de literaire kritiek 1898–1930* (Amsterdam: Sara/Van Gennep, 1992)
BRAAK, MENNO TER, 'De roman als document. M. H. Székely-Lulofs: De Andere Wereld', *Het Vaderland*, 11 March (1934)
——*Verzameld Werk. Deel 4* (Amsterdam: G. A. Van Oorschot, 1951)
BRUGGEN, CARRY VAN, *Eva* (Amsterdam: Querido, 1993)
BUCHANAN, IAN, *A Dictionary of Critical Theory* (Oxford: Oxford University Press, 2010)
BUIJNSTERS, P. J., 'Sara Burgerhart en de ontwikkeling van de Nederlandse roman', in *Nederlandse literatuur van de achttiende eeuw* (Utrecht: HES Uitgevers, 1984), pp. 199–222
CHAMPFLEURY [Jules François Felix Fleury-Husson], *Le realisme* (Paris: M. Lévy frères, 1857)
CIXOUS, HÉLÈNE and CLÉMENT, CATHERINE, *The Newly Born Woman*, trans. by Betsy Wing (Minneapolis and Manchester: University of Minnesota Press, 1986)
COUPERUS, LOUIS, *The Footsteps of Fate*, trans. by Clara Bell (London: William Heinemann, 1891), p. 46.
——*Extasy*, trans. by Teixeira de Mattos and John Gray (London: H. Henry, 1897).
——*Langs lijnen van geleidelijkheid (The Inevitable)* (Amsterdam: L. J. Veen, 1900).
——'Wonderlijke historiën. De badkamer', *Haagsche Post*, 20 January (1917)
——*The Inevitable*, trans. by Alexander Teixeira de Mattos (New York: Dood, Mead & Company, 1920).
——*De stille kracht* (Amsterdam: Querido, 1991)
——*Noodlot (The Footsteps of Fate)* (Wageningen: L. J. Veen, 1978), p. 92
——*The Hidden Force*, trans. by Alexander Teixeira De Mattos, with an Introduction by E. M. Beekman (London: Quartet Books Ltd., 1992)
CRARY, JONATHAN, *Techniques of the Observer: On Vision and Modernity in the 19th Century* (Cambridge, MA: The MIT Press, 1992)
CRENSHAW, KIMBERLÉ W., 'Demarginalizing the Intersection of Race and Sex: A Black Feminist Critique of Antidiscrimination Doctrine, Feminist Theory and Antiracist Politics', *University of Chicago Legal Forum* (1989), 139–67
DEKEN, AAGJE and WOLFF, BETJE, *De historie van mejuffrouw Sara Burgerhart* (Amsterdam: Wereldbibliotheek, n.d.)
DEKKER, RUDOLF, *Meer verleden dan toekomst. Geschiedenis van verdwijnend Nederland* (Amsterdam: Bert Bakker, 2008)
DEVENTER, C. TH. VAN, 'Een eereschuld', *De Gids*, 63.3 (1899), 205–57
DEYSSEL, LODEWIJK VAN, 'Over Louis Couperus', *Tweemaandelijksch Tijdschrift*, I. 4 (1895), 1–20
——'G. van Hulzen en Louis Couperus', in *Verzamelde opstellen*, VII (Amsterdam: Scheltema en Holtema's Boekhandel, 1904), pp. 1–10

D'HAEN, THEO, ed., *Europa buitengaats. Koloniale en postkoloniale literaturen in Europese talen* (Amsterdam: Bert Bakker, 2002)
DICKENS, CHARLES, *Sketches by Boz* (London: John Macrone, 1837)
DIJKSTRA, BRAM, *Idols of Perversity: Fantasies of the Feminine Evil in the Fin-de-siècle Culture* (Oxford: Oxford University Press, 1986)
DOEL, WIM VAN DEN, *Zo ver de wereld strekt. De geschiedenis van Nederland overzee vanaf 1800* (Amsterdam:Prometheus, 2011)
EAGLETON, TERRY, *Ideology: An Introduction* (London and New York: Verso, 2007)
EEDEN, FREDERIK VAN, *Deeps of Deliverance*, transl. from Dutch by Margaret Robinson (London: Fisher Unwin, 1902)
——*Het paleis van Kirké* (Amsterdam: Versluys, 1910)
——*Johannes Viator* (Katwijk: Servire, 1979)
——*Van de koele meren des doods* (Amsterdam: Querido, 1983)
EMMER, PIET, *De Nederlandse slavenhandel 1500–1850* (Amsterdam and Antwerp: De Arbeiderspers, 2000)
——'De Max Havelaar: een pleidooi voor meer kolonialisme', *Nieuw Letterkundig Magazijn*, 27.1 May 2010, p. 12
ETTY, ELSBETH, 'Liever dood dan (seks)slaaf', *NRC*, 17 May 2010
EVEN-ZOHAR, ITAMAR, 'Polysystem Studies', *Poetics Today*, 11.1 (1990)
FABRICIUS, JOHAN, *De scheepjongens van Bontekoe* (Amsterdam: Leopold, 2003)
FANON, FRANZ, *Black Skin, White Masks*, trans. by Charles Lam Markmann (London: Pluto Press, 2008)
FASSEUR, CEES, *Onhoorbaar groeit de padi. Max Havelaar en de publieke zaak* (Amsterdam: Huis aan de Drie Grachten, 1987)
——*Indischgasten* (Amsterdam: Bert Bakker, 1996)
FEENBERG, ANNE-MARIE, '*Max Havelaar*: An Anti-Imperialist Novel', *MLN* 112.5 (1997), 817–35
FENOULHET, JANE, *Making the Personal Political: Dutch Women Writers 1919–1970* (London: Legenda, 2007)
FONTIJN, J., *Tweespalt: Het leven van Frederik van Eeden tot 1901* (Amsterdam: Querido, 1990)
FOUCAULT, MICHEL, *The Archeology of Knowledge*, trans. by A. M. Sheridan Smith (London and New York: Routledge, 2002)
FRERIKS, KESTER, *Madelon: het verborgen leven van Madelon Székely-Lulofs* (Amsterdam: Conserve, 2005)
FREUD, S., *The Question of Lay Analysis*, trans. by N. Proctor-Gregg (London: Image Pub. Co., 1947)
FRIJHOFF, WILLEM and SPIES, MARIJKE, *1650. Bevochten eendracht* (Den Haag: Sdu Uitgevers, 1999)
GALEN, JOHN JANSEN VAN, 'De vrouw achter rubber', *Haagse Post*, 13 July 1985.
GERA, JUDIT, 'Beatrijs en haar latere zusters. Narratieve structuren van de vrouwelijke ontwikkleingsverhalen', in *Lage Lande Studies 6. Beatrijs de wereld in. Vertalingen van het Middelnederlandse verhaal*, ed. by Ton van Kalmthout, Orsolya Réthelyi, and Remco Sleiderink (Gent: Academia Press, 2013), pp. 369–84
GERA, JUDIT, 'Frederik van Eeden Van de koele meren des doods című regénye mint a holland századvég problémáinak művészi szintézise' (unpublished doctoral thesis, Eötvös Loránd University, Budapest, 1991)
——'Stages in the Development of Dutch Fiction', *Neohelicon*, 18.1 (1991), 225–38
——'Frederik van Eeden: Feminist of Antifeminist?', *Mededelingen van het Frederik van Eeden Genootschap*, 44 (1999), 20–27
——*Van een afstand. Multatuli's Max Havelaar tegendraads gelezen* (Amsterdam: Veen, 2001)
——'De stem van Kirke. Een feministische lezing van "De zwijnen van Kirkè" van Karel van de Woestijne', *Tijdschrift voor genderstudies*, 7.2 (2004), 15–26

——'(Anti-)Koloniale tekststrategieën in *Tjoet Nja Din*', in *Madelon Lulofs. Acta Neerlandica. Bijdragen tot de neerlandistiek in Debrecen* 5, (2007), 145–68

——'The Meaning of Silence in *Max Havelaar*', in *150 Jahre Max Havelaar. Multatulis Roman aus neuer Perspective*, ed. by Jaap Grave, Olf Praamstra, and Hans Vandevoorde (Frankfurt am Main: Peter Lang, 2012), pp. 125–32

——'Momenten van zelfreflectie. Maaike Meijer: De lust tot lezen. Nederlandse dichteressen en het literaire systeem, *Internationale Neerlandistiek*, 50 (2012), 82–84

——'De stille kracht van Couperus als roman van hybridisatie', *Acta Neerlandica, Bijdragen tot de neerlandistiek Debrecen*, 9 (2012), 87–96

——and A. Agnes Sneller, *Inleiding literatuurgeschiedenis voor de internationale neerlandistiek* (Hilversum: Verloren, 2010)

GOEDEGEBUURE, JAAP, '"Rubber", een bestseller uit de jaren dertig', *Literatuur*, 1 (1984), 22–27

HAASSE, HELLA S., 'Overeenkomstig en vergelijkbaar', in *Lezen achter de letters* (Amsterdam: Querido, 2000), pp. 7–24

HERMAN, LUC and VERVAECK, BART, *Vertelduivels. Handboek verhaalanalyse* (Brussels and Nijmegen: Vantilt, 2002)

HEYNDERS, ODILE, *Correspondenties. Gedichten lezen met gedichten* (Amsterdam: Amsterdam University Press, 2006)

HOMER, *The Odyssey*, trans. by Robert Fagles (London: Penguin Books, 1997)

HOMERUS, *Odyssee*, trans. by Imme Dros (Amsterdam: Athenaeum, 1996)

HULSMAN, G., 'Louis Couperus I–II–III', *Stemmen voor Waarheid en Vrede*, 33, March (1896), pp. 36–76; 113–52; 209–55

ISER, WOLFGANG, *The Act of Reading: A Theory of Aesthetic Response* (Baltimore and London: The John Hopkins University Press, 1978)

JAPIN, ARTHUR, *Een schitterend gebrek* (Amsterdam: De Arbeiderspers, 2003)

——*In Lucia's Eyes*, trans. by David Colmer (London: Chatto & Windus, 2005)

KELK, J. C., 'Historie contra heldendicht', *De Groene Amsterdammer*, 12 June 1948

KEMPEN, MICHIEL VAN, *Een geschiedenis van de Surinaamse literatuur* (Paramaribo: Okopipi, 2002)

KUNENE, DANIEL P., 'Deculturation — The African Writer's Response', *Africa Today*, 15.4 (1968), 19–24

KOUSBROEK, RUDY, 'De boekhouders van de Nederlandse literatuur' *NRC/Handelsblad*, 8 July 1983

KOUSBROEK, RUDY, *Het Oost-Indisch kampsyndroom* (Amsterdam: Meulenhoff, 1992)

LABRIE, A., 'Romantische politiek. Moderniteit en het ideaal van de zuivere gemeenschap', in *De zieke natie. Over de medicalisering van de matschappij 1860–1914*, ed. by Liesbet Nys, Henk de Smaele, Jo Tollebeek, and Kaat Wils (Groningen: Historische Uitgeverij, 2002), pp. 58–73

LACAN, JACQUES, *The Language of the Self: The Function of Language in Psychoanalysis*, trans. and ed. by Anthony Wilden (Baltimore: Johns Hopkins Press, 1968)

LANSER, SUSAN S., 'Toward a Feminist Narratology', in *Feminisms: An Anthology of Literary Theory and Criticism*, ed. by R. R. Warhol and D. Price Herndl (New Brunswick, NJ: Rutgers University Press, 1991), pp. 674–93

LINSCHOTEN, JAN HUYGEN VAN, *Itinerario, voyage ofte schipvaert naer Oost ofte Portugaels Indien* (Den Haag: Martinus Nijhoff, 1955)

LOOMBA, ANIA, *Colonialism/Postcolonialism* (London and New York: Routledge, 1998)

LULOFS, F., 'Inleiding', in *Beatrijs* (Leiden: Martinus Nijhoff, 1983), pp. 7–24

MAAS, NOP, *Multatuli voor iedereen (maar niemand voor Multatuli)* (Nijmegen: Vantilt, 2000)

MARRES, RENÉ, 'Is de antikoloniale roman Rubber van Székely-Lulofs racistisch?', in René Marres, *Zogenaamde politieke incorrectheid in Nederlandse literatuur, ideologiekritiek in analyse*

(Leiden: Internationaal Forum voor Afrikaanse en Nederlandse Taal en Letteren, 1998), pp. 74–81

MEIJER, MAAIKE, 'Vrome en geleerde hartsvriendinnen in de achttiende eeuw in Nederland', in *Onder mannen, onder vrouwen: Studies van homosociale emancipatie*, ed. by M. Duyves, G. Hekma, and P. Koelemij (Amsterdam: SUA, 1984), pp. 167–78

——*De lust tot lezen: Nederlandse dichteressen en het literaire systeem* (Amsterdam: Sara/Van Gennep, 1988)

——*In tekst gevat: Inleiding tot een kritiek van representatie* (Amsterdam: Amsterdam University Press, 1996)

MEIJERS, C. M., 'Intree in de maatschappij', in *Van moeder op dochter: De maatschappelijke positie van de vrouw in Nederland vanaf de Franse tijd*, ed. by W. H. Posthumus-van der Groot and others (Nijmegen: Sun, 1968), pp. 109–218

MEULEN, DIK VAN DER, *Multatuli. Leven en werk van Eduard Douwes Dekker* (Amsterdam: Sun, 2002)

MILLER, NANCY K., *The Heroine's Text: Readings in the French and English Novel, 1722–1782* (New York: Columbia University Press, 1980)

MONT, POL DE, 'Louis Couperus', in Louis Couperus, *Een zieltje* (Gent: Hoste, 1893), pp. 1–2

MOORMAN, E. M. and UITTERHOEVE, WILFRIED, *Van Achilleus tot Zeus: Thema's uit de klassieke mythologie in literatuur, muziek, beeldende kunst en theater* (Nijmegen: Sun, 1987)

MORRISON, TONI, *Playing in the Dark: Whiteness and the Literary Imagination* (Cambridge, MA, and London: Harvard University Press, 1992).

MULTATULI, *Max Havelaar of de koffiveilingen der Nederlandsche Handelmaatschappij* (Amsterdam: Wereldbibliotheek, 1932)

——*Max Havelaar or the Coffee Auctions of the Dutch Trading Company*, trans. by Roy Edwards (Leiden: Sijthoff; London Heinemann, London House & Maxwell New York, 1967)

MUSSCHOOT, ANNE MARIE, 'Karel van de Woestijne en het symbolisme', in *Op voet van gelijkheid. Opstellen van Anne Marie Musschoot*, ed. by Yves T'Sjoen and Hans Vandevoorde (Gent: Studia Germanica Gandensia, 1994), pp. 101–24

NIEKERK, C. H., 'Race and Gender in Multatuli's Max Havelaar and Love Letters', in *One Hundred Years of Masochism: Literary Texts, Social and Cultural Contexts*, ed. by M. C. Finke and C. H. Niekerk (Amsterdam and Atlanta: Rodopi, 2000), pp. 171–90

NIEUWENHUYS, ROB, 'De onbegrepen stille kracht', *Haagse Post*, 37 (1974), pp. 46–49

——*Oost-Indische spiegel. Wat Nederlandse schrijvers en dichters over Indonesië hebben geschreven vanaf de eerste jaren der Compagnie tot op heden* (Amsterdam: Querido, 1978)

——, PAASMAN, BERT, and ZONNEVELD, PETER VAN, *De geschiedenis van de Indisch-Nederlandse letterkunde. Oost-Indisch Magazijn* (Amsterdam: Bulkboek, 1990)

NOUHUYS, W. G. VAN, 'De stille kracht', *Het Vaderland*, November 1900

OKKER, FRANK, *Tumult. Het levensverhaal van Madelon Székely-Lulofs* (Amsterdam: Atlas, 2008)

OOSTRUM, D. C. VAN, 'Sneezes and Lies: Female Voices in Multatuli's Max Havelaar', in D. C. van Oostrum, *Male Authors, Female Subjects: The Woman within/beyond the Borders of Henry Adams, Henry James, and others* (Amsterdam: Rodopi, 1995), pp. 47–69

OVERSTEEGEN, J. J., 'De organisatie van Max Havelaar', *Merlyn*, 1 (1962–63), 20–45

——*Vorm of vent?* (Amsterdam: Athenaeum, 1969)

——'Uit de donkere dagen van voor Freud', in *De Novembristen van Merlyn. Een literatuuropvatting in theorie en praktijk* (Utrecht: HES Uitgevers, 1983)

PAASMAN, BERT, 'De Indisch-Nederlandse literatuur uit de VOC-tijd', in *Europa buitengaats. Koloniale en postkoloniale literaturen in Europese talen*, ed. by Theo D'haen (Amsterdam: Bert Bakker, 2002), pp. 33–97

PATTYNAMA, PAMELA, 'Secrets and Danger: Interracial Sexuality in Louis Couperus's *The Hidden Force* and the Dutch Colonial Culture around 1900', in *Domesticating the Empire:*

Race, Gender and Family Life in French and Dutch Colonialism, ed. by Julia Clancy-Smith and Frances Gouda (Charlottesville and London: The University Press of Virginia, 1998), pp. 84–107

PETERSON, KARIN, 'Feit en fictie. De verbeelding van de Atjeh-oorlog in de romans van Madelon Székely-Lulofs', in *Atjeh: de verbeelding van een koloniale oorlog*, ed. by Liesbeth Dolk (Amsterdam: Bert Bakker, 2001), pp. 117–28, 211–12

PIETERSE, SASKIA, *De buik van de lezer. Over spreken en schrijven in Multatuli's Ideën* (Nijmegen: Vantilt, 2008)

PORTEMAN, KAREL and SMITS-VELDT, MIEKE B., *Een nieuw vaderland voor de muzen. Geschiedenis van de Nederlandse literatuur 1650–1700* (Amsterdam: Bert Bakker, 2008)

POTGIETER, E. J., *Liedekens van Bontekoe* in E. J. Potgieter, *De werken. Deel 12. Verspreide en nagelaten poëzy*. Deel 2. (Haarlem: H. D. Tjeenk Willink, 1896), pp. 1–52

PRAAMSTRA, OLF, and PUSZTAI, GÁBOR, 'Een "lasterlijk geschrijf": kritiek en (zelf)censuur in de Nederlands-Indische literatuur; de ontvangst van László Székely's Van oerwoud tot plantage (1935)', *Indische Letteren*, 12 (1997), 98–124

PRAAMSTRA, OLF and TERMORSHUIZEN, GERARD, 'Inleiding', in Madelon Székely-Lulofs, *Doekoen* (Leiden: Koninklijk Instituut voor Taal- Land- en Volkenkunde, 2001), pp. 7–22

——'Madelon Székely-Lulofs en het koloniale discours', *Indische Letteren*, 22 (2007), 209–39

PRATT, MARY LOUISE, 'Arts of the Contact Zone', *Profession*, 91 (1991), pp. 33–40

PUSZTAI, GÁBOR and TERMORSHUIZEN, GERARD, 'De tweede man. Het huwelijk van Madelon Lulofs en László Székely', *Acta Neerlandica. Bijdragen tot de Neerlandistiek Debrecen*, 5 (2007), 49–62

RAEMDONCK, BERT VAN, ed., *Niks geniaal vandaag. De briefwisseling tussen Karel van de Woestijne en Emmanuel de Bom* (Kapellen: Pelckmans, 2010)

ROEPER, VIBEKE, 'Inleiding', in *Het Journaal van Bontekoe* (Amsterdam: Athenaeum–Polak & Van Gennep, 2001)

ROEPER, VIBEKE and WILDEMAN, DIEDERICK, 'Schipper Bontekoe', in *Bontekoe. De schipper, het journaal, de scheepsjongens*, ed. by K. Bostoen and others (Amsterdam: Scheepvaartmuseum; Zutphen: Walburg Pers, 1996), pp. 9–34

SAID, EDWARD, *Orientalism* (London: Vintage Books, 1979)

SALVERDA, REINIER, 'Beeld en tegenbeeld van het koloniale verleden', in *Rekenschap 1650–2000*, ed. by D. Fokkema and F. Grijzenhout (Den Haag: Sdu Uitgevers, 2001), pp. 71–114

SICKING, J. M. J., *Overgave en Verzet: De levens- en wereldbeschouwing van Carry van Bruggen* (Groningen: Passage, 1993)

SÖTEMANN, A. L., *De structuur van Max Havelaar* (Groningen: Wolters-Noordhoff, 1981)

SPIVAK, G. C., 'Can the Subaltern Speak? Speculations on Widow-Sacrifice', *Wedge*, 7/8 (1985), 120–30

STERNE, LAWRENCE, *The Life and Opinions of Tristram Shandy* (Harmondsworth: Penguin Books Ltd, 1983)

SWINNEN, AAGJE, *Het slot ontvlucht. De 'vrouwelijke' Bildungsroman in de Nederlandse literatuur* (Amsterdam: Amsterdam University Press, 2006)

SZÉKELY-LULOFS, MADELON, *Koeli* (Bussum: F.G. Kroonder, 1931)

——*Rubber, roman uit Deli* (Amsterdam: Het Wereldvenster, 1931)

——*De Hongertocht* (Amsterdam:Elsevier, 1936)

——*Tjoet Nja Din. De geschiedenis van een Atjehse vorstin* (Den Haag: Thomas & Eras, 1985)

——*Weet je nog wel ... een boek vol pluche en pleizier* (Den Haag: De Bezige Bij, 1957)

TALLY, ROBERT T., *Spatiality: The New Critical Idiom* (London: Routledge, 2013)

VALENT, MARION, 'Over "De stille kracht" van Louis Couperus', *Literatuur*, 1 (1984), 203–09

VANDEVOORDE, HANS, 'De onmacht die hem sarrend sloeg. Over Karel van de Woestijne', in *Brussel en het fin-de-siècle. 100 jaar Van Nu en Straks*, ed. by Frank de Crits (Antwerp and Baarn: Houtekiet, 1993), pp. 105–16
VEER, P. VAN 't, 'De biografie van J. A. Kegge (1796–1854)', *Hollands Maandblad*, 15.312 (1973), 39–42
VERSTEEG, COOS, 'Een doodgezwegen roman herdrukt', *Haagsche Courant*, 31 May 1985
VINCENT, PAUL, 'Louis Couperus (1863–1923), Dutch Novelist, Short Story Writer and Poet', in *Encyclopedia of Literary Translation into English: A–L*, I, ed. by Olive Classe (London: Fitzroy Dearborn Publishers, 2000), pp. 314–15
WIJNGAARD, COCK VAN DEN, 'Madelon Lulofs (1899–1958)', *Bzzlletin* (1983), 110
WOESTIJNE, KAREL VAN DE, 'De zwijnen van Kirkè', in K. van de Woestijne, *Verzameld Werk*, III: *Verhalen en parabelen* (Bussum: C. A. J. van Dishoeck, 1947), pp. 120–37
WRIGHT, E., 'De kolonisatie van de tekst', in *Literatuur in psychoanalytisch perspectief: een inleiding met interpretaties van Multatuli's 'Saïdjah en Adinda'*, trans. by J. C. van Meurs, ed. by H. Hillenaar and W. Schönau (Amsterdam and Atlanta: Rodopi), pp. 148–64
ZOOK, DARREN C., 'Searching for *Max Havelaar*: Multatuli, Colonial History, and the Confusion of Empire', *Modern Language Notes*, 121.5 (2007), 1169–89
YARNALL, JUDITH, *Transformations of Circe: The History of the Enchantress* (Urbana and Chicago: University of Illinois Press, 1994)
ZONNEVELD, PETER VAN, *De Romantische Club: Leidse student-auteurs 1830–1840* (Leiden: Athanae Batavae, 1993)

INDEX

Abel, E., Hirsch, Marianne and Langland, E. 161, 162, 170
  The Voyage In: Fictions of Female Development 187 n. 1
abolition 39, 60
Alpers, Svetlana 24, 61
  The Art of Describing: Dutch Art in the Seventeenth Century 35 n. 16
Alphen, Ernst van 3, 6
  Bang voor schennis? Inleiding in de ideologiekritiek 9 n. 9
Amir 135
Austen, Jane:
  Mansfield Park 7, 51

Bakhtin, Mikhail 5, 162
  'The Bildungsroman and its Significance in the History of Realism: Toward a Historical Typology of the Novel' 187 n. 6
Bal Mieke, 4, 6
  De theorie van vertellen en verhalen. Inleiding in de narratologie 10 n. 11
  'Notes on Narrative Embedding' 160 n. 12
Balakian, Anna 6, 45
  'The Unfamiliar Literatures' 6, 10 n. 16, 61 n. 14
Barend van-Haeften, Marijke 14, 15, 34
  'Van scheepsjournaal tot reisverhaal: een kennismaking met zeventiende-eeuwse reisteksten' 35 n. 6
Barth, Roland 4
Bastet, F. L. 106, 107, 119
  Louis Couperus. Een biografie 120 n. 15
Batavia 13, 18, 19, 20, 21, 28, 106, 108, 111, 114, 133
Beatrijs 8, 162, 164, 165, 185, 186, 187
Beecher Stowe, Harriet:
  Uncle Tom's Cabin or Life among the Lowly 39
Beek, Relus ter 122
Beekman, E.M. 92
  Troubled Pleasures: Dutch Colonial Literature from the East Indies 1600–1950 99 n. 76
Beets, Nicolaas 7, 37, 40, 42, 43, 45, 46, 48, 50, 51, 56–61, 93
  life 42–43
  reviews/criticism 43–51
  style of writing/themes 51–61
  works:
    Camera Obscura 40, 42, 43, 45, 50, 54
    'De Bevrijding der Slaven' 60
    'De familie Kegge' 7, 40, 51
    'De familie Stastok', 45, 48–49
    De Nederlanden 58
    'Een onaangenaam mensch in den Haarlemmerhout' 46, 48
    'Proeve eener hulde aan Sir Walter Scott' 42
Bel, Jacquelin 7, 107
  'Mansfield Park versus de Camera Obscura. "De familie Kegge" als koloniaal verhaal' 61 n. 8
  Nederlandse literatuur in het fin de siècle. Een receptiehistorisch overzicht van het proza tussen 1885 en 1900 120 n. 19
  'De mystiek in de Nederlandse letterkunde rond de eeuwwisseling' 188 n. 17
Berg, Willem van den , Eijssens, Henk, Kloek, Joost, and Zonneveld, Peter van 7
  'Inleiding' 10 n. 18.
Bettelheim, Bruno 165
  The Uses of Enchantment: The Meaning and Importance of Fairy Tales 187 n. 10.
Bexc, Jeronimus II. 12
Bhabha, Homi K. 8, 110, 112, 116
  ambivalence 8, 102, 110–14, 118, 119
  hybridity 8, 101, 112, 114, 115, 117, 118, 119
  The Location of Culture 120 n. 23
  mimicry 8, 112, 113, 114, 118, 119
Bible 15, 26, 58, 94, 95, 181, 184
Bilderdijk, Willem 42, 43
Bildungsroman 161
Blau DuPlessis, Rachel 162
  Writing beyond the Ending: Narrative Strategies of Twentieth-Century Women Writers 187 n. 5
Bom, Emmanuel de 151
Bontekoe, Willem Ysbrandtszoon 7, 11, 16, 18, 19, 20, 21
  life 16–18, 21, 24
  reviews/criticism 16–21
  style of writing/themes 24–32
  Journael 7, 11, 16, 19, 20, 21, 24, 25, 27, 28, 31, 32, 34
Bork, G. J. van 56
  'Enkele sociale aspecten van de "Familie Kegge" 62 n. 23
Bostoen, Karel 19, 34
  'Held in een bloedstollend drama' 35 n. 9
bourgeois 43, 51, 78, 96, 166, 172, 175
Braak, Menno ter 64, 69, 105, 124
  'Multatuli, Droogstoppel, Havelaar' 98 n. 14

'De roman als document. M. H. Székely-Lulofs: De Andere Wereld' 147 n. 5
Brooshooft, Pieter:
'De ethische koers in de koloniale politiek' 102
Bruggen, Carry van 8, 178
life 178
style of writing/themes 178–81
Eva 8, 178, 181
Bulwer-Lytton, Edward:
The Student. Tales and Essays 45

canon 72
literary 7, 16, 40, 66
Cappelle, J. P. van:
Bijdragen tot de Geschiedenis der Wetenschappen en Letteren in Nederland 33
Chalon, Louis 151
Champfleury:
Le réalisme 43, 61 n. 13
Circe 8, 149–59, 171
citoyen 78
Cixous, Hélène 150, 157
with Clément, Catherine, *The Newly Born Woman* 160 n. 4
Coeman, Jacob 13
The Batavian Senior Merchant Pieter Cnoll and his Family 13
Coen, Jan Pieterszoon 13, 19, 20, 21, 24, 25, 30, 34, 133
Colijn, Hendricus 34
(post)colonial 1, 3, 6, 7, 9, 11, 34, 66, 67, 73, 74, 91, 92, 102, 110, 112, 116, 126, 138, 140, 142, 146, 149
Compagnie 139
van Verre 12
Vereenigde Oost-Indische 12, 70, see also: VOC
West-Indische 37
contact zone 7, 9, 21, 30, 34, 55, 133, 134
corresponding reading 8
Costa, Isaäc de 56
'1648 en 1838' 56
Couperus, Louis 7, 51, 101, 102, 104, 105, 106, 107, 108, 115, 119, 129, 131
life 102–04
reviews/criticism 104–08
style of writing/themes 108–19
works:
De stille kracht 7, 101, 102, 115, 117, 119, 131
Eline Vere 104, 105, 108
Epiloog 105
Extase 105
Illusie 105
Langs lijnen van gelijdelijkheid 108
Majesteit 105
Noodlot 104, 108
Raadsels 105
'Wonderlijke historiën. De badkamer' 120 n. 17

Crary, Jonathan 50
Techniques of the Observer: On Vision and Modernity in the 19th Century 61 n. 21
Crenshaw, Kimberlé 73
'Demarginalizing the Intersection of Race and Sex: A Black Feminist Critique of Antidiscrimination Doctrine, Feminist Theory and Antiracist Politics' 98 n. 18
cultuurkamer 127, 136
cultuurstelsel 63
Curie, Eva 135

Daendels, Herman Willem 82
Damsté, H.T. 134, 135
Darwin, Charles 173
Daum, P.A. 51, 129
Debussy, Claude 154
Deken, Aagje and Wolff, Betje: 8, 166, 168
life: 166
style of writing/themes 167, 168–72
works:
Historie van mejuffrouw Sara Burgerhart 8, 166, 168, 170, 186, 187
Historie van den heer Willem Leevend 166
Historie van mejuffrouw Cornelia Wildschut 167
Deutel, Jan Jansz. 16, 19, 20, 21, 24
De Huwelyckx Weeg-schaal, 19
Een kort tractaetje tegen de toovery 19
Deventer, Ch. T. van: 101, 105, 106
'Een eereschuld' 101
Deyssel, Lodewijk van 104, 105, 106
'Over Louis Couperus' 119 n. 9
G. van Hulsen en Louis Couperus' 119 n. 11
D' haen, Theo 20
Europa buitengaats. Koloniale en postkoloniale literaturen in Europese talen 35 n. 12
Dickens, Charles 43, 50
Sketches by Boz. Scenes, Tales, Characters 45
'London Recreations' 45–46
Disraeli, Benjamin:
Tancred 80
Doel, Wim van den 129
Zo ver de wereld strekt. De geschiedenis van Nederland overzee vanaf 1800 61 n. 4
Doppelgänger-motif 96
Dostoevsky, F. M. 78
The Double 98 n. 26
Dekker, Eduard Douwes 72, 77; see also Multatuli
Dekker, Rudolf 11, 63
Meer verleden dan toekomst. Geschiedenis van verdwijnend Nederland 35 n. 2
Dijkstra, Bram 151
Idols of Perversity: Fantasies of the Feminine Evil in the Fin-de-siècle Culture 160 n. 5
Dokarim 134, 135, 139, 143
Hikajat Prang Kompeuni 134

Drees, Willem 147
Druten, Jan van 34
Dutch colonization 11, 18, 21, 24, 37, 72, 101, 134

Eagleton, Terry, 2
 Ideology: An Introduction 9 n. 3
East Indies 11, 12, 16, 18, 20, 21, 24, 25, 27, 28, 34, 38, 39, 72, 88, 92, 124, 142
 Dutch 4, 13, 63, 64, 70, 71, 75, 81,82, 84, 101, 102, 105, 106, 107, 111, 115, 116, 117, 119, 121, 122, 124, 127, 129, 130, 132
Eeden, Frederik van 8, 173, 175, 178
 life 173–75
 style of writing/themes 175–77
 works:
  Johannes Viator 178
  Van de koele meren des doods 8, 173, 175, 186, 187
Eighty Years War 12, 25
Emants, Marcellus:
 Een nagelaten bekentenis 171, 172
Emmer, Piet 11, 77
 De Nederlandse slavenhandel 1500–1850 11 35 n. 1
 'De Max Havelaar: een pleidooi voor meer kolonialisme' 98 n. 24
Engels, Friedrich 173
ethical politics 101, 102, 107, 111, 121
Etty, Elsbeth 94, 95, 96
 'Liever dood dan (seks)slaaf' 97 n. 8

Fabricius, Johan:
 De scheepjongens van Bontekoe 33
Fanon, Franz:
 Black Skin, White Masks 115
female development 8, 161, 162, 164, 170, 172, 178, 181, 185, 186
feminist criticism 4
Fenoulhet, Jane 9, 178
fin-de-siècle 8, 132, 151, 153, 158, 175, 189
focalizer, 4, 157
 embedded 81
focalization, 4, 80, 81, 91, 141, 162, 186
Foucault, Michel 39, 67, 102
Freriks, Kester 124–26
Frijhoff, Willem and Spies, Marijke 38
 1650. Bevochten eendracht 61 n.1.

Gamond, Isabelle Gatti de 153
Genette, Gerard 4, 5
gender 2, 3, 4, 5, 6, 8, 57, 73, 74, 82, 85, 91, 94, 110, 144, 149, 156, 157, 159, 161, 185
Goethe, Johann Wolfgang 43, 161
 Wilhelm Meister's Apprenticeship 161
Graaff, Nicolaas de:
 Reisen en de Oost-Indische Spiegel 15
Greimas, Algirdas Julien 162
Groot, Hugo de 33

Haasse, Hella S. 91
 'Overeenkomstig en vergelijkbaar' 99 n.75
Hacker, Arthur 151
Herman, Luc, 4
 with Vervaeck, Bart 4
 Vertelduivels. Handboek verhaalanalyse 10 n. 12
heteroglossia 92
Heutsz, J. B. van 102, 121, 122, 124, 128, 133, 136, 138, 146
 De onderwerping van Aceh 133
Heyden, Jan van der:
 Stilleven met rariteiten 27
Heynders, Odile 185, 186
 Correspondenties. Gedichten lezen met gedichten 24 n. 10
Heisterbach, Caesarius 164
Hildebrand 43, 45, 53, 56, 57; see also Nicolaas Beets
Hoëvell, Walter Robert van 13, 39
 Slaven en vrijen onder de Nederlandsche wet 39
Hoffmann, E.T.A. 78, 105
Homer 88, 150, 151, 155, 156, 157
 Iliad 151
 Odyssey 150
Hooft, Pieter Cornelisz. 19, 33
 Nederlandsche Historiën 19
Huizinga, Johan:
 Herfsttij der Middeleeuwen 131, 132
Hulsman, Gerrit 104, 105, 108
Hurgronje, C. Snouk 132, 134, 142
 De Atjehers 132
hybridity 8, 101, 112, 114, 115, 117, 118, 119

ideology 1–4, 6, 9, 13, 86, 126, 147
 colonial 16, 18, 20
 critical 67, 74, 75
 critique 13

Irving, Washington:
 The Sketch Book of Geoffrey Crayon, Gent. 45
Iser, Wolfgang 91

Japin, Arthur 8, 181
 style of writing/themes 184–85
 Een schitterend gebrek 8, 181, 186
Jonkman, J. A. 129
Joyce, James:
 Ulysses 150

Kempen, Michiel van 39, 40
Keyzer, Thomas de:
 Portret van Constantijn Huygens en zijn secretaris 27
Kloos, Willem 105
Kol, Henri van:
 Land en volk van Java 101
Koninklijk Nederlandsch Indisch Leger (KNIL) 64
Kousbroek, Rudy 124

Labrie, Arnold 52
  'Romantische politiek. Moderniteit en het ideaal van de zuivere gemeenschap' 62 n.24.
Laforgue, Jules:
  Moralités légendaires 154
Lanser, Susan S. 4, 5, 6, 8, 149, 156
  'Toward a Feminist Narratology' 10 n. 13
Lenthe, Alard van 122
Lessing, Gotthold Ephraim:
  Nathan, the Wise 88
Linschoten, Jan Huygen 11, 12, 15, 28
  Itinerario 11, 15
  Reys-Geschrift van de Navigatiën der Portugaloyers 12
Lipsius, Justus 19
locus amoenus 94
Loomba, Ania 81, 85, 86
Lukács, Georg 6

Maeterlinck, Maurice 151, 154
  Pelléas et Mélisande 154
Mallarmé, Stéphane:
  L'après-midi d'un faune 154
Marx, Karl 78, 173
Mary miracle 8, 164, 186
  legend 164
Meijer, Maaike, 2, 6, 8, 126, 138, 172
Merlyn 2, 64 188 n. 15
Miller, Nancy K. 162
mise en abyme 54, 80
mission civilisatrice 129
Mont, Pol de 105
Montaigne, Michel de 181
Morrison, Tony 8, 138
  Playing in the Dark 8, 138
Multatuli 7, 32, 51, 63, 64, 66, 67, 69, 72, 73, 74, 75, 77, 80, 82, 84, 86, 88, 89, 93, 94, 95, 97, 101, 111, 117, 119, 124, 129, 131 (see also Douwes Dekker)
  life 69–73
  reviews/criticism 64–75
  style of writing/themes 75–97
  works:
    Max Havelaar 7, 32, 63, 64, 66, 67, 73, 74, 90, 111, 124, 131, 142
    Ideën 84
Multatuli Genootschap 67
Musschoot, Anne Marie 154

narration 4, 5
  private 5
  public 5, 177, 178
  semi-private 177, 185
narrative level 5
  extradiegetic 5
    narrator 80, 156
  intradiegetic 5
    narrator 53
  metadiegetic 5

narratology 3, 4, 6
  classical 4
  feminist 4, 5, 6, 8, 149
  post-classical 3, 4
  traditional 5
Nederlandsche Handel-Maatschappij 63, 69
New York 37
Nieuw-Amsterdam 37
Nieuw-Holland 37
Nieuw-Nederland 37
Nieuwenhuys, Rob 106, 124, 135
Nijgh Lennaart 34

Okker, Frans 126
Oldenbarnevelt, Johan van 12
Oostrum, Duco van 93, 94, 95
Orange, Willem of 33, 53
Ortelius:
  Theatrum Orbis Terrarum 85
Oversteegen, J. J. 64, 66, 91, 171, 172
  Vorm of vent? 97 n. 2
  'De organisatie van Max Havelaar' 98 n. 23
  'Uit de donkere dagen van voor Freud' 187 n. 14

Paasman, Bert: 20, 21
  De Indisch-Nederlandse literatuur uit de VOC-tijd 20
palimpsest 128
Pattynama, Pamela 8, 110, 111, 112, 119
  interracial sexuality 8, 111
Perron, Edgar du 64, 124
Peterson, Karin 135
Pieterse, Saskia 66, 84, 85
plot 5,6, 8, 53, 54, 75, 107, 135, 136, 139, 155, 161, 162, 168, 167, 184
Poe, Edgar Ellen 105
politionele acties 127
Pope, Alexander:
  Essay on Man 166
Post, Elizabeth Maria:
  Reinhart, of natuur en godsdienst 32
Potgieter, Everhardus, Johannes 32, 33
Praamstra, Olf 124, 126, 130
Pratt, Mary Louise:
  'Arts of the Contact Zone' 35 n.15
Protestantism 12, 25
Pusztai, Gábor 124
Puteh, Njaq 134

Remonstrants 18
  anti-Remonstrants 18
Richardson, Samuel 168
  Clarissa 168
Ridder, André de 151
Roemer, Astrid 40
Roeper, Vibeke 16, 18, 34
Rops, Félicien 151
Rosenboom, Thomas 34

Ruusbroec, Jan van 151

Said, Edward 3, 7, 39, 51, 61, 73, 91, 92, 110, 126, 129
  Culture and Imperialism 51
  Orientalism 61 n. 3, 73, 110
Salverda, Reinier 131
Second World War 8, 71, 124, 127, 128, 135, 161
Sicking, J.M.J.:
  Overgave en Verzet: De levens- en wereldbeschouwing van Carry van Bruggen 188 n. 25
Slauerhoff, Jan Jacob:
  Jan Pietersz. Coen 34
slavery 21, 38, 39, 43, 61 n.1
Smeeks, Hendrik:
  Beschryvinge van het Magtig Koningryk Krinke Kesmes 15
Sötemann, A.L. 66, 74, 91
Spivak, Gayatri Chakravorty 86
Staten-Bijbel 15
Staten-Generaal 12, 37
Sterne, Laurence 48
  The Life and Opinions of Tristram Shandy 48, 50
  A Sentimental Journey through France and Italy 48
Stevenson, R. L. 78
Stevin, Simon 33
Stinstra, Johannes 168
Stradanus:
  Vespucci discovers America 85
subject position 8, 74, 162, 177, 184, 185, 186
subjugation 7, 9, 13, 53, 59, 60, 73, 77, 81, 84, 86, 149, 161, 171
Surinam 4, 37, 39, 40
Swinnen, Aagje 172
  Het slot ontvlucht. De 'vrouwelijke' Bildungsroman in de Nederlandse literatuur 187 n. 2
symbolism 8, 154
Székely, László 8, 124
Székely-Lulofs, Madelon 8, 51, 121, 124, 126, 127, 128, 129, 130, 131, 132, 133, 134, 135, 138, 142, 147
  life 129–130
  style of writing/themes 131–35, 136–47
  reviews/criticism 135–36
  works:
    Hongertocht 127
    Koelie 124, 138
    Rubber 124, 126. 138
    Tjoet Nja Din 8, 121, 124, 128, 129, 130, 131, 136, 138, 142, 147
    Weet je nog wel? 130
Taine, Hyppolite 104, 173
Termorshuizen, Gerard 124

text:
  euphoric 162
  dysphoric 162
Thoreau, Henry David:
  Walden or Life in the Woods 173
Tolstoy, Alexej 135

Udemans, Godfried:
  't Geestelyck roer van 't Coopmans Schip 38
  Practyce van de Christelijcke hooft-deugden 38
  'utile et dulce' 15

Valent, Marion 106
Vandevoorde, Hans 8, 149, 158
  'De onmacht die hem sarrend sloeg. Over Karel van de Woestijne' 149
Vereenigde Oost-Indische Compagnie 12; see also VOC
Versteeg, Koos 135
Vliet, H.T.M. van 108
VOC 12, 13, 14, 18, 19, 20, 21, 24, 25, 37, 63, 70, 71
Vos, Jan:
  Aran en Titus 19
Vries, Theun de 127, 135

Wagner, Richard 154
Waterhouse, John Williams 151
West India Company see WIC 37, 38
West Indies 4, 24, 37, 39, 40, 51, 54, 55, 58, 60
Wildeman, Diederick 16, 18, 34
Wilhelmina, Queen 34, 101, 122
Woestijne, Gustave van de 151
Woestijne, Karel van de 8, 149, 151, 153, 154, 155, 157, 158, 159
  life 151–54
  style of writing/themes 154–59
  works:
    'De zwijnen van Kirkè' 8, 149, 151
    Interludieën 151
    Janus met het dubbele voorhoofd 151
Wolff, Betje 8, 166, 168
Woolf, Virginia:
  The Voyage Out 161, 165
Wright, Elizabeth 92, 95
writing beyond the ending 162

Yarnall, Judith 156
  Transformations of Circe: The History of an Enchantress 160 n. 9

Zook, Darren C. 92

www.ingramcontent.com/pod-product-compliance
Lightning Source LLC
LaVergne TN
LVHW061251060426
835507LV00017B/2006